In the second half of the nineteenth century a number of women, sponsored by the Female Middle Class Emigration Society, left Britain to seek a better life in the colonies. Unmarried and unemployed, they were among the many educated genteel women who were endeavouring to find work as governesses, then one of the few occupations open to them.

In letters back to the Society these women reported on life as they saw it in the colonies during the years 1862–1882. They tell of their travails; of their adjustments to strange and often hostile environments; of their loneliness, their failures and their successes.

Most importantly, they give fresh and disarming views on colonials and colonial society, touching on aspects of pioneering experience and on life in the towns of seven countries during a fascinating period in history.

Patricia Clarke, journalist and historian, is the author of *A Colonial Woman*, the biography of the pioneering Mary Braidwood Mowle 1827–1857, and *Pen Portraits*, a surprising account of the many women writers and journalists in colonial Australia. She has also just completed *Her Brief, Bright Day* (forthcoming), the story of Louisa Atkinson, the first Australian-born woman novelist and a noted naturalist, and is compiling, with Dale Spender, a collection of letters and diaries written by women during Australia's first half-century.

Actively involved in heritage issues and in local and family history, Patricia Clarke is the Editor of the *Canberra Historical Journal*.

The Governesses

LETTERS FROM THE COLONIES 1862–1882

Patricia Clarke

ALLEN & UNWIN
Sydney Wellington London Boston

To the governesses of the Female Middle Class Emigration Society, the fortuitous preservation of whose letters made this book possible. They all may have not found the El Dorado they were seeking, but they had the courage to venture far.

First published in 1985 by
Hutchinson Publishing Group (Australia) Pty Ltd

First paperback edition published 1989 by
Allen & Unwin Australia Pty Ltd
8 Napier Street, North Sydney NSW 2059 Australia

Allen & Unwin New Zealand Limited
75 Ghuznee Street, Wellington, New Zealand

Unwin Hyman Limited
15-17 Broadwick Street, London W1V 1FP England

Unwin Hyman Inc.
8 Winchester Place, Winchester, Mass 01890 USA

National Library of Australia
Cataloguing-in-Publication entry:

Clarke, Patricia.
The governesses: letters from the colonies 1862-1882

Bibliography.
Includes index.
ISBN 0 04 442125 7.

1. Female Middle Class Emigration Society. 2. Governesses -- Australia -- Correspondence. 3. Australia -- Social conditions -- 1851-1891. I. Title.

371.1'0092'2

Produced by SRM Production Services Sdn Bhd, Malaysia

Contents

Acknowledgements vii
Sources ix
Introduction xi

1 Genteel Emigrants 1
2 The Voyage Out 24
3 The First Arrivals 49
4 A Mixed Reception 62
5 Life with the 'Nouveaux Riches' 82
6 Station Life 103
7 Hard Times in Depressed Years 118
8 Disappointments and Difficulties 128
9 The Last Emigrants 140
10 Following Miss Rye to New Zealand 151
11 A Challenging Life in South Africa 174
12 Venturers to Alien Lands 203
Epilogue 215

Appendix: Female Middle Class Emigration Society Letter-books — List of Correspondents, 1862–1882 217
Bibliography 225
Index 231

Acknowledgements

I gratefully acknowledge assistance from the staff of the National Library of Australia, Canberra, in the compilation of this book, particularly from Mrs Margaret Brennan and Mrs Jean James and other staff of the Petherick (Australian Studies) Room, who could not have been more helpful. I also wish to thank the staff of the Newspaper and Microfilm Reading Room, where I read the Female Middle Class Emigration Society's records and letter-books; Ms Mary Ann Pattison, the Australian Joint Copying Project Officer; and the staff of the Pictorial Collection, where I selected most of the illustrations.

The records of the Female Middle Class Emigration Society were microfilmed in London in 1963, as part of the Australian Joint Copying Project, when they were held by the Women's Migration and Oversea Appointments Society. They now are held by the Fawcett Library, City of London Polytechnic, and I am happy to acknowledge all quotations from the FMCES records to that source.

My thanks also to my editor, Bridget Everett, who was most helpful and suggested many lines of enquiry, and prodded me on to find out more about the governesses and their fate.

I am grateful to the following organisations and individuals for help in obtaining valuable information and/or illustrations, particularly honorary office-bearers and members of local historical societies, who have been very generous in giving their time to answering my queries: Alexander Turnbull Library, National Library of New Zealand, Wellington; Angaston District Council; Archives Authority of New South Wales; Ballarat Historical Society (Research Librarian, Katrine E. Kelly); J. S. Battye Library of West Australian History, Library Board of Western Australia, Perth (Acting Principal Librarian, Christopher Coggin, and Film Archives Officer, Jack Hannibal); Berrima District Historical Society (Research Officer, Edward Marriott); Mrs Peter Isobel Bright, Rainbow Beach, Qld; Diocese of Brisbane (Diocesan Archivist, Mrs Patricia Ramsay); Diocese of Chicester; Church of England Children's Society, London (Archivist, Mrs Miranda Melbourn); CSR Limited (Administration Officer, Miss Dorothy J. Howard); Current Book Distributors, Sydney; Archdeacon Ted Doncaster, Anglican Parish of Floreat Park, WA; Durban Municipal Library (Librarian, Mrs M. H. Kennedy); Mrs Catherine Foggo, Singleton, NSW; Graaff-Reinet Publicity Association (Chairman, E. S. Whitlock); Hastings District Historical Society (Chairman, Records and Research Division, F. Rogers); Heritage Society, Graaff-Reinet (Mrs R. B. Kingwill); La Trobe Library, State Library of Victoria (Manuscripts Librarian, Tony Marshall); Joseph J. Mack, Surrey Hills, Vic.; Diocese of Melbourne (Registrar, R. F. S. Crosbie); Mitchell Library, State Library of New South Wales; Monash University, Education Faculty (Ms Marion Amies); Narrabri Historical Society (John Brooks); *Natal Mercury* (Editor, J. O. McMillan); Diocese of Peterborough (Diocesan Registrar, Raymond Hemingray); St George's Cathedral, Perth (Dean, Very Rev. David Robarts); Sale Historical Society (J. O'Connor); Scone and Upper Hunter Historical Society (Acting Assistant Secretary, Anne McMullin); Singleton Historical Society (Mrs Dot Clayworth); South African Embassy, Canberra (Information Attaché, Mr Aubery Dwyer); Tretyakovsky State Gallery, Moscow (Scientific Secretary, V. M. Petyushenko); University of Natal (the Campbell Collections), Killie Campbell Africana Library (Africana Librarian, Ms J. F. Duggan); and Mrs Doris Wilson, Durban.

Finally, I am very grateful for the kindly interest and support of my husband Hugh, and our friends Helen and Richard Pape, all more familiar than I am with the stresses of writing a book.

Sources

The main sources used for this book were the records of the Female Middle Class Emigration Society (FMCES), particularly some hundreds of letters written to the Society by those women the Society assisted to emigrate.

Other FMCES records that provided important information were the four annual reports published by the Society between 1862 and 1886, and the addresses given by Maria Rye and Jane Lewin in the early 1860s to the congresses of the National Association for the Promotion of Social Science. Miss Rye's address at the Dublin Congress in 1861 was the catalyst for the formation of the Society.

As the governesses' letters often give only minimal information regarding employers and addresses, and this sometimes in not readily decipherable handwriting, it was necessary to refer to other general reference works, local histories, directories, and even births, marriages and deaths records. These, together with information supplied by local historical societies, were helpful in the detective work that was necessary to follow the movements of many of the emigrants and to provide background on the people who employed them and the economic and social life of the places where they lived.

Apart from the deletion of some personal items, details of routine arrangements or repetitious material regarding the repayment of loans, the letters selected have been reproduced without alteration. However, some obvious spelling errors have been corrected, including the names of people and places (it is assumed that these mistakes occurred in the copying of the letters into the Society's letter-books) and to some extent the punctuation has been amended, although not in such a way to affect the writing flow.

Introduction

This book records the aspirations, achievements and vicissitudes, the successes and failures, of a group of educated women who, having found it difficult or impossible to support themselves in nineteenth-century Britain, took the courageous step of emigrating to the colonies, in the hope of finding work as governesses. In a class-conscious age, they spurned the help available to working-class emigrants through government agencies and instead borrowed money to finance their ventures.

The loans they raised were made available to them through the Female Middle Class Emigration Society, founded in London in 1862. When repaying the money lent to them, many of the recipients wrote letters to the Society. Some of these were little more than polite acknowledgements, but many of the women also wrote of the shocks, disappointments and joys of life in strange and often isolated places.

These letters, very fortunately, have been preserved. The aim has not been to interpret the letters, but to let the governesses speak for themselves. At their best, the letters contain genuine, immediate impressions of people, places and society, seen through the eyes of a particular type and class of British woman of that era who experienced emigration at a time when long sea voyages were hazardous and knowledge of life in the colonies often rudimentary.

The majority of the governesses came out to Australia, and the book mainly concerns them. Some went to New Zealand

and South Africa, and their often very different experiences are recorded also. The final chapter concerns the few who emigrated to other countries, particularly two women who ventured much further in a cultural sense, one to India and the other to Russia.

1 Genteel Emigrants

'Amongst no class does greater distress exist than amongst the class of poor governesses . . .'

Jane Lewin, London, 1863

When Emily Streeter, a young, vulnerable but spirited girl, landed in Sydney from London on the *Rachel* in September 1861 in search of employment as a governess, she symbolised the hopes of many women in Great Britain for a better life overseas. Educated and genteel, but unmarried and unemployed, they hoped that their services would be in demand in the British colonies in one of the few congenial occupations then open to them. In England, women like Emily Streeter faced lives of quiet desperation as they searched for employment in an overcrowded market. Their hopes of finding a governess's paradise in the colonies often were not realised, but the more adaptable found a measure of success.

Emily Streeter, one of a group of six women who pioneered a scheme for the emigration of governesses from Great Britain, was not immediately successful in her search for work. However, after a worrying five weeks in Sydney, which exhausted her financial resources, she found a position with a grazier's family in the isolated district of Jerry's Plains on the Upper Hunter, teaching five children aged five to eleven.

Many others followed. Miss A. H. Jackson went to South Africa, to Verulam, near Durban, in 1863 and was catapulted into an unfamiliar world of green mamba snakes, native servants, houses with thatched roofs and canvas ceilings, Natal sores and dysentery. Laura Jones found herself working as an assistant teacher and living in a six-foot-square hut in a small mining-town in northern Victoria. Ostracised because of her religious beliefs, she was forced to resign her position and earned a precarious living doing needlework for the miners' wives.

Marion Hett travelled the last three miles of her journey to Tutu Totara, a station on New Zealand's North Island, by bridlepath. Louisa Geoghegan left Melbourne on Christmas Day 1866 to travel to a sheep-station in the Wimmera, near the South Australian border, a journey that took six days of hard driving with early morning starts, rests in the heat of the day and more riding in the evening. Soon after she arrived, one of her charges died tragically of measles and was buried in a grave near the lonely homestead.

Elizabeth Mitchinson, in the late 1870s, went to Bedford, in the eastern part of Cape Colony, South Africa, where she taught five pupils English, French, Latin, music, drawing and painting. There she did not undress to go to bed, for fear Zulus would attack during the night. Augusta McNeill travelled two days on an overladen bullock-dray to get to a situation north of Christchurch, New Zealand, where she taught six children, cleaned the schoolroom, collected wood, lit the fire, scrubbed the floors, washed dishes, sewed for the family and played the piano three hours a night for their entertainment.

At least Augusta had a job. Others were not so lucky. Ellen Ollard, in Melbourne in the 1870s, earned only £13 in two years and Agnes Macqueen, in Brisbane in 1865, endured great hardships and existed only by selling her drawings.

The emigration of these and other governesses in the latter part of the nineteenth century, to the British colonies in Australia, New Zealand and South Africa, and to the United States and Canada — also to more exotic destinations, including India and Russia — was financed by the London-based Female Middle Class Emigration Society. The Society's purpose was to lend money and give other assistance to educated women of good character, to enable them to pay their passages to places overseas where prospects of obtaining employment as governesses were believed to be favourable.

Over its twenty or so years of operation, the Society assisted approximately 300 emigrants, an insignificant number among the human tide of millions who left the British Isles to begin new lives in the colonies. The importance of this tiny, atypical group of women rests on the fact that so many of them recorded their feelings about emigration and their observations on the places to which they emigrated. Because they had borrowed money, they were obliged to communicate regularly with the Society and many, when they repaid part or all of their loans, wrote lengthy and informative letters. This correspondence was encouraged by the Society, particularly letters from those women who reported in any depth on conditions in the colonies, for the Society was looking continually for openings for further emigrants. These letters from the governesses, laboriously transcribed into letterbooks by an office worker in London, have survived.

What emerges from the best of the letters are fresh perceptions on life in Australia and the other countries of destination between 1862 and 1882, when in the dying years of the Scheme, the letters (or the recording of them) petered out. They also provide a fascinating perspective on the attitudes and the prejudices of the type of British middle-class women who were attracted to the Scheme.

The Female Middle Class Emigration Society began as a result of the exertions of Maria S. Rye, who was born in Chelsea in 1829, the eldest of nine children of Edward Rye, a London solicitor of Norfolk origin. One of her brothers, Edward, was an entomologist and author of a book on British beetles and another, Walter, was a voluminous writer on Norfolk history.

Maria Rye, although generally a woman with a moralistic and conservative outlook, held advanced views regarding female employment. In English society, lower-class women traditionally had worked for a living — as domestic servants, and as farm and field workers, particularly during harvest time. Later, they slaved in the notoriously cruel conditions of the early factory system. However, the avenues for employment open to women of the middle and upper classes were almost non-existent. These women were expected to marry and then manage households of their own. Nineteenth-century Britain, however, did not provide all women with the opportunity for marriage and for many the situation was desperate. A substantial surplus of women dimmed the prospects of marriage and middle-class pretensions and educational status posed insurmountable barriers to acceptance of work as shop-assistants or servants. As a result, many middle-class and upper-class women were doomed to a life as unpaid household drudges in their own families or with their relatives. The surplus of women was attributed to losses of men in wars and the effect of migration by far greater numbers of men than women. On the other hand, the colonies were promoted continually as places that needed more emigrants, and particularly women, to balance the surplus of men. This combination of lack of opportunity for marriage or for work in the home country, and the need for women in the colonies, was remarked on by many observers, but one who acted was Maria Rye.

In 1861, and then in her early thirties, Maria Rye was a prominent member of the Society for Promoting the Employment of Women and, in her own right, ran a law stationery service where she employed women to copy legal documents by hand, a new field for women's work. An advertising handbill for the firm described her as:

> LAW STATIONER,
> Office: 12, Portugal Street, Lincoln's Inn, W.C.
> LAW PAPERS of all kinds carefully and skilfully copied at the usual charges.
> DEEDS engrossed on parchment and stamped.
> CHANCERY BILLS printed.
> SPECIFICATIONS copied.
> CIRCULAR LETTERS written 1*s.* 6*d.* per dozen.
> ENVELOPES addressed 5*s.* per 1000.
> SERMONS AND PETITIONS copied.

Maria Rye's experience in this business reinforced her appreciation of the great numbers of educated women who were desperate for employment. Her office was beseiged every day by applicants for work, many the daughters of professional men from towns, cities and counties all over the British Isles.

Other similar establishments associated with the Society for Promoting the Employment of Women — for example, the Victoria Press run by Emily Faithfull, who was printer to Queen Victoria, the Register Office run by Miss Crowe* and the Telegraph Station run by Mrs Craig — reported similar numbers of applicants. In 1861, 810 women applied for one situation at one of these establishments for which the pay was £15 a year. Another 250 applied for a vacancy at £12 a year. Another similar establishment received 120 apparently

---

*It is not known if this Miss Crowe is Catherine Crowe who emigrated to South Africa in 1862. Certainly, there is no indication of this in her letters to the Society.

unsolicited applications in a single day when there was not even a vacancy. When Emily Faithfull opened her printing office, she received seventy-eight written and more than one hundred personal applications, but she could employ only twenty women.*

As a partial solution to the problem of surplus women, Maria Rye turned to emigration. Using her own resources and private donations from others of similar views, she began providing loans for passage money to enable small numbers of educated women to emigrate to the colonies.

At this time, middle-class women generally were considered to be outside the scope of government-assisted migration schemes, unless they were prepared to swallow their pride and describe themselves as servants. These schemes, financed by the colonial governments and run from London by the Colonial Land and Emigration Commissioners, varied in detail but were based on supplying the type of emigrants most needed in the colonies: usually labourers, artisans and female servants. Miss Rye described the orders from the colonial governments specifying the types of migrants required as being 'as peremptory and as defined as that of any Melbourne merchant writing to the corresponding house in London, about Manchester cottons or Bermondsey boots'.

There were continual complaints from the colonies that the women who were arriving as emigrants did not fit the category of servant. As early as 1852, the Immigration Agent in Victoria, Edward Grimes, complained that there was no demand for nursery governesses, companions to ladies or artificial flower-makers, after a number who had so described themselves arrived in Melbourne. Another report on immigration the following year stated that openings in the colonies for persons of an educated or half-educated class were not as good as for unskilled workers. At the same time, there were persistent and tantalising reports of the lack of women in the

---

*Although unable to provide work for more than a handful of the young women who applied, these enterprises were forerunners of the move by women into office work. The electric telegraph, for instance, opened up a new field of work for women and their eventual employment in the Civil Service. Women were first employed as telegraph clerks in 1854, when Queen Victoria's speech at the opening of Parliament was telegraphed to the Continent by girls who were supervised by a woman telegraphist. When the privately owned telegraph-stations were taken over by the government in 1870, some of the employees, including some women, became civil servants.

colonies. Miss Rye, in a paper read at the Social Science Congress at Dublin in 1861 on 'Emigration of Educated Women', gave the total deficiency of women in New Zealand as 11,161; in Victoria, 138,579; in South Australia, 1,889; and in Western Australia, 4,207. She continued:

155,636 fewer women than men in the two islands of which we alone possess statistical accounts! What would the disproportion be if we could include Natal, Canada and Columbia, in the reckoning? Of the fearful reverse of this picture as exhibited in England it would be superfluous to speak; and if the vice and immorality on either side of the Atlantic is ever to be uprooted, it must be by some further extension of emigration, by the steady departure from these shores of our superfluous workers, and by an influx into the colonies of a body of women infinitely superior by birth, by education, and by taste, to the hordes of wild uneducated creatures we have hitherto sent abroad.

She saw the solution in convincing the colonies that the introduction of such a class of women would 'not only be a relief to England, but an actual benefit to the colonies themselves — an elevation of morals being the inevitable result of the mere presence in the colony of a number of high-class women'.

Despite the official reports, which were unanimous in discouraging the migration of women looking for more refined employment, Maria Rye, by corresponding with prominent members of society in the Australian colonies, managed to get some influential backing for her scheme. Edward Willis, a pioneer settler at Port Phillip, offered to have the question raised in the Victorian Legislative Assembly. He agreed with Miss Rye: 'This is a most excellent cause you have in hand. Qualified teachers and governesses are *very much wanted indeed* in Australia. Those going out have a very fine field before them.' He added that as there were various grades of society in Melbourne, each with different requirements and wants, it was 'scarcely fair and just to confine the advantages of free emigration to women of the lowest attainments and capacities'. However useful and necessary such a 'substratum' of workers might have been at the start of colonisation, the time had passed for female emigration to be exclusively confined to the servant class.

Mrs Thomas Turner à Beckett, a prominent member of

Melbourne society, was more in the mainstream of colonial opinion. She replied that the colonies would be very interested in any scheme for sending out a 'higher class of servant'.

The most promising response came from the Anglican Bishop of Sydney, Bishop Frederic Barker, and his wife. A letter written on the Bishop's behalf, and quoted by Miss Rye in her paper, stated:

> We shall be very glad to assist in finding situations for educated women of respectable character, provided they could be sent out to Sydney by a fund raised in England. The Bishop begs me to tell you that if two or three persons qualified for teaching parochial schools for girls or infants could be sent here, there would not be any difficulty in providing situations for them. They should have some certificates of their competency, and be not under twenty or more than two or at most five and thirty years of age. Should the plan suggested meet with the approbation of your ladies' committee, we must ask you to apprize us of any persons likely to come out and in what vessels their passages are taken, in order that arrangements may be made for their reception in Sydney, and for their future destination as teachers. We have been greatly interested in the various schemes now at work in London and elsewhere for the protection and employment of women. The colonies ought to assist largely in such a work, but you know the many difficulties and evil influences that have to be encountered here; and how we have suffered from swarms of ignorant women, who are a misery to any place. But if respectable, well-taught persons could be introduced in any numbers they would, as you say, be of incalculable benefit to the colony.

There were also enthusiastic responses from Adelaide and Durban, in South Africa. From Adelaide, Miss Rye said she had heard 'that large incomes are earned there by many highly accomplished women'. She added: 'It is true that there are all kinds of incongruities in colonial life', but how preferable such a life, to the homeless condition of nine governesses out of ten in this country?'

Maria Rye's views reached a much wider audience when she addressed the Social Science Congress at Dublin in 1861. In her address, she described graphically the desperate unemployment and hopelessness faced by many educated women in England, the real or perceived limitations to the emigration of such women under existing assisted schemes and the imbalance between the sexes in the colonies, with the implied prospects of marriage, as well as employment, for emigrant women. The advice she had had from all quarters, Maria Rye said, was: 'Teach your protégées to emigrate; send them where the men want wives, the mothers want governesses, where the shopkeepers, the schools, and the sick will thoroughly appreciate your exertions, and heartily welcome your women'.

Her solution was the establishment of a loan fund from which suitable applicants for emigration would be lent passage money, repayable after two years and four months.

> There are two great advantages in this system — firstly, we shall, by lending instead of giving, be able to assist a class of persons who, however poor they may be (and I believe not one person in a thousand has the very faintest idea how absolutely poor the *women* in this class are) would object, and very properly object, to being treated as paupers; secondly, this money, although always changing hands, would, with proper management, scarcely diminish or, at any rate, the losses would be so small that an insignificant subscription would amply cover them.

The printing of this address by the Victoria Press and its distribution, together with a letter by Emily Faithfull, published in the London *Times* of 4 December 1861, resulted in donations towards the establishment of a fund to assist educated female emigrants. The theme of Maria Rye's address also was taken up in a letter signed 'S.G.O.', the well-known initials of Lord (Sidney) Godolphin Osborne, philantropist and Anglican clergyman, published in *The Times* on 3 April 1862 under the heading 'Sisters Help Sisters'. The letter commended Miss Rye's scheme and solicited donations, stating that educated women were 'the very class much wanted in Australia and at Natal'.

A series of letters to the editor of *The Times* followed, some critical of the plan to send governesses overseas. In *The Times* of 23 April 1862, an anonymous writer ('B.'), who had recently returned from Australia, warned:

> Bearable situations as a governess are by no means so easily to be obtained as residents in England imagine; and the position of such a lady sent out in search of such a situation, but who fails to obtain it, or who even experiences long delay in obtaining it, is, in a country so expensive and so far from home, lamentable indeed.

This was followed on 24 April by a poignant letter from 'J. K.', 'A Returned Australian Governess', who wrote:

Sir, — Having experienced all the disappointment and trials attendant on emigrating to Australia as a governess, hoping to get speedy and remunerative employment in that capacity in the colony, perhaps a few words on the subject will strengthen your correspondent 'B.'s' excellent advice to those who are so kindly intending emigration assistance for the above object.

Early in 1858 I emigrated to Melbourne (leaving a position in a family as governess for the purpose), on the encouragement and advice of a friend in the colony, taking with me the highest testimonials and a letter of introduction to the Bishop's wife. On arrival I could not obtain a situation, though that lady, with others, interested themselves most warmly for me; and having no funds, I consequently had no home, and, after enduring much distress, could only obtain employment as daily needlewoman, the pay of which was inadequate to meet the still expensive rate of board and lodging in the colony.

Suffering much, my health entirely failing from disappointment, &c., some friends kindly made up a subscription, and sent me home to meet the reproaches of those who, knowing scarcely anything, and nothing practically, of the colony, blame me for not having succeeded. . . .

Maria Rye replied the next day in a letter which began: 'J. K., having given her melancholy experience, and forwarded her four-year-old news about Melbourne, allow me to make a few extracts from letters received by the last mail, which will place the picture in another, and, happily, in a brighter light'. Then followed extracts from letters written by FMCES emigrants Caroline Heawood and Maria Barrow from Melbourne and Gertrude Gooch from Sydney, who had written to the Society in favourable terms of their experiences since coming to the colonies.*

On 30 April, another correspondent, 'C.L.T.', also a former resident of Australia, warned that there were large numbers of young women of 'superior class' in Australia 'without proper means of subsistence'. They had been induced to migrate by the hope of instant employment and a much higher rate of remuneration than in England, but instead were reduced to their last pound and to save themselves from starvation had to take in washing or needlework to earn a precarious existence. The writer concluded:

---

*See Chapter 3, pages 54–7 and Chapter 4, pages 63–5.

I think it should be fairly laid before these ladies, that their going to the colonies is like a raffle in which there are 50 blanks to one prize, and that, although that very humane, and I have no doubt most well-intentioned lady, Miss Maria Rye, is enabled to produce a few letters from governesses who have succeeded, there are now, at this moment, ten times as many who have not even the means to pay the postage home of their letters to England, which would plainly prove the inexpediency of any number of these ladies emigrating to the colonies. Hundreds there are, believe me, who will never be heard of; thousands there are who will never have, like 'J. K.', the helping hand extended to them to enable them to rejoin their friends and families in England, whom they have quitted without properly weighing the subject of emigration before it was too late.
To all governesses I say, reflect, consider how you will be placed if you don't get a situation. What then?

In *The Times* of 26 April, there had appeared an official warning from Stephen Walcott of the Government Emigration Board in London. He wrote that there was no demand for governesses in New South Wales, Victoria or South Australia. He quoted the Immigration Agent in Victoria, in a communication dated 25 January 1862, as saying 'no demand whatever exists for the superior class of emigrants, such as clerks, shopmen, &c., and the same remark applies to the corresponding class of females, such as governesses, milliners, &c. I would strongly dissuade such from coming hither, unless they may have been invited to join friends already settled here'. Walcott concluded: 'A small number, especially of those who have friends in the colony prepared to receive and protect them till they can obtain situations, may, perhaps, succeed; but we are convinced that a large emigration, should it take place, will only result in disappointment and disaster'.

An equally long letter from Maria Rye and Jane Lewin, published in *The Times* on the same day, acknowledged subscriptions totalling more than £300. Another letter two days later from Miss Rye showed she was unconvinced that there would be any problems arising from her scheme for the emigration of governesses.

I not only believe, but am confident, that there are vacant situations in the colonies for many hundreds of women vastly superior to the hordes of wild Irish and fast young ladies who have hitherto started as emigrants. If these women of mine work, it will be well; if they marry, it will be well; whichever happens, good must arise for the colonies, for our countrywomen and for commerce.

She contrasted the desperate employment situation in England with the colonies, where, she said, barely competent women were receiving £124 to £130 a year as governesses.

Maria Rye's unshakeable confidence, and the support of influential people, led to the formation of the Female Middle Class Emigration Society in May 1862, with the Earl of Shaftesbury, the great social reformer, as one of the patrons. Other patrons were Lord Brougham, former Lord Chancellor and President of the National Association for the Promotion of Social Science; the Right Reverend the Lord Bishop of Sydney, Bishop Barker; Sir William à Beckett, formerly Victorian Chief Justice; the Honourable Arthur Kinnaird, later Lord Kinnaird, M. P. and philanthropist; and R. Monckton Milnes, later Lord Houghton, M. P. and a president of the Social Science Congress. The patronesses were the Honourable Mrs Locke King, Lady Young, Mrs H. Alers Hankey, Mrs Fynes Webber, Lady Franklin, Lady Dowling, the Honourable Mrs Egerton, Miss B. R. Parkes and Miss Isa Craig. The honorary secretaries were Maria S. Rye and Jane E. Lewin.

The colonial correspondents who acted as representatives of the Society were named in the Society's first annual report as: Mrs Barker, Mrs Gordon and Mrs A. Dillon in Sydney; Mrs T. T. à Beckett, Mrs Gatty Jones, Mrs Perry and E. Willis, Esq. in Melbourne; Mrs Clarke in Adelaide; Mrs R. Acutt, Mrs Brickhill, Mrs Churchill, Mrs Lamport and Mrs McArthur in Natal; and in British Columbia,* Governor Douglas, Bishop Hills, Archdeacon and Mrs Wright and Colonel and Mrs Moody.

The FMCES adopted as its rules:

1 The Society confines its assistance entirely to educated women — no applicants being accepted who are not sufficiently educated to undertake the duties of nursery governess.

2 Every applicant is examined as far as possible, with regard to her knowledge of cooking, baking, washing, needlework and housework, and is required to be willing to assist in these departments of labour should it be necessary.

3 Applicants are required to give the names and addresses of four persons as referees, from whom the Society can obtain information

*Despite the high-powered nature of this committee, few emigrants went to British Columbia under the Scheme.

respecting the position, character, strength, qualities, and general suitableness of the applicant for a colonial life, two of these referees to be ladies with whom the applicant has held situations, and two to be her personal friends. The references are, if possible, taken up personally by the Secretaries, and the Society hopes, by establishing correspondents in the chief provincial towns, to ensure in all cases a personal interview with the applicant, if not with her referees.

4 If the information obtained is satisfactory, the applicant, being accepted by the Society, receives all possible needful assistance. Should she be unable to pay the entire cost of outfit and passage money, the Society advances the deficient amount, a legal agreement to repay within two years and four months being signed by the emigrant, and two respectable householders as securities. Should an approved applicant not require a loan, she is equally entitled to the advantages of the Society's care and protection.

5 The Society secures all passages and purchases cabin fittings on behalf of the emigrants, thus saving much trouble and time. It is also enabled by the liberality of shipowners and outfitters to effect a considerable saving of expense.* The Society's assistance to emigrants is given free of any charge whatever.

6 The Society has established regular correspondents at most of the colonial ports. As soon as a party leaves England, notice of their departure is sent by the Overland Mail to the correspondent at the port to which the emigrants are bound, a list of their names and qualifications, together with copies of the testimonials of each applicant, are sent at the same time and as the notice is received six weeks before the emigrants arrive, there is time to make preparations for their reception, and even to seek for situations.

In practice, some of these rules were unrealistic. As some of the women applied because they were unemployed — gentlewomen in distressed circumstances — they would have had difficulty in complying with the requirement for employers' references. Also, as their plaintive complaints bear

---

*The Society gave the cost of a second-class passage and cabin fittings 'as generally about £25'. A contemporary publication, S. W. Silver's *Emigration Guide*, quoted the following prices:

London to	*3rd class*	*2nd class*	*1st class*
Sydney	£18 and upwards	£30 and upwards	£40 and upwards
Melbourne	£14	£25	£40
Auckland	£16	£25	£40
Wellington	£18	£30	£42
Cape Town	£20	£30	£35
Natal	£25	—	£35

out, any idea that they were prepared to combine the duties of adaptable housekeepers with governessing, as envisioned by the rules regarding ability to cook, wash and sew, proved optimistic. They were women deeply ingrained with ideas of their 'place' in the rigid caste system of nineteenth-century Britain. They had the usual attainments of their class and sex: the ability to read and write as a minimum, together with varying degrees of training in cultural subjects, such as French, music and drawing — although, as it turned out, some were found wanting in these accomplishments. In addition, some of the emigrants were too old and too set in their ways to adapt to the more demanding and less stratified life of the colonies.

The FMCES's first annual report, dated 28 October 1862, stated that the aim of the Society was to ensure that:

> women who are superior in birth and attainments to most of those who have hitherto been sent to the colonies, might receive protection and assistance to emigrate, and thus lessen the number of our ill-paid and starving, *because superfluous,* workers at home.

Miss Jane Lewin, sole secretary in Miss Rye's then absence overseas, was able to report success:

> The first party, consisting of six ladies, sailed for Sydney in June 1861.* Since then 54 persons have been sent out by the Society, all, with five or six exceptions, of the governess class, many of whom had spent months trying in vain to obtain a situation, all from whom there has been time to hear have speedily obtained employment at salaries varying from £20 to £70 per annum.

The Society's report documented the fates of fourteen women sent to Australia and Africa during 1861, together with their initial salaries, if known, and comments, including in some cases a statement on the contrasting lack of employment in Britain:

*Although the Society's work did not begin formally until May 1862, emigrants assisted through Miss Rye's efforts and by donations before that date were regarded as Society emigrants.

LIST OF EMIGRANTS

No.	*Destination*	*Date of Sailing*	*Salary Obtained in the Colonies*	*Remarks*
1	Australia	1861	£70	Was nursery governess in England, at £20 per annum.
2	Australia	1861	—	Very young and inexperienced, obtained situation after a time.
3	Australia	1861	£60	Had failed entirely to obtain employment in England, from inability to teach music.
4	Australia	1861	£35	The climate caused severe headaches, which much affected her success.
5	Australia	1861	—	Married directly, and returned to England.
6	Australia	1861	£45	Obtained situation immediately.
7	Africa	1861	£25	Obtained situation shortly — very comfortable and happy.
8	Africa	1861	£20	Obtained situation with family returning to India.
9	Australia	1861	£50	Got employment as daily governess, three days after arrival.
10	Australia	1861	£50	Obtained employment as daily governess immediately.
11	Australia	1861	£60	Had experienced great difficulty in obtaining employment in England, on account of slight deafness.
12	Australia	1861	£40	Obtained comfortable situation, two months after landing.

13	Australia	1861	—	Went to live with a brother.
14	Australia	1861	—	Obtained situation as shopwoman, but lost it through mis-conduct.

At the time of this report, Maria Rye was on her way to New Zealand and the Australian colonies, where she planned to investigate female emigration and complete the Society's colonial organisation. The work of the Society, from the time of her departure, was largely in the hands of Jane Lewin, who developed a rapport with many of the emigrants. Although not such a public figure as Maria Rye, Jane Lewin (who was a niece of the historian and Member of Parliament, George Grote) was to become a key member of the FMCES.

Already in 1862, Miss Rye had assisted, independently of the Society, 315 persons to emigrate, including several families. The greater number were domestic servants, shop-women and packing operatives from Manchester, where on a visit to that distressed city, she had been beseiged by two thousand applicants for emigration.

In an address to the Social Science Congress in October 1863 on 'Female Middle Class Emigration', Jane Lewin explained the difference between the work of the FMCES and the work of emigration undertaken separately by Maria Rye, and the misunderstandings that had occurred. In the latter part of 1862, she said, Miss Rye had dispatched large parties of working women to Queensland, New Zealand (Miss Rye herself had accompanied this group) and British Columbia on assisted passages offered by the colonial governments. These parties had consisted entirely of servants, dressmakers and others, and were sent out through Miss Rye's personal exertions.

Miss Lewin referred to the confusion that had arisen regarding these separate activities, including criticism of the Society for allegedly sending ninety-six governesses to Queensland: these were, in fact, factory or domestic workers. She said: 'The Society rarely sends more than six of its emigrants in one party and far more generally only two at intervals of two to three months'. And she added:

... it is not only amongst the least educated class of females that great distress exists, nor is it the poorest only that are entitled to the benefits of emigration, nor indeed is it the most ignorant and unintelligent who are the most wanted in the colonies. Amongst no class does greater distress exist than amongst the class of poor governesses; and Miss Rye's efforts are specially directed to the emigration of governesses and of the better class of servants.

. . . In all cases, however, the Society requires education of the hands, as well as of the head; and the most highly accomplished applicant would be rejected were she to profess total ignorance of household work, cooking and the like, or to refuse to assist in domestic matters in the event of her being called upon to do so. It is hardly necessary to add that all possible precautions are taken to ensure good moral character in those who are sent out.

According to Miss Lewin, the Society fulfilled the two things required by 'struggling educated women': loans to pay passages when they were unable to pay for these themselves, and someone to meet them, to obviate the 'risk of landing in a distant country unknown and unprotected, ignorant where to turn for a night's lodging or a little friendly counsel, for it must always be remembered that no existing immigration agency, public or private, helps this class of women.' She continued:

The Society supplies the first of these requirements by granting loans, on sufficient security, to accepted applicants, and the second by establishing correspondents in every colonial port to which it sends. These correspondents, generally ladies of good position, receive the immigrants on their arrival, direct them to respectable lodgings and assist them in obtaining employment.

Official reports continued to be sceptical of the existence of openings in the colonies for educated females. The 1863 report of the Colonial Land and Emigration Commissioners made the sweeping comment that there were no openings for this class in Australia, British North America, the Cape of Good Hope or Natal. However, the report admitted that 'an opening for one or two governesses might from time to time be found' and that 'a few thoroughly educated ladies who would be willing to go into the bush and not object, in addition to their educated duties, to assist occasionally in domestic matters (female servants being scarce) might meet with comfortable homes and that possibly a very limited number might obtain engagements in Sydney'. Nevertheless, the Society continued to sponsor small numbers of governesses and, generally, was able to report at least their initial success.

As a result of the frequent absence of Miss Rye and her absorption in other schemes, together with the illness of Miss Lewin, the Society's next annual report was not issued until 1872. By then, 158 women had sailed for Australia, New Zealand, South Africa, British Columbia and the United States with the assistance of the FMCES. The 1872 report included a short account of the fortunes of the women who had emigrated and a reminder from Miss Lewin that 'governesses will never be wanted anywhere, in large numbers; so that our emigrants will never be reckoned by hundreds, although the Society may be doing very active and very useful work, among the class for which it is specially designed'.

In the following two years to the end of 1874, a further 21 women emigrated with the Society's assistance, bringing the total to 179 and by the end of 1879, the number had risen to 215.

During the 1870s, a paid secretary, Mrs Sunter, who had been associated with the running of Miss Rye's law-copying firm, was appointed to assist Miss Lewin. She was succeeded in about 1880 by Miss Strongith'arm. Jane Lewin remained honorary secretary until about 1882, when she joined Maria Rye on the Committee.

In its next report, issued at the end of 1882, the Society stated that the number of its emigrants had reached 260 and they had, for the most part, done remarkably well. One success story cited was of a lady who emigrated to New Zealand in 1866 and had been able to retire on an income of £150 per annum, derived from her savings during a period of fifteen years. 'Such a fact is most encouraging, as shewing the possibilities open to a woman of energy in the Colonies'.

In accordance with the Society's practice of preserving the privacy of emigrants, the successful lady's name is not given. Five FMCES emigrants went to New Zealand in 1866 and the Society reported on them as follows:

No.	*Salary in Colony*	*Remarks*
101	£60 per year	Went out to a situation which she kept some years, left to open a School which is doing well.
106	£60 per year	Went out to a situation but found it filled. Afterwards obtained good engagement.

107		Very moderately qualified, took needlework as more lucrative than teaching.
112	£120 per year	First engagement at £40, then £80 in Otago, afterwards Government school.
113		Failed through misconduct. Died in hospital of consumption.

The most likely success story is No. 112, who does not appear to have written to the Society. Next seems to be No. 101, who was probably Martha Wyett, whose experiences are described later.*

There is an apparent contradiction in the fact that the Society was able to report on the success or otherwise of most of its 302 emigrants (although it does record 'nothing known' about some) while recording letters from only 113. It only can be assumed either that some emigrants recorded the outcome of their movements in note form when they returned their loans, and these notes were not regarded as letters, or the information was obtained from their relatives or the people who guaranteed their loans.

The last letter in the Society's second letter-book is dated 1882 and the Society's final report was issued in 1886. By then, the work of other societies largely had taken over the role of the FMCES. The Society's report for 1886 announced that the work of the FMCES had been transferred to the Colonial Emigration Society, whose honorary secretary, Julia Blake, would act for both societies.

The report warned 'half-educated women teachers' against emigrating, since 'the distress occasioned by the keen competition' was as 'extreme and despairing in the large and old-settled towns of the Colonies as in England'. A letter from an emigrant to Sydney was quoted: 'I have *heard* of this keen competition in London. I never expected to *see* it in Sydney! The lady I went to had had 90 ladies already. The avenue to her house was peopled with girls.' The correspondent added that if teachers wanted work, they must go 'up country', must accept the life of the family without other society, and must share the household work with the mother and family.

---

*See Chapter 10, pages 159–60.

'It is dull', she said, 'but teachers won't find work in the towns, which are overstocked'.

The report advised half-educated teachers to turn to any other means of living, such as a 'Mother's Help', rather than face competition from colonial teachers, who by this time were emerging well-trained from local teachers colleges and universities.

In all, 302 women were sponsored by the FMCES, including those women sent out in 1861 and the early part of 1862, before the formal commencement of the Society. The records of the destinations of these female emigrants are not complete, however, the years 1873 to 1879 inclusive being missing. To the end of 1872, 158 emigrants were assisted by the Society. Of these, 87 went to Australia, 33 to New Zealand, 20 to South Africa, 9 to Canada, 8 to the United States and 1 to India. For the years 1880 to 1885, 86 were assisted, 42 to Australia, 15 to New Zealand, 12 to South Africa, 14 to Canada, 2 to the United States and 1 to Russia.

Over the years of its existence, the FMCES operated on a small budget. Its main expenses were payments for passages for intending emigrants, usually ranging from £200 to £400 a year, and cabin fittings. The main receipts were the payments emigrants made towards their passages (some did not need to borrow the full amount of their fare and others were able to pay their fares, only taking advantage of the other services offered by the Society), the repayments of loans and subscriptions and donations. Each year, repayments reached a substantial figure: for example, from 1 July 1864 to 1 July 1865, repayments totalled £196 0s 10d, payments by emigrants towards their passages were £121 11s 11d, and subscriptions and donations, £77 2s 0d. Expenditure on passages was £230 and on cabin fittings, £12 11s 5d.

The Society's accounts do not indicate the writing-off of any loans as bad debts. Extensions of the time in which repayments had to be made often were granted, but apparently even long-standing debts were regarded as being recoverable, either from the governess herself or from her guarantors.

As the emigration of educated females fostered by the FMCES proceeded, albeit low-key and in small volume, for two decades, controversy continued to surround Miss Rye and her involvement in female emigration schemes. Part of this controversy was a result of confusion about the different schemes in which she was engaged, so that some criticism directed against her mistakenly assumed that her dispatch of some hundreds of females at particular times was in an endeavour to place them as governesses, when usually they were going as domestic servants.

Miss Rye did little to sort out this confusion. She was ever ready to spring into print, as the following extracts from a letter published in the London *Times* on 5 September 1862 show:

> A few days since a letter (written at Melbourne) was placed in my hands, in which the writer very pathetically and very emphatically urged the necessity of my being stopped and prevented 'sending out a quarter of a million of educated women'. Hydras, gorgons, and chimeras dire! If such is the impression abroad no wonder *Argus* rolls his eyes and sounds the alarm.
>
> Heaven forbid that I should refuse to listen to any voice of real warning, let the voice sound from what quarter it may; but as long as every girl we send abroad gets comfortably placed within a few hours after landing, receives a fair sum for her services, and continues to write home happily, I shall consider myself perfectly justified in considering my work a success. By the July mail we received £10 from a young governess, part of the loan lent her to reach Sydney. This girl had been out of a situation in England six months before starting, and yet within a year after landing in Australia she could save the sum named out of her salary. Does not this fact speak for itself? . . .
>
> I shall conclude my letter by quoting the *Melbourne Herald* of the 14th of June, as the advice tallies with the suggestions embodied in my paper on the subject read at the Guildhall this summer, in which I particularly dwelt on the necessity of women working, whether at home or abroad, more honestly and earnestly at domestic work. The *Herald* says: 'If a lady is not afraid of work she will have little difficulty in obtaining employment in a respectable household in some domestic capacity. If she is content to earn a comfortable livelihood in some capacity not exactly menial, but yet not quite that of companion to the mistress of the house, she will find her services in eager request at good wages. This is the kind of help which ladies in Australia require. We do not like to use the word 'servant', for that implies the kitchen, and the scullery, and the laundry; but it is the something between servant and governess that is really wanted here (e.g. middle-class girls), and for which liberal remuneration would be paid. A well-educated, handy, thoroughly useful young lady, who would aid the overworked housewife in her multifarious labours, who would keep the young ones in the nursery in order, teach the four-years-old the rudiments

of learning, be an intelligent companion for an elder daughter — who would be, in a word, like a good maiden aunt in the house, would be valued in scores of colonial homes as a real treasure. This is precisely the class of young ladies which, next to domestic servants, we want most sadly in the colonies. If Miss Rye and her friends at home will favour us by sending us a few candidates for emigration of that stamp we shall promise to receive them with open arms and to obtain for them instant and well-paid employment.'

Miss Rye quotes this editorial with approval, but the *Herald's* views were not those of most of the FMCES emigrants, who saw their role as being above any involvement in domestic duties.

As a class, the English governess was a strong element in a class-conscious society, in which she held an ambivalent position. Governesses were expected to be well-bred and genteel, yet materially they were poor and deprived. Charlotte Bronte, who had experience as a governess, summed up society's attitude to these women in *Shirley*:

The daughters of tradespeople, however well-educated, must necessarily be underbred, and as such unfit to be the inmates of OUR dwellings, or guardians of OUR children's minds and persons. We should never prefer to place those about OUR offspring who have not been born and bred with somewhat of the same refinements as OURSELVES.

The governesses who ventured abroad went complete with an inner consciousness of and acceptance of strong class divisions. They almost all objected to travelling second class — although they had to borrow money to buy even second-class tickets — not mainly because of the discomfort, but because they felt superior to the people with whom they had to mix. Once settled in their new homes, they were very conscious of any attempts to involve them in duties they considered beneath them. In short, they often were unfitted for the more egalitarian colonial society.

Some women, however, adapted well, while those who were unsuited to their new lives can be contrasted to those who were exploited. In all the countries to which they emigrated, these women entered a buyer's market: there were always more governesses seeking employment than there were jobs available, and in times of economic depression, so widespread in the 1860s and 1870s, the market for their skills dried up almost completely. They had practically no bargaining power over wages (some were reduced to taking unpaid jobs in order to get accommodation); only the highly accomplished who were able to teach a range of subjects, such as French, German and sometimes Latin, music, singing and drawing, could command reasonable salaries. These women, although not under as much pressure to take any job offered, compared with those less qualified, were still vulnerable to finding themselves employed in an uncongenial, or at worst intolerable, family situation. Further, they could be located in an inaccessible part of the country, perhaps up to a week's journey by coach and steamer from town, and requiring relatively a large amount of money for the return fare, should they manage to extricate themselves.

Even when employed in a relatively good position, a governess often was expected to do some domestic work and light sewing, as well as to teach five or six children of different ages and at varying levels. Depending on the circumstances, domestic work could be a pleasant way of occupying the time or a most resented imposition.

A governess also was extremely vulnerable to financial and other changes in her employer's situation. Most of all, she was vulnerable to the devastating effect of illness, which not only could involve loss of income but loss of accommodation and, sometimes, a quite desperate struggle merely to survive. Such illness often was a result of the abnormal stresses of leaving family and friends (usually for ever), the worries of a long sea journey at a time when shipping disasters were common and the trauma of adjusting to a new life in a very different environment, a life that may bring unemployment or cruel treatment by an employer and often required demanding tasks for low pay. Those women who had relatives to rely on for moral and material support were fortunate.

A poignant description of the trauma that resulted from arriving at a new position as a governess was written by Mrs Thomas, one whose arrival in Australia predated that of the first of the FMCES emigrants by almost two decades, but whose experiences spanned the same period and, in some cases, the same households. Writing under the pen-name 'Lyth', she said: 'One of the greatest trials of my life had been the inevitable feeling of utter loneliness when first entering a family as a stranger, where they were all so familiar, so bound up together by the ties of home affection'.*

Although she remained associated with the FMCES during its existence, Maria Rye, after her return to England in 1865 from a trip to New Zealand and Australia, turned the major part of her interests to the emigration of destitute and neglected children. She purchased and lived in Avenue House in the then semi-rural district of Peckham, where she took in girls from workhouses and the slums to train in domestic work.

Maria Rye continued this work until the late 1890s. She then retired to Hemel Hempstead, in Hertfordshire, where she died on 12 November 1903 at the age of seventy-four. In a long obituary, published on 17 November, the London *Times* said of her: '[Miss Rye] was of a very strong character and physique and held intense religious convictions'. The obituary dealt mainly with her efforts in promoting the emigration of destitute girls, but also mentioned her efforts in providing work for women of the governess class by starting a law stationers' firm, in association with Jane Lewin, and in the formation of the Female Middle Class Emigration Society, also with Jane Lewin. Of this work, the obituary recorded that Miss Rye 'visited, between 1860 and 1868, Australia, New Zealand, and Canada, her aim being to study the problem of emigration from the colonial standpoint. She met with cordial support from leading colonists, and during those years — largely owing to the advocacy of *The Times* and to the efforts of Miss Lewin — Miss Rye was instrumental in transferring to the Colonies numbers of girls of the middle classes'.

*'Lyth' (Mrs Thomas), *The Golden South: Memories of Australian Home Life from 1843 to 1888*, Ward & Downey, London, 1890, p. 173.

2 *The Voyage Out*

'. . . *no* Lady *should come out on those emigrant ships*'.

I. M. Cary, Dunedin, 1863

Before confronting the problems of adjustment in a sometimes hostile environment, the governesses who decided to forsake their families and friends in Britain, in the hope of achieving happiness and prosperity overseas, also had to face the daunting prospect of a long sea voyage.

Travel by sea in the nineteenth century was often a hazardous undertaking, and for emigrants travelling as far as Australia and New Zealand, it was especially so. The voyage, usually by sailing-ship, rarely took less than three months and often much longer; it traversed extremes of climate from the intense and humid heat at the Equator to the icy gales and storms of the southern ocean; it was usually uncomfortable, cramped, regimented and tedious; the food was dreary and monotonous, if not actually lacking in essentials; and severe seasickness and serious epidemic diseases were common.

Like all migrants to Australia, New Zealand and South Africa, the FMCES emigrants approached the long sea journey with much trepidation. Those who experienced a comfortable and not overlong voyage were happy to write a favourable report to the Society, reports into which can be read a good deal of relief that they had managed to survive the journey. Those who did not suffer from seasickness, were happy to record the fact.

Most, however, had complaints to make, usually about the physical discomforts of the trip and the necessary association with people of all classes, particularly emigrants of the lower classes. Both complaints resulted from the fact that most governesses travelled second class. This was not nearly as spartan or uncomfortable as that provided for the great bulk of migrants who travelled steerage, where they were herded in extraordinarily over-crowded, often dirty and wet conditions, below the waterline, and were supplied with only a minimum of basic food-stuffs, from which they had to prepare their own meals at communal fires. However, although second-class passengers were spared some of these indignities they were not nearly as comfortably provided for as those who travelled first class. The evidence of the governesses letters indicates that in second class, there were often too many passengers to a cabin and any small material comforts, so necessary on a long sea voyage, had to be provided by the passengers themselves.

Despite these conditions, many of the emigrant governesses reported favourably on their voyage. Fanny Giles, who arrived in Sydney on 3 August 1864 on the *Spray of the Ocean* after a voyage of fourteen weeks, during which they at first had 'beautiful weather', then 'heavy gales and contrary winds', said, in a letter dated 10 September, she suffered 'but little' from seasickness and liked the voyage so well she would 'not mind having another were it necessary'. She evidently was a brave and intrepid traveller, for a report on this voyage published in the *Sydney Mail,* quoting Captain Slaughter, said that on 22 June, south-west of the Cape of Good Hope, the ship had been struck by a heavy gale from the north-west, which lasted four hours. This fell suddenly to a calm with very heavy turbulent seas, resembling the middle of a cyclone. The ship had been unmanageable, the seas falling heavily on stern and bow continually, carrying away the jib boom and doing much other damage.

Florence Allen, who landed at Albany on 22 January 1880, reported in a letter dated 10 March, from Perth, that she had had a fair' voyage with 'only a moderate amount of rough weather, pleasant travelling companions and the kindest of chaperones and a hearty welcome from my sister and her friends .

Emily Streeter, travelling to Sydney on the *Rachel* in 1861, said in a letter dated 18 January 1862 that she had had 'on the whole a very favourable voyage'. The captain and the mates 'were very kind and attentive and did all in their power for our comfort'. Elizabeth Boake, in a letter dated 23 March

1867, said of her voyage of three and a half months in the *Forest Rights,* which arrived in Melbourne on 13 January 1867, that it was long and pleasant, 'my fellow passengers and the Captain were all so kind and attentive that the time seemed to pass quite quickly'. An *Argus* report of this voyage said that it had been protracted, mainly because of light winds and exceedingly fine weather. The passengers praised Captain R. H. Carey's courtesy and attention to their comfort.

Jane Finch, who arrived in Sydney on 8 July 1864 on the *Bucton Castle* with Miss Edwards, said in a letter dated 21 September that their voyage had been perfectly safe, but 'long and tedious'. The ship took three months on the voyage from the Downs to Sydney, carrying among her fifteen passengers two Primitive Methodist pastors.

Mary Bayly, who arrived on the *Nourmahal* on 28 November 1866, had a 'pleasant voyage although a slow one. I . . . enjoyed it greatly, indeed I was almost sorry when we came to land.' Like several others, Mary Bayly mentions in her letter of 21 December, in almost surprised tones, that she was 'quite well the whole time' on the voyage. The *Sydney Morning Herald*'s account of the voyage reported that the ship struck an easterly gale with heavy rain near Cape Otway and later was becalmed at the Dromedary off the south coast of New South Wales for twenty hours, during which time 'a great many whales' played around the ship.

Louisa Geoghegan, who arrived in Melbourne a few days before Christmas 1866, after a 'pleasant and favourable voyage', sent a cutting from the Melbourne *Argus* describing the voyage in a letter dated 19 February 1867 to the Society. The newspaper reported the arrival of 'the celebrated clipper ship of Messrs Green's Blackwall line', *Swiftsure,* on 20 December, 'after an excellent fair weather passage during which some splendid sailing was achieved'. The *Swiftsure* left Plymouth on 23 September and passed the meridian of the Cape of Good Hope on 23 November; 'for nearly 40 consecutive days the ship achieved an average of 236 knots, on a subsequent day she performed the not very common feat of 364 knots — a pace which is rarely equalled even on the long voyage'.

Mrs Margaret Allen, who arrived in Melbourne on the *Dover Castle* on 30 September 1864, was also happy with her voyage. Bishop Perry and Mrs Perry, returning to Melbourne after a trip to Great Britain, were first-class passengers on the same ship. In a letter dated 21 October, Mrs Allen wrote:

I have great pleasure in informing you I had a delightful passage on the *Dover Castle* and should occasion require, you need never fear sending any Lady out second Class while Captain Ayles has the Command. I cannot express the gratitude I feel to him and Mrs Ayles for their Kindness, their own dear little girl slept in the next Cabin to mine; as soon as we left Plymouth, the Captain ordered two berths to be taken out of my Cabin, so I had with me but one person, a quiet religious young woman, nurse to a family, who left at six in the morning and did not come in till nine at night so I had plenty of room and every comfort possible. We landed on Thursday 30 September. My son came in a boat to meet the Ship before we anchored.

The Bishop had prayers twice a day, regularly gave lectures and did all he could to instruct and entertain every one· we had a peaceful and pleasant time, no serious illness or accident.

Other governesses were less happy about their crossing. Many were critical of their accommodation, their treatment during the voyage and their fellow passengers, particularly those they considered to be of a lower class. Filth, drunkenness, swearing and 'horrid' people were only some of their complaints. Miss A. H. Jackson, who emigrated to Natal in March 1863 on the *Durban* said, in a letter dated May 1863, 'the ship was very badly provisioned and badly appointed and the filth disorder and confusion were monstrous'.

Maria Barrow, who arrived in Melbourne on 28 January 1862 with other FMCES emigrants including Caroline Heawood, on the *Dover Castle* 'certainly did not like the voyage' and did not think anything 'would ever induce me to try the Sea again under similar circumstances'. She continued, in her letter of 17 February:

Miss Heawood was unwell several times, but generally we were pretty well, though I oftener than not had a headache and now and then a small disaster — once, for instance, I put my foot into a can in the dark and fell head forward into the Cabin and sprained my finger rather badly — I have not recovered the use of it yet and it was six weeks before I left the Ship. Another time when we shipped a Sea, Miss H. and I had a famous tumble into our Cabins — it quite shook the breath out of my body. *She* knows best about *hers*, but I don't fancy she enjoyed it much — I can afford to laugh at it now, but I assure you we could not force a smile at the time. I think we had a great deal of rough weather; at any rate we had plenty of wet and were reported in the paper to have had a wet and rough passage.

Catherine Crowe, who arrived with her sister at Durban on the *Dudbrook* on 2 June 1862, described their trip, in a letter dated 1 July, as 'a most tedious, disagreeable voyage in consequence of contrary winds and calms'. They had to put into Algoa Bay on the west coast for provisions and water, but these again ran short before they reached Natal. However, she reported they had the most comfortable sleeping cabin on the ship, thanks to Miss Rye.

There is no record of any of the emigrant governesses being lost in a shipwreck, but the fear of that fate hung heavily over all who travelled in sailing-ships and reports of shipping disasters were common.

Kate Brind, writing from New Zealand to Miss Lewin in a letter dated 27 July 1873, nearly a year after she left England, said: 'Have you sent many young ladies out since I left? The shipwrecks we read of now are something terrible, it almost makes one dread the idea of going on a sea voyage.' Emily Nelson wrote from South Africa, in a letter dated 29 February 1876: 'We had a long voyage, but we reached Port Elizabeth in safety at last, after a good many stoppages and after having nearly run aground on a small Island near the Cape'.

One who came very close to disaster was Miss M. Crowley, who travelled from England to Sydney under sail in 1881. This was unusual in itself, for steamships and steam-assisted vessels by then had been carrying most Australian-bound travellers for some years, particularly after the wreck of the clipper-ship *Loch Ard* on the southern coast of Victoria in 1878, when only two of the fifty-two passengers and crew were saved. Miss Crowley's voyage went well until the ship neared Melbourne, then:

We were eleven weeks on the way, and with the exception of two severe storms, the passage was a good one, till within 40 hours' sail of Melbourne when she stranded and after five hours' signalling, firing and waiting, three steamers came alongside; the passengers were all transferred to one of them and safely landed in Melbourne, where I had to stay a week till I got my boxes from the ship, only losing what was left in the Cabin.

How very insignificant *everything* but sweet life appeared to me that morning when I scrambled down the side of that splendid ship and got into the small boat; they did not know at what moment she might break up. The passengers' baggage was taken off in tugs and a great deal of valuable cargo thrown overboard.

Miss Crowley's adventurous arrival in Australia most probably took place aboard the iron barque *Hereford,* which ran aground on the Victorian coast on a reef near Swampy Creek, about twenty-four miles from Geelong, on 9 January 1881, after being becalmed off Cape Otway. She remained stuck all night, bumping heavily in the swell. After some delay, all fifty passengers and Captain McCarthy were landed near Anglesea and found shelter at residences nearby. Some passengers travelled by buggy to Geelong and coaches were sent from there for the others. Some were later taken to Melbourne on the coastal ship the *Edina* and others travelled from Geelong by train.

On 18 January, a seaman and a policeman, who had been on board the *Hereford,* were drowned when a wave capsized a boat carrying nineteen men from the ship to the shore. The *Hereford* was sold, her remaining cargo was unloaded and she was pumped dry before being towed clear of the reef on 17 February by the Melbourne tug *Albatross,* which had come to the rescue. During the tow to Melbourne, she became unmanageable and the steamer *Nelson* stood by until she passed through the Heads, where the tug *Racer* joined in towing her to port.

Although the *Hereford* seems to be the only shipwreck that took place at approximately the right time and place to fit Miss Crowley's description, she is not listed in newspaper reports among the passengers on the ship. However, she may have been the unnamed 'servant' listed among the first-class passengers who accompanied Mr and Mrs Steward and their two children. When the passengers arrived in Melbourne, those who were unable to arrange their own accommodation, were put up at either the Immigrants' Home (women and children) or the Model Lodging Home (men), before going on to their original destinations. Miss Crowley said she travelled to Sydney by steamer.

Eliza Maria Ford also described a dramatic voyage to Sydney with her sister and Caroline Lash in 1864, aboard the *Caroline Coventry,* when, she said, the crew of the ship mutinied. She wrote, in a letter dated 1 November 1864 from Cleves, Ryde, near Kissing Point, Sydney:

My voyage out was in every respect a most disagreeable one; we encountered very bad weather with heavy gales. The sailors took offence at some orders of the Captain's and mutinied. They not only refused to work but threatened to murder the Captain and the Chief Officer. They were, of course, put in irons until they promised to return to their duty, which was not until the end of the week.

Her critical comments on her fellow passengers reflect those made by some other governesses:

The Cabin passengers were also extremely disagreeable, so that I can with truth say I had not one pleasant day during the whole of the four months' voyage.

The other FMCES passenger on the *Caroline Coventry* who wrote to the Society, Caroline Lash, did not mention a mutiny. In fact, in her letter dated 21 September from Miller's Point, Sydney, she said she enjoyed her voyage 'very much and arrived quite safely and in health'. She continued:

Our passage was prolonged as we were compelled to go round Tasmania, which added 700 miles to the voyage — the latter part was very rough indeed, the last gale we experienced was of 48 hours' duration without a single lull. The greater part of the Bulwarks were washed away, which gave free admission to Neptune and kept the deck continually wet. We 'hove to' off the Heads in the Gale. I like the Captain and his Wife very much, they were most kind to me in every way. There was a very kind Portuguese Lady on board who was very kind to me; I liked the other Ladies very much.

The voyage of the *Caroline Coventry*, which ended in Sydney on 3 September 1864, was quite hazardous, according to a report by Captain Jones published in the *Sydney Mail*, although his account does not include a mutiny. The Captain said the ship had struck a succession of heavy gales from all points of the compass, from the Cape of Good Hope to Cape Leeuwin. During a violent gale, a heavy sea had broken on board, filling the decks and cabin and washing away the bulwarks on both sides and doing other damage. The vessel was making water and 500 barrels of flour stowed in the afterhold had to be thrown overboard, which made the vessel easier to handle and decreased the leakage of water. Later, a gale that lasted four days forced Captain Jones to go south of

Tasmania and he had rounded the South West Cape on 28 August. On the way up to Sydney, he had struck another furious gale.

The McGillivray sisters also had a stormy passage while travelling on the *Result* from Scotland to Melbourne, where they arrived on 27 August 1862. They met continuous gales and tempestuous weather from the Cape of Good Hope to Port Phillip Bay. Ships at this time usually followed the Great Circle route through the southern ocean, sailing into Antarctic waters to latitudes as far as 55° south, to shorten the journey between the Cape of Good Hope and the Australian west coast. Writing to Miss Rye in a letter dated 24 September 1862, Isabella McGillivray said of the voyage she made with her three sisters:

You will be glad to learn that we have all arrived in safety with the *Result* after a very quick passage of 69 days. We had a very pleasant run from Plymouth till we came near the Cape, winds fair and no calm, except for one day or part of a day. Rations abundant and excellent of their kind, although we never got to take some of the things, and the Cabin was always very dirty owing to the stupidity of a conceited boy who acted the part of an experienced steward with very poor success. When nearly off the Cape we encountered a dreadful gale with very heavy seas from the meeting of the Oceans and after that till we got within the Heads we had a succession of gales, tempestuous weather, wind and rain all the way. The *Result* must be a fine vessel to have passed through what it did without injury and I feel I would not like to say a word against the good ship that has brought us through such troublous waters — Captain Dickinson is a very prudent and cautious commander, too much so in some people's estimation, who thought we should [have had] many times much more sail on, but *we* felt comfort in thinking that what could be done for safety had been done — I cannot say he is a popular Captain but everyone acknowledges that he takes good care of the Ship. So far as my Sisters and I were concerned he was always kind and Mrs Dickinson very kind and friendly. We have met them several times when crossing to Melbourne since our landing.*

We got into the Bay on the 27th August, but one of my sisters only went on Shore as the Sea was rough and the wind high and another of my sisters, Caroline, was very ill and we had to wait till the Ship would come up to the pier, which it did next morning. She

---

*The McGillivrays lived at Williamstown on Port Phillip Bay, to the south-west of Melbourne, to which they travelled by ferry across the bay.

had got cold during the hot weather and when the Storms came on there was no comfort and her cold incurable, so that she was very ill indeed and we could not have the same treatment at Sea that she would have required, blistering etc., besides nourishing food. She was able to walk on Shore a quarter of a mile.

Although many of the governesses complained about having to travel second class, the Society remained in favour of second-class travel, no doubt because this limited the amount the emigrants needed to borrow for their fares and kept their repayments within reasonable bounds. Often the complaints about second-class travel related to fellow passengers rather than to any actual discomfort in the accommodation. Many of the governesses felt their natural and rightful place was with the type of people who travelled first class, and some thought that travelling second class would hinder them in obtaining good positions in their adopted countries.

On a few occasions, the Society apparently was able to obtain first-class passages at no extra cost, sometimes by arranging for a governess to travel as a companion to another passenger. This was the case with Annie Davis, who arrived in Melbourne on the *Revenue* on 27 July 1863, as companion to Miss Bryant, the only female first-class passenger. Although not listed as a first-class passenger, by sharing a cabin with Miss Bryant, she would have had all the advantages of first-class travel. Annie then travelled on to Sydney, from where she wrote, in a letter dated September 1863:

It has been undoubtedly a great advantage for me having come *first* class. Messrs Foulders behaved very generously in their arrangements, though in some respects it was a mutual advantage, for my fellow passenger would not have sailed in the *Revenue* had she been the only Lady passenger; anyhow, it materially increased the comfort of my voyage.

The *Revenue* arrived in Melbourne after a voyage of 13 weeks and 2 days. We found on coming into Port and comparing notes with other vessels that ours was a singularly favourable voyage; the majority of ships then arriving having met with severe disasters. For the first six weeks out we were favoured with glorious weather and a rapid course, for the remainder of the time we had variable light winds, calms, etc., also two most severe gales.

I suffered very little from seasickness. I was very glad when the voyage was over for, at the best, a long voyage is wearisome. I and the other Lady shared a Cabin; the arrangements were very comfortable, the rooms being unusually large and airy. I cannot speak too highly of the Captain and Officers; they were very kind, also my fellow passengers. I enjoyed my stay at Melbourne very much. I had letters of introduction there and found some kind friends. I was there from Monday 27 July to Thursday 30. I received every attention from Messrs Foulders' Agents there — Henty and Co. I took a First Class passage from Melbourne to Sydney — the fare for it £7, of which I paid £4, the fare is exorbitant for the two days' passage, but everything provided is '*first class*'. I enjoyed the trip to Sydney exceedingly. I was so inured to the sea that even a screw steamer and rough weather did not affect me.

Annie Davis's trip to Sydney was made, as a first-class passenger, on the *Rangatira,* which arrived on 2 August.

A first-class passage to Melbourne also was arranged for Annie Hunt, who arrived on 21 September 1869 on the *Highflyer*. A fellow passenger, however, made the voyage unpleasant by implying that she was a recipient of charity. As she reported to Miss Rye in a letter dated 11 October:

You will be glad to hear I have arrived quite safely at my journey's end after a very rapid passage, in fact the shortest made . . .

I have been very ill the greater part of the voyage, but received every kindness and attention and, as far as possible, comfort, though, of course, you know from experience this last commodity is difficult to obtain on board ship. However, here again I am deeply thankful to you for the happy change in my Cabin, for had I travelled as arranged I really do not think I should ever have reached Melbourne alive. They were such a dirty, inferior sort of people there.

[Firstly,] my voyage was extremely unpleasant as there was only one other Lady and, secondly, because one of the passengers found out that through your kindness I was travelling first class and, in consequence of this, he took every occasion to insult me by talking to others about me before my face and not even sparing my good name, seeming to think you employed your energy and [?time in] reformatory work and that I was one of its objects. On many such occasions I had to rise and leave the table because I would not speak to such a man and knew it would be no use to cause further words. However, I had a very pleasant friendly companion, a Mrs Tait, and a very kind friend in the Doctor, whom I could not thank enough for his trouble and attention. On more than one occasion he wished me to let him mention my unpleasant situation to the Captain, but I thought, as it would only last a few short weeks, it would be best to let it pass unnoticed if possible, and when this man found I treated him with contempt he got tired out before the voyage was quite over and wanted to be quite polite to me, so I was. I had not mentioned anything about it and I hope you think I acted right in doing so.

The first-class passengers who arrived on Green's Blackwall Line ship the *Highflyer*, under Captain William Harrison, were the Reverend George Tait and Mrs Tait, Miss Hunt, Dr Penfold, and Messrs Alex Leeper, Gage and Littlewood. The *Argus* reported that the ship had made a 'very excellent passage' and continued: 'The *Highflyer* has ever held premier rank with regard to rapid sailing and her present voyage out accomplished in 69 days from the Lizard to Cape Otway, has tended to confirm her already established and well acquired reputation'.

Another who travelled first class, although how this was arranged is not clear, was Mrs Lucy Phillips, who emigrated to Melbourne in 1873, accompanied by her small son. She arrived on 24 June on the *Carlisle Castle* and wrote from South Yarra, on 12 August:

. . . let me express my gratitude through you to Mr Henry Green for so very kindly and unexpectedly giving me a *First Class* passage with my dear little Boy. It was not until I was actually on board on the Monday, that I knew of my piece of good fortune, and I was some time before I could rest satisfied that there was not some mistake in the matter. However, my doubts were dispelled when Mr Green and Son came into my Cabin, and told me himself about it.

Was it not a pity about all my fittings? Most of them are perfectly useless of course, and I had no alternative but to dispose of them to the Chief Steward, whom I found out when it was too late to be a fearful rogue. He only gave me 30/- for the whole lot.

Rosa Phayne, who arrived in Melbourne on 24 May 1869 on the *Roxburgh Castle* and who hated the voyage, as she was to hate everything about life in Australia, nevertheless realised that travelling second class had at least saved her from incurring a greater debt. She was apparently one of the Society's emigrants who had enough money to pay her fare, but used the other services offered by the Society, such as the arrangement of favourable rates for fares and cabin fittings, and introductions to representatives in the country of destination. In a letter dated 13 August, she wrote:

Our voyage was an extremely protracted one, so very long, so often a calm. The passengers I detested beyond words; they were so very low and horrid a set. I regretted greatly coming second class; still, now I am so glad I have no debt on my mind.

Maria Atherton, who with her sister and another governess, Jane Smith, had a particularly bad experience on her trip to Brisbane on the *Young Australia* in 1862, was so incensed at her treatment that she wanted the Society to try to get a refund from the shipping company. Her letter, dated 'August and 2 September 1862', did not arrive in London until 30 January 1863, after being saved from the wreck of the *Colombo*, a reminder of the hazards of sea travel. She wrote to Miss Rye:

You will no doubt have heard of the arrival of the *Young Australia* after a favourable passage of 85 days from Plymouth; *speedy* I should say rather than favourable . . .

We were treated very unjustly on board the ship, as the other parties can fully testify and, if properly represented to the Black Ball Co. and Mr Jordan,* I think they cannot fail in *common justice* to return us £5 each of the passage money. We should have had much better accommodation in the intermediate than in the second Cabin.

Being short of room they placed four of us in a Cabin *not so large* as the others which contained *only two persons*. We had *no light* and *no air* and were therefore quite unable to retire to our berths and though we were the only parties deprived of a seat at the Table in the second Cabin and obliged to stand or seat ourselves on boxes, which was objectionable to others. Then we were frequently deprived of water and rations as we were unable to fetch them ourselves and there was no one to get them for us. The last week we were almost starved (and our appetites were never very large); we had neither flour nor meat nor, in fact, anything at all but a few Stale Biscuits. — The Stores were abundant enough, but the others got the Lion's Share.

I have enclosed you the 'Lay of the 2nd Cabin'** in which I have just *sketched out* a little of our life on board the *Young Australia*. The Saloon Passengers objected to the 2nd Class on the Poop (rather unusual exclusiveness, I believe), consequently a large number of free Emigrants and Passengers were huddled together in a dense mob on the decks and the noise, filth, drunkenness and swearing

---

*Henry Jordan, Queensland government emigration agent in London.

**Unfortunately, not included in the FMCES records.

were altogether frightful. True they cleared a small space for a 2nd class Poop in the Tropics and this was a relief, but it did not suit in rough weather. Providence was very gracious to us or with such a reckless, drunken mob, we should never have reached our destined port safely . . .

My sister and I were never sea-sick and should have enjoyed the passage if there had been any decency or order but, huddled together as we were, it was perfectly *miserable* and we should have been glad even to have been in steerage where there *was more ventilation and light* . . .

If the Black Ball Co. will return some of the passage money, and we surely cost them very little and had wretched accommodation for £60, will you please pay the Bill at Silver's [for cabin fittings] and forward the balance per next Mail . . .

The *Chatsworth*, which left Liverpool a month before we sailed, reached Moreton Bay only two or three days before us and, having been in quarantine, only lands her Passengers today.

Miss I. M. Cary had a similar experience when she travelled to Dunedin on the *Telegraph*, which left England in March 1863 on a voyage that took 104 days. She found her cabin so unsatisfactory that, after sitting up for two nights, she complained to the captain. He moved her to another cabin, which she shared with a young English farmer and his two young sisters, where she got more air, being near the door. This apparently strange arrangement for those circumspect times was accepted by Miss Cary without question, perhaps an indication of how unbearable her original accommodation must have been. She wrote to Miss Lewin on 18 October 1863:

I can assure you, to me the passage was most trying. We had food enough, I had so many things of my own, I did not suffer as much as others, but oh Miss Lewin, no *Lady* should come out on those emigrant ships.

Travelling on ships carrying government-assisted emigrants was a particular cause of concern to some governesses. Marion Hett, who had a fast trip of only eighty-one days when she arrived on the *Ramsey* at Christchurch in June 1870, was one of these. In a letter dated 23 June, from Lyttleton Harbour, she reported:

Certainly if one could choose one would not select a ship which carried Government emigrants. The girls were always on the poop

Maria S. Rye *Church of England Children's Society, London*

Mrs Jane Barker, wife of Bishop Barker, one of the FMCES's Sydney representatives who assisted the emigrant governesses.
National Library of Australia

with us, and often annoyed us extremely by their levity of conduct. They ought never to come out in a ship with mixed passengers, but, if possible, emigrants should have a vessel to themselves, for, however steady girls might be before starting, a voyage like this must inevitably spoil them.

Fanny Cross, destined for Dunedin in 1879, apparently as a third-class or steerage passenger, also found the passengers 'very common' and '[it was] quite impossible for me to live three months with them'. According to her letter of 16 July 1880, written from 143 George Street, Dunedin, she and her mother apparently inspected the ship before the sailing date and her mother decided to pay extra money to allow Fanny to travel second class. As Fanny wrote: 'They built at Falmouth a little cabin, so I was very comfortable, besides the Captain was a gentleman and made it very comfortable for me as I was the only one travelling alone'. This speedy change in accommodation probably would have been achieved by putting up a partition in an already existing cabin.

The governesses who enjoyed themselves most were those who joined in the social activities of shipboard life. Eliza Walpole, who emigrated to Victoria on the *Result*, which arrived in August 1863, under Captain H. T. Dickinson, wrote a detailed description to Miss Lewin in a letter dated 21 September 1863, from 'Musk Cottage', near Ballarat:

I am sure you will be glad to hear that of God's great mercy the *Result* with all on board anchored safely in Hobson's Bay on the 27th* of last month, having made the passage from Plymouth in 70 days. The first night after leaving Plymouth we had a severe gale, which lasted 24 hours, and again we had heavy weather for a few days before we anchored. With these exceptions we had incessant fine weather, indeed it was a most wonderful and agreeable voyage. Of course, we had the extremes of heat and cold, with a few calms. On these occasions boats were lowered and the gentlemen passengers rowed about and around our splendid vessel.

Through your kindness, Mr Selfe** saw everything was comfortably arranged for me on board. I had a berth in one of the largest and most airy Cabins. There were two passengers in the

---

*According to the *Argus*, the ship arrived on 29 August.

**Mr Selfe (or Self, according to another writer), apparently was an employee of either the Blackwall Shipping Line or S. W. Silver & Co., which arranged cabin accommodation.

Cabin with me, a kind, motherly woman and her daughter from Jersey. She was coming to join her husband who is a brick-layer and has been in these Colonies for some years. In the next Cabin was a very nice, well-educated Swiss lady, who had lived as Governess for some time in the Dean of Westminster's family. She was coming out to be married. I made a friend of her, and rarely spoke to any of the other passengers. Mr Cooper (the First Officer) was extremely kind and attentive to me, and anything I wanted I had only to ask him and he would be sure to see to it for me — I can never speak in too high terms of the kindness and gentlemanly manner in which the Captain and Officers treated me; the comfort of all on board was studied by them in every way.

During the voyage a fancy bazaar was held on board in aid of the funds of the Poplar Hospital.* There were two stalls of fancy and useful articles, and one of refreshments. It was held in the Saloon and the wonderful sum of £28–10–0 was raised. It afforded a great deal of pleasure and occupation for all who worked for it. The Captain said such a thing had never been heard of before as a Fancy Fair on board ship. It will, therefore, make the *Result* famous in the annals of the Poplar Hospital.

I am sorry not to have been able to send a few lines to you as you wished from Plymouth. I had written, but the Pilot went off leaving all our letters, which carried great disappointment to the passengers.

The *Argus* reported that the Blackwall ship *Result* had made a clipper passage of seventy-one days, sailing from Plymouth on 16 June. It had had generally fine weather during the voyage. The *Argus* described Captain H. T. Dickinson, as it had when the *Result* arrived in Melbourne a year before, as a 'gentleman well known in this trade' and added that on arrival he had been presented by his passengers with 'a very handsome address, expressive of their thanks for the great interest manifested and unremitting care displayed throughout the passage'.

Rosarie Winn, who emigrated to Durban in Natal in 1862, was a similarly happy passenger on the ship she refers to as the 'dear old *Dudbrook*'. She wrote from Durban, in a letter dated 25 June 1862:

We brought out a Paper called the *Dudbrook Chronicle* weekly, which I used to help the Captain to write and to which I contributed

*This hospital is situated in the docks area of East London, at 303–315 East India Dock Road, E14.

an article every now and then. The Farewell Letter, which is copied from our paper and appears in the *Natal Mercury*, is written by one of our Lady Passengers and Captain Duncan [*sic*] who was the Editor and used to read the Papers to us writes the concluding Lines so that he may not appear to be sounding his own praises. We used to have a Debating Society on board which met twice a week to discuss different topics and we kept it up during the whole voyage, but only the Gentlemen, of course, carried on the debates, so you see Miss Rye our time was well employed at Sea. I think all our papers ought to be printed and sent home for really there are some capital productions in them in the shape of Poetry, Critiques, etc. which are very good.*

Rosarie Winn described her voyage as being 'happy, prosperous and fair', taking seventy-eight days from the Downs, in contrast to her fellow passenger, Catherine Crowe, who found it tedious and disagreeable. Strikingly different comments on the same voyage are not uncommon and most probably can be attributed to the nature, expectations or health of the travellers. Those who were happy and sociable by nature, or were among friends, appeared to find even difficult voyages bearable, while others who perhaps suffered more from seasickness or were more distressed at leaving their homes and families and more apprehensive about the future, often found the voyage out unpleasant.

Another traveller to help raise money for charity on board ship was Louisa Dearmer, who arrived in Melbourne on 19 May 1868 aboard Green's Blackwall Line ship the

*The *Natal Mercury* of 21 June 1862 reported: 'The fine bark *Dudbrook*, Capt. Deacon, reached the outer anchorage, where she now lies, on Friday last, after a fine passage of 74 days from the Downs, all well. . . . The passengers had all disembarked by Saturday night, and are unanimous in their praises of both their ship and commander.' The *Mercury* said that it had 'been favoured with copies of the *Ocean Times* and the *Dudbrook Chronicle*, regularly issued on the voyage, which are both highly creditable productions', and went on to quote from the concluding article in the *Chronicle* written by 'a lady passenger': 'Dear Friends and Neighbours, — The scenes are rapidly closing, and the curtain will very shortly fall on our stage of life on board the *Dudbrook*. We must . . . thank that good Providence which has preserved us through our long and perilous voyage, and to Him commit our future lives and cares, praying for His blessing on our labours in our new home. . . . Before concluding, we will just turn, in quiet thought, to dear Old England. . . . We will not sigh, but go and make, as well as we can, another English house in another country. The reality is "work, work, work", persevere and be not down-cast at early difficulties. Let us separate in friendship, forgetting each other's faults and failings, and . . . be ever ready to lend a helping hand to one another. May success and happiness attend all in their separate vocations. . . . Farewell, Farewell, Farewell! . . .'

Anglesey, captained by Captain W. H. Mutter. She was one of six first-class passengers, the others including Deputy-Assistant Commissary-General Myddleton and Mrs Myddleton. Two days later, Louisa Dearmer left on the *City of Melbourne* for Sydney, where she arrived on 23 May 1868. In a letter dated 14 December, she wrote of her voyage on the *Anglesey*:

> Would you kindly do me the favour to ask Mr Self if he would send me the yearly report of the Merchants Seamen's Orphan Home? I want the one which will contain the subscription we got on board the *Anglesey*; it was £17. I have got the tin box which was nailed to the Mast of the *Anglesey*. Captain Mutter allowed me to have it to get it filled here if I can.

Passengers had to provide their own cabin fittings for the trip and one of the services provided by the Society was to arrange for the purchase and installation of these fittings for its emigrants. From the number of times it is mentioned, it seems that the Society used the London firm of S. W. Silver & Co. to supply such requisites.

Silver's, a well-known firm of outfitters, particularly of emigrants and travellers, had shops at 3 and 4 Bishopsgate and 66 and 67 Cornhill, London. The Bishopsgate establishment, the Emigration Warehouse, advertised a 'complete assortment of all requisites for the Voyage and the Colonies, namely — Warm and Light Clothing, Waterproof ditto, Shirts, Hosiery, Bedding, Mess Utensils, Lamps and Candles, Cabin Boxes, Flotable Mattresses & Life Belts (warranted), Rhodes' Patent Tents, &c.' It also offered to have 'Cabins secured and Fitted Up. Luggage Stored and Shipped'.

In a further advertisement, not likely to allay apprehension in intending travellers, Silver's advised it was the sole licensee of Laurie's Patent Flotable Mattresses, pillows, life belts and sundry buoyant articles, designed 'to preserve life in shipwreck'. Each mattress 'will sustain eight persons in water for an indefinite period ... Every pillow or seat cushion will sustain one or more persons. The life belts are preventives to sinking, the cheapest yet submitted, very portable, and applied in an instant in case of accident.' At the Bishopsgate Street address, opposite the London Tavern, 'a comfortable fit out for a month's voyage may be procured for 4 Guineas, including a Sinking-Preventive Mattress'.

Silver's also advertised that it had ladies' outfits suitable for Home, the Colonies and the Continent at its Cornhill warehouse, where ladies were waited on by female attendants. The company also supplied clothing for naval and army officers and the firm has continued to the present time as military outfitters.

One complaint about Silver's came from Emilie Glen, who arrived in Natal in 1866 after a passage of seventy-two days. In a letter dated 27 October from Verulam, Natal, she charged:

> Silver's did not send all the things I paid for. There was no toilet pail and the looking glass was about half the size of the one I paid for. I found the cupboard ordered was not needed as there was one in the ship, so the Carpenter, whom they sent, took it back with him.

When the travellers arrived at their destination, they had to dispose of their cabin fittings. Although some of the items were suitable for life in their new homes, the larger items could not be transported easily, so the governesses had to dispose of them as best they could — by sale or sometimes by literally throwing them overboard.

Cécile Nagelle, who travelled out on the Blackwall Line's *Anglesey* (bringing her canary Dickie with her), wrote at length on this problem of disposal of fittings. The *Anglesey* arrived in Melbourne on 20 December 1873, having left London on 11 September, but being becalmed for the first six days out. The *Argus* of 22 December reported that the ship had a chequered reputation, complaints having been made about her condition on the last voyage to England. She had since been caulked, overhauled and recoppered and had come out with a full complement of passengers and a 'large and valuable cargo'. An advertisement stated that the 'saloon cabins are fitted with cabin furniture and are *roomy*, well ventilated and lighted. Ladies and Gentlemen's bathrooms are provided. The Second and Third Class accommodations are fitted with every convenience for passengers.'

The conveniences provided in second class could not have included a mattress, since Cécile Nagelle had to dispose of hers on arrival. She travelled second class, unlike another FMCES emigrant, Edith Jadis, who was listed among the cabin passengers. Cécile Nagelle wrote from Melbourne, in a letter dated New Year's Eve:

Now as regards my Bedding, I sold my mattress on Board to one of the Passengers, of course, very much under value — also my water can-hook pot, cups and saucers — the wash basin, lantern, pillow and blankets I have kept — if I had not been able to sell the mattress I would have left it to the Carpenter as a perquisite, as he was so very obliging. I asked the Chief Mate what was generally done with the bedding etc. and he said it was thrown overboard. Mrs Roe* asked me to mention this to you, always to warn young ladies against bringing too heavy luggage as transport is so very expensive. Railways are not yet open everywhere . . .

I think Messrs Green have been very careless as regards my Contract Paper; they never sent one, after you had paid them the passage money; they knew very well I could not get my luggage without it, and how was I know? It was their business to attend to it. I had a great deal of work about it — was obliged to go again on Board the *Anglesey* to get an order from the Captain — then to the Agents for endorsement of the same, again to the station to claim my luggage, all this walking about has done me much harm, so far that it increased both pain and swelling in my leg, which I hurt very much through falling down a ladder a few days' previous to our landing. I was forced to get medical advice and the Doctor ordered me rest for one week, and to apply cold water to the bruise . . .

I tell you about the contract paper as it may be a warning to others and I think Messrs Green ought to be told of it. If ever I go back to England I hope I shall not be obliged to travel second class; it is very unpleasant and uncomfortable, for a single Lady particularly. As far as the Cabin is concerned, it was very nice and, indeed, I am glad I had it all to myself with Dickie to keep me company — but he did not take up much room — I am so glad I got him with me; he was no trouble either going on board, or on shore — he looks so handsome and sings so well. I think the Sea air has done me much good, I am reaping the benefit of it now; I never felt better.

Martha Wyett, who arrived in New Zealand in January 1866 to work at Wairarapa, gave her cabin fittings away, but regretted this later, as she reported in her letter of 10 February:

. . . the bed, pillow, chair and carpets I gave away, but I should have found them exceedingly useful had I brought them with me . . .

The voyage I enjoyed especially to the Cape for the weather was warmer, but never did I find the heat so great as to be oppressive

---

*Mrs Roe was matron of the Governesses' and Servants' Home, Melbourne.

and uncomfortable, from the Cape to Wellington we had not one warm day, to me it was painfully cold.

Few commented on the impact of the unfamiliar scenery of new lands. One who did was Sarah Hammett, who arrived in Melbourne as a cabin passenger on the *Orwell* on 22 February 1870, being described on the shipping-list as a thirty-year-old governess. Her arrival took place during the bush-fire season and on 28 February, she wrote:

It has not been hot here since my arrival — but I hear that it was almost unbearable a short time before, indeed, we were pretty sure that it was so before we came up as the 'Otway' and 'King Island' seemed to be all on fire. I hope we shall get some rain — everything looks so parched and withered.

Another, Mrs C. Barton, travelled on the *Blackwall* around Tasmania, arriving in Sydney on 7 January 1864. 'With Sydney Heads I was enchanted', she wrote to Miss Lewin in a letter dated 18 January, 'also the Southern Coast of Tasmania'.

I know you will be glad to hear of the safe arrival of the *Blackwall* and its Company; we reached this on the 7th after a very prosperous voyage — I can speak in the highest terms of Captain Hanson's kindness and consideration, also of the good ship *Blackwall*, in which we all (humanly speaking) felt secure.

Fanny Thomas found the approaches to Port Chalmers and Dunedin very beautiful when she reached New Zealand in 1864. In a letter of 12 July, she reported:

Of course you will have heard what a long passage we had. I was very glad when we anchored at Port Chalmers. I think you would very much like New Zealand. That is if you . . . admire wild scenery. The sail from the 'Heads' into Port Chalmers was very beautiful; the high Hills on either side and the pretty little wooden houses along the shore presented a very pretty appearance. On the left as we entered is the Maori Settlement. The Missionary has his house in the middle of their huts. The town of Port Chalmers is small and peculiarly situated, the houses are so scattered, and the streets are very steep, the harbour is small and both difficult and dangerous to enter on account of the bar and sandbanks, which have made the passage up very narrow. The sail from Port Chalmers to Dunedin is equally as pretty as in some parts the banks are thickly wooded, some of the shrubs were very peculiar. The Fern trees were a great height; the trees retain their foliage all the year round. I would very much like you to see the Bush.

First-class passengers dined at the captain's table; however, for others, the food and drink provided on board ship was very basic and many governesses advised intending emigrants to bring some supplies of their own, to add variety to the shipboard meals. S. W. Silver's *Emigration Guide* listed the allowance of food in second class, intermediate and steerage per week per adult as:

Preserved Meats and Soups 2 lb; Beef 1¼ lb; Pork 1 lb; Bread 3½ lb; Flour 3 lb; Oatmeal 1 lb; Rice ½ lb; Peas ½ lb; Preserved Potatoes 1 lb; Suet 6 oz; Cheese 8 oz; Butter 12 oz; Tea 2 oz; Coffee 4 oz; Sugar 1 lb; Loaf Sugar 6 oz; Raisins ½ lb; Pickles or Vinegar 1 gill; Mustard ½ oz; Pepper ¼ oz; Salt 2 oz; Lime juice 6 oz; Water 21 quarts.

But even first-class passengers felt the monotony of shipboard food. Elizabeth Boake, writing of her voyage to Melbourne as a first-class passenger on the *Forest Rights*, in her letter dated 23 March 1867, said: 'I would certainly advise a supply of medicines and some kind of pleasant drink, such as raspberry vinegar for variety; one gets so tired of lime juice!'

Jane Kidson, who arrived in Melbourne on the *Alfred* on 8 October 1863, advised other travellers, in a letter dated 23 October, to do as she did and bring with them on board ship 'Jam, Eggs, Potted Meats, Potatoes, Onions', to supplement their shipboard meals. She added:

. . . the living is so very different to what we are accustomed to that we felt the want of some little things. I cannot speak too highly of the attention of the head Steward; he sent us so many things to our comfort. I consider we were very much favoured — so I may safely say the voyage was a very happy one.

Margaret Pyman, writing from 11 Macquarie Street, Sydney, on 18 August 1865, after thanking Miss Lewin for securing her a pleasant companion and a comfortable ship, the *Dover Castle*, under Captain R. K. Deacon, which arrived in Melbourne on 8 August, said:

By some mistake Miss Booty and myself did not receive the same advantages as the other passengers, being obliged to purchase our wine, while those who paid precisely the same as ourselves and had equally good Cabin accommodation were allowed a bottle of sherry each week. It was not that I cared for or required it, but I did not choose to be deprived of my rights. The Captain was civil, and contributed to our comfort as far as lay in his power, and the officers were gentlemen in every sense of the word — the passengers we had no reason to complain of, although there were two among our class who proved to be dishonest and worthless and they are now reaping the reward of their misdemeanours . . .

It is, I find, a great mistake to come out second class and I sincerely regret not making full fare first class passage . . . I should have been a considerable gainer in many ways.

Her companion, Louisa Booty, who went on to Bendigo, also complained about not receiving wine. In an undated letter, written from Sandhurst, she said that 'even the third class had wine and they had only paid £18. Had I known before I could have taken some with me, ship fare not being too nice.' In an account of this voyage of the *Dover Castle*, the *Argus* said the ship had made an excellent passage of eighty-two days and the passengers had spoken highly of the trip.

A description of a voyage made by Mary Richardson on the *Cornwallis*, which arrived in Sydney on 29 November 1862, is notable for its account of the very poor food. Mary Richardson travelled out with Miss Quilton and Miss Pool* (neither of whom wrote to the Society) and her letter is notable also for the intense dislike she displays towards Miss Pool. Whether this was due to Miss Pool's eccentric behaviour — which may have been aggravated by her companions' antipathy — or to Miss Pool apparently being an Irish Catholic is not clear. There is no indication that any of the other FMCES governesses were Catholics, the overwhelming majority being firm adherents of the Church of England. In a letter dated 13 February 1863, Mary Richardson said:

Our chief friend was Mr Peake, the 2nd Officer, he was really very kind, but for him I don't know what we should have done — The Captain [E. Pryce] spoke an occasional half dozen words to us sometimes, but you will scarcely credit when I tell you that Mrs Price [Pryce] never spoke to us the whole voyage, except *one morning* for about two minutes.

---

*Ellen Quilter and Miss Poole, according to the shipping records.

We never had a piece of fresh meat for dinner the whole way, although they had more sheep and pigs than they could use for the 1st Cabin. Miss Quilton and I have often made our dinner of two or three potatoes; we never touched the Salt Beef from the first; we did eat a little of the pork sometimes. All the rice was used before we got to the Cape. We were very fortunate in having fine weather as far as the Cape, but from there it was very stormy . . . It cost Miss Quilton and me about 30/- to have our luggage removed from the ship to our Lodgings; we paid 10/- for a boat to bring it on shore and we paid a guinea a week for staying with a family on the Surry Hills.

Miss Quilton and I gave up all idea of the Governesses' Home before we arrived at Sydney on account of Miss Pool. We were so thoroughly disgusted with her that we determined as soon as ever we left the ship never if possible to come in contact with her again, her conduct on board the ship was such as I think you could not believe without having witnessed it. — We were very uncomfortable in our Cabin, but she made it doubly worse, in fact, became so abusive at last we were obliged to make a formal complaint. I wrote a Note to the Captain requesting a private interview, which was immediately granted. The result was she was turned out of our Cabin and put into a kind of little closet by herself where she was eventually locked up for misconduct. She was threatened with irons several times. I am happy to say I have not seen her since I left the Ship, although I have heard some rather strange stories. I suppose she applied at the Roman Catholic Refuge for assistance a few days after she left the Ship. I think the party who sent her from Ireland acted very wrongly. She certainly is a most improper character to be sent from her own Country. I have not heard whether she has met with a situation yet or not; so far as character is concerned she is not fit for a family. Miss Quilton and I have been sworn friends ever since we left London. She is in a situation in Sydney. We feel it very much being so far parted after being so inseparable for four months; we were always together on board ship it became quite proverbial.

The *Cornwallis*, the new iron clipper ship on which Mary Richardson and her friend travelled, was described by the *Sydney Mail* of 29 November 1862 as one of the finest ships ever to enter Sydney. She made the journey in ninety-nine days, including a 'splendid' run of twenty-five days from the Cape of Good Hope to Van Diemen's Land. Later, the ship was detained on the New South Wales south coast by heavy gales. The building of the *Cornwallis* was superintended by Captain Pryce, who was part-owner. Her cabins and saloon were fitted 'with a degree of elegance seldom seen in merchant vessels, with ample ventilation and every accessory for the comfort of passengers'.

Arabella James, who arrived in Auckland on 31 October 1864 with her sister to join her father, another two sisters and her brother, described the trials of a long voyage, particularly as the ship did not call at any ports on the way. On their voyage out, the first land they sighted after they left England was the southern coast of Tasmania. She wrote to Miss Lewin in a letter dated 4 November:

> We received the greatest attention from all, especially from the Captain, who was most kind to us and was a very nice man. We had very few Cabin passengers, a Mrs Clapton, a widow and two daughters were I think the most ladylike people on board, the Doctor's wife was not a very amiable person and was not generally liked, but fortunately we managed to steer clear of all the quarrelling which seems to be attendant on a long voyage; certainly it is a great trial sometimes to be in such close quarters with different families day after day . . . The first land we sighted after leaving England was Tasmania, which we saw quite plainly. The three Kings off the coast of New Zealand were very beautiful looking rocks. You may imagine how we enjoyed seeing land after such a long voyage. The coast of New Zealand is very pretty and mountainous looking. We had a nice view of Auckland from the harbour, and we were agreeably surprised in the town; there appear to be some very good shops, although we did not see much of them being Sunday.

The forlorn fate of those who arrived alone and were not met by friends, relations or representatives of the Society is captured in a letter from Ellen Ollard, who arrived in Melbourne on the *Shannon* on 1 November 1874. In a letter to Mrs Sunter dated 4 August 1876, nearly two years later her arrival remained vivid in her memory:

> The voyage was a very pleasant one and I need hardly tell you that I was very sorry when it came to an end, and I found myself for the first time in my life at the mercy of strangers.
>
> We anchored in the Bay on Saturday the 1st of November at about half past one in the afternoon and, never while I live, shall I forget the feeling of despair that took possession of me when I saw everyone on board talking to their friends who had come to meet them. Miss Davis (my cabin companion) came out to be married and her intended husband took her away in a little yacht and Mrs Thomas, the only remaining lady, went away in the Steamer with her husband and, of course, all the gentlemen got away as

soon as they could and I was left to indulge my grief and to wonder what would become of me in this strange land. On Monday morning one of the passengers who had been very kind to me during the voyage offered to go to the Home with me.

Perhaps an indication of the apprehension with which the emigrant governesses approached their journey is shown by the number who thanked God for their safe arrival. Sarah Webb, who travelled with Mary Hughes on the *Lady Melville*, under Captain H. Gimblett, from whom, and from Mrs Gimblett, she said they had received 'great kindness', was one of these. On 25 April 1863, she wrote from Bendigo to Miss Lewin:

Through the tender mercies of our heavenly Father our good ship landed all her passengers safely at Melbourne on March 28th and to my great joy my brother met me.

The voyage from England was a challenge and adventure for some governesses; for others, it was a disagreeable and far too egalitarian an experience. The governesses' reactions to their new homeland varied similarly. As they stepped off the ships that brought them to their new homes, the governesses faced not a temporary three or four months' adaptation to life aboard ship, but, in most cases, a lifetime in strange and challenging surroundings where their livelihood was by no means as assured as they had hoped or expected.

3 *The First Arrivals*

'. . . I am now beginning to understand something of Colonial Life'.

Gertrude Gooch, Sydney, 1862

The pioneer group of six governesses sent to Australia by Miss Maria Rye prior to the official formation of the FMCES scheme, arrived in Sydney on 20 September 1861. As one was to write, Sydney was then nearing the seventy-fifth anniversary of its foundation. It had outgrown the frontier atmosphere common to young towns in new countries and for those with sufficient money, it provided a comfortable life. Its population of about 95,000 lived in the city and in the surrounding suburbs of Woolloomooloo, Surry Hills, Paddington, Pyrmont, Camperdown, Chippendale, Redfern and Glebe. Farther out were the villages, such as Ashfield and Burwood. In the suburbs, the streets were still undrained, but behind the small cottages stood the stately mansions of the wealthy in landscaped English gardens, away from the noise and dust of the city. Glebe was densely covered with exotic trees and part of the original bush, behind which were elegant residences.

The University had first accepted students in 1852. A railway began to run from Redfern to Parramatta Junction in 1855 and three years later, Sydney was connected to Melbourne and Adelaide by electric telegraph. Late in 1861, a horse-drawn tramway from Circular Quay along Pitt Street opened for traffic, taking passengers to and from the railway station at Redfern. The tramway had a short life: its raised lines were said to be the cause of traffic accidents and it was removed in 1865. Horse-drawn omnibuses and hansom cabs took over again until a steam tramway began running in 1879.

Melbourne had gained great wealth from gold, but Sydney with its extensive pastoral hinterland was the wool centre. Darling Harbour was crowded with ships, the big, square-rigged overseas traders and the smaller coastal vessels all evidence of its importance as a long-established port.

An era of substantial building had begun in the 1860s and the erection of wooden structures was no longer permitted in the city. St Andrew's Anglican Cathedral was consecrated by Bishop Barker in 1868 and six years later, the building of the Town Hall was completed, soon followed by the new Post Office.

Sydney in the 1860s was also a city of poverty. The Report of a Select Committee on the Condition of the Working Classes of the Metropolis in 1860 found a great deal of distress because of unemployment. This was not confined to the unskilled, many persons 'of better education and social habits' being 'reduced to much suffering for want of any kind of employment for which they are fitted and who make their distress the more severe by their struggle to conceal it. There appear to be competent clerks and accountants who cannot obtain situations.'

At the time the governesses arrived, education in New South Wales was a haphazard affair. There were five school systems, one National (Government) and four denominational (Anglican, Catholic, Presbyterian and Methodist), all receiving some government funds, but educating, in all, fewer than half the children of school age. There were also many hundreds of small private schools of variable quality. Many middle- and upper-class children were educated at home, but in the poorer parts of Sydney and the newly settled farming districts, large numbers of children received no schooling. Although changes in the provision of education were to come later and were to affect the demand for private schooling, the first group of FMCES governesses arrived in September 1861 in high hopes that their services would be in great demand. The group — Emily Streeter, Georgiana Mounsdon, Ellen Ireland, Gertrude Gooch, Mary Phillips and Miss Butterfield — had left England just over three months earlier aboard the *Rachel*, a ship of 567 tons, which carried a small number of first- and second-class passengers.

The reception the governesses received was not what they had expected, following the enthusiastic tone of the exchange of correspondence between Miss Rye and Bishop Frederic Barker, Anglican Bishop of Sydney. They were surprised when they were not met at the ship; they were disconcerted that Bishop and Mrs Barker, to whom they had letters of introduction, were away from Sydney; and they spurned the offer of the Dean, William Macquarie Cowper, that they should stay at the Governesses' and Servants' Home. This establishment was to prove unacceptable to most of the early arrivals, who regarded it as more suited to servants than governesses.

Fortunately for the new arrivals, and for those who followed, one of the governesses, Emily Streeter, found a friend in Mrs Augustus Dillon, the wife of a Sydney Post Office clerk, who helped this group and later arrivals to find accommodation and attempted to place them in situations, after they had registered with her employment agency. She proved to be of more practical assistance than the other members of the FMCES's Sydney committee, including Mrs Jane Barker, whose other duties as a bishop's wife, frequent travels around the diocese and a trip to England during 1862–64, all combined to prevent her from giving the governesses the individual attention they expected on arrival.

Of the six women who arrived on the *Rachel* in September 1861 one, Miss Mounsdon, married a fellow passenger, Edward Andrews, and returned to England soon after. On her marriage certificate, Georgiana Amelia Drake Mounsdon does not give an occupation and there are no details of her parents or her birthplace in England. Edward Andrews is described as a gentleman. The marriage was performed by the Reverend Thomas Hayden, M.A. at St John's Anglican Church, Darlinghurst, on 23 January 1862. None of the other travellers on the *Rachel* was a witness to the marriage. For governesses, the possibility of marriage in the colonies was one of the reasons for leaving the security of England, and in this Georgiana Mounsdon achieved notable success with her shipboard romance. Perhaps jealousy was the reason she was not popular with some of the other governesses.

The fortunes of four of the other women are documented in the letters they wrote to the FMCES from their new homes in New South Wales: Emily Streeter, who wrote two letters; Ellen Ireland, who wrote three; and Gertrude Gooch and Mary Phillips, who wrote only one. By no means all the FMCES emigrants wrote to the Society — for example, Miss Mounsdon and Miss Butterfield; of the 302 emigrants, letters were recorded from only 113. The usual reason for writing was to accompany repayment of a loan or part of a loan. Some of the governesses, however, did not require loans, merely taking advantage of the Society's other services, such as travel arrangements and letters of introduction to people in the colonies. Others repaid their loan without an accompanying letter or through the agency of family members or guarantors.

Emily Streeter, described (by her initials only) in a FMCES report as being unable to teach more than the rudiments of English, French and music and who had been unsuccessfully seeking employment in England for six months before her departure, went at first as governess to the children of a grazier at Jerry's Plains, a small settlement in the Patrick's Plains district on the Hunter River, west of Singleton. She probably reached her destination by way of steamer to Newcastle, rail to Maitland and then coach through Singleton. A letter from S. Emily Streeter, 'Carrington Cottage', Jerry's Plains, Upper Hunter, dated 18 January 1862 and addressed to Miss Rye, is the first to appear in the letter-books of the Society. She wrote:

We were greatly disappointed to find on our arrival that the Bishop and Mrs Barker were from home and would not return for three months. On the following day the Dean sent us a letter saying we might board at the Governesses' and Servants' Home for 12/- a week, which we all declined, excepting Miss Mounsdon. Fortunately a friend of mine, a Mrs Augustus Dillon, whose sister I have known intimately for years in England, came to see us and promised to assist us all she could. Miss Ireland and myself obtained board at £1/1/0 a week a few doors from where Mrs Dillon resides. After waiting five weeks and getting very anxious for all my money, as you may suppose, was nearly exhausted, I obtained my present engagement as Governess to Mrs Edward Parnell's children, five in number varying from 11 to five years. Miss Gooch, Miss Phillips and Miss Butterfield upon their arrival went to their friends. They have all obtained engagements, excepting Miss Butterfield, but Miss Phillips and Miss Mounsdon have, I believe, left their engagements.

Jerry's Plains is almost 150 miles from Sydney. It is a very small

Bishop Frederic Barker of Sydney (*first left*) and Bishop Charles Perry of Melbourne (*third from left*), two Anglican clergymen who were prominent in giving assistance to the emigrant governesses. They and their wives are mentioned often in the governesses' letters.
National Library of Australia

Some governesses preferred the relative independence of starting a small school of their own. A group from Miss England's High School for Girls on a picnic at Dixon's Creek, near Stanthorpe, Queensland.

Greenwood/Gillstrom Collection, National Library of Australia

village and we have a very nice Clergyman, but only have Service every other Sunday for he has two Parishes and they are widely scattered.

Mr Parnell* is what they call a Grazier and holds about a thousand acres of land. They are exceedingly kind and I am very comfortable and should I remain 12 months I shall be enabled in that time to repay the £20 so kindly lent. There is not the opening here for Governesses that you supposed, but still I think one or two sent out at a time might do very well, but they ought to have the means of living for at least two or three months. If you wish to know more about the matter you could not do better than correspond with my friend Mrs A. Dillon, 19 Macquarie Street South, Sydney, for she is engaged in education and has been some years in the Colony. I think she would be better fitted, for she would give it her attention, whereas Mrs Barker has so much on her hands that she is obliged to leave it to others. You will I know forgive my suggesting such a thing, but I am anxious to save other ladies the annoyance we experienced.

I bless God for permitting me to come out here and I shall ever feel deeply grateful to you and Miss Lewin for your kind assistance; will you kindly remember me to her and thank her for me.

Four months later, on 20 May, Emily Streeter wrote from Sydney, repaying £10 of her loan and promising to send the remainder as soon as she could possibly manage it, 'if it is only £5 at a time'.

---

*Emily Streeter's employer, Edward Parnell, was born at Richmond on the Hawkesbury River on 24 October 1818. He managed stations for his father in the Namoi River valley at Gunnedah, Tulcumbah and Weetalibah, and then became owner of several other properties before purchasing Carrington Park at Jerry's Plains. On 30 January 1849, he married Caroline, second daughter of Simon Kemp of Newcastle, at Newcastle Cathedral. They had two sons and five daughters. Five of the children were baptised at St James's, Jerry's Plains: Emma, born on 24 September 1851; Caroline Charlotte, born 3 May 1855 (and died 30 April 1856); Edward Carrington, born 29 March 1857; Walter Herbert, born 16 September 1859; and Edith Blanche, born 10 June 1863. Another son was born at Jerry's Plains on 16 September 1860, but apparently was baptised elsewhere. The Parnells had a town house in King Street, Newcastle. The family lived at Jerry's Plains until June 1867, when they moved to Newcastle.

The Parnell family was associated with Jerry's Plains from the earliest days. Edward Parnell's father, Thomas, received a land grant of 630 acres in the Parish of Milbrodale, County of Northumberland, and the first house in the district was known as 'Parnells'.

Edward Parnell was a prominent worker for the Anglican Church and a brother, the Reverend Charles Parnell, was the minister at Milbrodale, south of Singleton.

I am now on a visit to my friend Mrs Dillon, where my friend Miss Ireland is now staying. Her health has been very indifferent ever since she left England, but I am happy to say she is rather better now and will not return home yet as she first thought she must do. She is most valuable to Mrs Dillon, but I am anxious that she should now take another engagement.

I suppose that long before you receive this letter you will have seen Mrs Andrews (Miss Mounsdon that was). I have never seen her since we landed and never wish to meet *that Lady* again. Miss Phillips has, I believe, an engagement at Goulburn. Miss Gooch has for a time left her engagement owing to her Brother's illness and is now staying with her Nephew at Maitland. Miss Butterfield is now seeking an engagement as Nursery Governess and that is the extent of the information I can give you of my fellow passengers. And now dear Miss Rye please accept my sincere thanks for your kindness in assisting me out here. I do not at all regret the step I have taken in coming out here for, although there are many disagreeables, still I am quite sure I could not have done so well at home and I have met with very many kind friends.

I am sorry to tell you that I have left my first engagement after a stay of only six months, but my slight knowledge of French is my great difficulty, but I am now working it up with Mrs Dillon. I have however another engagement in view to which I am going in a few days; it is at Penrith, only a short distance from Sydney by Rail. If this should not succeed I should most certainly become a candidate for the Government Schools, for they are much better paid than private Governesses.

Gertrude Gooch had obtained a situation with Mr Alexander Learmonth of Learmonth, Dickinson and Co., importers, of Charlotte Place, Sydney, through the good offices of Captain Acock of the *Rachel*, which had carried a consignment for the firm. The Learmonths, who lived at 'Yasmar', Parramatta Road, Ashfield, paid Gertrude a yearly salary of £70. She was then over thirty years of age and had been receiving only £20 a year in England. Among the most perceptive of the governesses in her comments on Australian life, she wrote to Miss Rye from Ashfield on 17 February 1862, commenting on, among other things, the visit of the first 'All England' cricket team, under the captaincy of H. H. Stephenson of Surrey, which toured Australia in 1861–62.

I think I may venture to send you a letter, as I am now beginning to understand something of Colonial Life. In the first place we had a tolerably good passage, but a very slow one, just 100 days from Gravesend and on my arrival I was engaged as a Governess to a family by the name of Learmonth. We had on board the *Rachel* some consignments for Mr Learmonth's house of business in Sydney and I have to thank the Captain of the *Rachel* for my situation as he saw Mr Learmonth at his Office in Sydney. I have been so very much engaged that I have not even thought of any of the letters I took to the Bishop. I know he is going to England soon; I am not likely to have anything to do with Clergy here. I had an offer of [several] situations in one month so I would not accept a School. I did not make an effort to obtain the situation I now hold. Miss Mounsdon is married to one of the Gentlemen Passengers who came out with us. Miss Phillips obtained a situation, but was discharged on account of her ignorance after a month's trial. Miss Ireland is in a very good situation, but she is afraid the climate will be too hot for her. Miss Streeter also had a situation and Miss Butterfield we safely handed over to her relations, . . . a short distance from Sydney. We often thought whether any more ladies followed us and as you may perhaps be glad to have the address of someone whom you could tell Ladies coming out here to call upon, I send you one. I am perfectly disinterested in doing so as the Lady is no friend of mine, but she is very clever and could do much for a stranger; her name is Mrs Augustus Dillon, 19 Macquarie Street South, Sydney, and it would be better for them to go direct to her on arriving here. I understand in the District Schools they prefer married people as it is protection for the woman.

I could have obtained a post at Newcastle, but I do not care for anything in that way now. All Sydney has been quite diverted from business by the 'All England Eleven'. It was a pretty sight and the Australians have been fairly beaten* . . .

This is a wonderful country and certainly must one day become considerable amongst the Nations of the World. It was only 74 years this January since it was colonized and it is something quite extraordinary what has been accomplished in that time. It has now during the last expedition [of Burke and Wills] been fairly crossed by John King, there were about twelve in the expedition, but he is the only Survivor; some were murdered by the blacks and two of the Leaders died. The difficulty in the interior is want of water and the immense extent of bush.

---

*In the game played between the 'All England' X1 and the team representing New South Wales at the Domain on 29 January 1862, the Englishmen won by 49 runs (175 and 66 against 127 and 65).

There is a great deal to learn to become fitted for active life here. Australian ladies are very different to English and they dislike, as they term it, our particular ways. One thing is the climate is so very different. They are certainly very indolent and untidy. Children are very much indulged and have no energy nor application, do not like the least trouble. All Australians ride like Arabs, love luxury and money. They live very much out of doors and eat great quantities of fruit. Beef and Mutton are very cheap here, rice is eaten as a vegetable and tea is very much taken. It is a great mistake to bring clothes with you, they can be bought reasonably and warm clothing is very little required here, boots and shoes are expensive and a stock of them would be very useful. It is also a mistake to bring furniture from England as a house must be furnished suitable for the climate. We have had intensely hot weather ever since we arrived, scarcely any rain, the air is cooled by hurricanes, they come on very suddenly and are very violent. We never see such thunder and lightning at home as we have here. The climate varies very much as the country is so large and a man's possessions will sometimes be as large as a county at home.

People are wanted here, but not of any sort; people who come here should be intelligent. And Capital is another thing. The worst sort to come are such as Miss Phillips, fit for nothing, and that will not do for Australia.

Australians are keen and very quick and fair judges of English people. Governesses *well* educated generally find situations, but they can do better at home when they are not well qualified. Australian children are just like the vegetation here for neither appear to submit to much control. Pineapples, peaches and the finest fruit grow in open air without care and the children are equally wild and impetuous; you meet with very few quiet patient girls here; they like no trouble, nor will they take any about anything. The floor is the place for everything and it is no use making yourself unhappy because they will not acquire English manners for they do not like them and you can soon see the difference between an English and Australian Lady, but it is very natural. Mothers prefer you to fall into their ways in preference to introducing your own and they do not like to be made to feel inferior.

I found all my relations. My poor brother I am afraid is dying.*

---

*Henry Gooch, spirit merchant, died on 24 March 1862 at Melbourne Street, East Maitland, aged fifty-three. He was born in Norfolk, England, the son of Henry Burton Gooch, spirit merchant, and Mary Ann Reed, and had lived in New South Wales since 1835. In 1838, he married Mary Ann Barnes in Sydney and they had one son, Henry Mansfield Gooch, who was twenty-two at the time of his father's death. Henry Gooch was buried on 26 March, in the Presbyterian Burial Ground, East Maitland.

I am certain it will be a long while before I see the Old Country again, perhaps never. I love it as ever, but I can earn more money here and I expect always [will] find something to do. There are enough of us at home. I often think of you, our old Ship, the Voyage and many other things and cannot yet believe I am 17,000 miles away from Old England . . .

P. S. . . . I have spoken to many people of the voyage and most people think when it can be conveniently done that it is far better to come out First Class; two or three ladies could join and engage one Cabin.

Mary Phillips, regarded by Gertrude Gooch as ignorant and the worst sort of person to go to Australia, wrote herself from Cooper (? Cowper) Street, Goulburn, on 16 June 1862, a year after she had sailed from England. In its early years, Goulburn, 138 miles south-west of Sydney, had been a garrison town. The main road south was built by a convict gang stationed at the nearby Towrang Stockade, which in the decade from 1833 was the chief penal settlement in the southern districts. Police parties searching for bushrangers also made their headquarters at Goulburn. Free settlers began arriving in the district in greater numbers in the 1860s and Goulburn became a market centre for the surrounding district and the areas farther south.

Commenting on an article that appeared in the London *Times* on the work of the FMCES, Mary Phillips wrote to Miss Rye:

A year has now elapsed since I left England to become a Governess in Australia. Whether you have heard from Miss Gooch I do not know, but an Article I read in the 'Home News' suggested the thought to me of writing to you — as you still appear sanguine of success in your endeavours to persuade Governesses to emigrate to these Colonies.

Miss Gooch gave us to understand that she only was expected to give you an account of our voyage, success, etc., so I had no thought of doing so till I read the Article before stated — the *Times* I think was right, there is no opening here for a number of educated Females — a few who have friends may do very well. I know from my own experiences that anyone coming here without friends must fare very badly. Had it not been for my friend Mr Pearce (who still continues his kind interest in me) and with whom I stayed five weeks before I obtained a suitable engagement, I should have felt deep regret for the step I had been persuaded in taking. You will I suppose have had an interview with the Bishop before you receive [this]; he was absent at the time of our arrival, but my friend introduced me to his Lordship immediately on his return and as I was going to Goulburn to undertake the duties of teaching, which engagement I obtained by answering an advertisement in the *Sydney Herald*, his Lordship gave me an introduction to the Revd. Sowerby,* and the Dean of Sydney, one to the Revd. Leigh;** from the latter I have received the greatest kindness, the situation I had taken proving a most miserable affair and I leaving after a stay of three weeks. Mrs Leigh invited me to stay with her and after a pleasant week spent with her she obtained me an engagement which I am now filling and still bears a kind regard for me.

I am now acquainted with all the Goulburn Society and have a few friends to whom I am attached. So I may say I have been fortunate, but by all I hear from persons of considerable experience and good standing it is not advisable to send a number of Governesses out here, there really being no demand for them — in Sydney I can assure you the difficulty of obtaining an engagement appeared to me the same as in England and with regard to the voyage I must say that we were exceedingly uncomfortable† and had it not been for the kindness of two of the first class passengers, I don't know what I should have done, the fare being bad and the house constantly wet from the time we rounded the Cape — but I have no doubt the Bishop has informed you of the true state of things here and by the manner His Lordship expressed himself at the interview I had with him, I do not think he would advise any more being sent out as we were.

I hope his Lordship will enjoy his visit to England, many many here feel his absence and likewise Mrs Barker's very much.

I do not know where Miss Gooch is, but as you have heard all particulars from her, I will not say more. Trusting you and Miss Lewin may enjoy many years of health and happiness and wishing you success in all your efforts for the welfare of others, I remain . . .

---

*William Sowerby, born in England in 1799, was appointed first Anglican clergyman at Goulburn in 1837 and created Dean of Goulburn in 1869.

**Richard Leigh was curate at Goulburn from 1858 to 1864, mainly assigned to country work in the Crookwell, Binda, Taralga and Lake Bathurst districts. He was incumbent of North Goulburn from 1864 to 1871, and later held several parishes in south-eastern New South Wales, including that of the Candelo parish in the Bega district. He was created Canon in 1897.

†Mary Phillips' account of the voyage out on the *Rachel* differs markedly from Emily Streeter's comments that the voyage was on the whole very favourable. See Chapter 2, page 25.

The remaining member in the first group to write to the Society, Ellen Ireland, seemed the least able to cope with life in a new country. She was often sick and at one stage spent some months at Mrs Dillon's home being nursed back to health. Her first letter, dated 18 February 1862, was written from Newcastle, where she was employed as governess to a solicitor's family.

I should have written to you before, but my health has been and still continues so bad that I hardly know what to do; it is certain this climate does not suit me. But I must say wherever I have been I have met with the greatest of kindness, am now in a very nice family, only one dear little girl to teach, eight years of age, very forward, but I am now on the Doctor's List and have been ever since I have been in this country which has been a great drawback to me.

I went to Goulburn first and glad I was to get away from there. I never met such rude children in all my life. The Bishop and his wife visited that City while I was there and I was introduced to them by the Rev. Leigh, Clergyman there, at a public Meeting and Mrs Barker called on me before they left Goulburn; they were very kind indeed. I am now in a Solicitor's family receiving 40 guineas a year, but I fear my poor head will not let me remain; however, I must do something for I shall not be happy until I have paid my debt. On my landing I lost my purse with all my money, but fortunately some honest person picked it up and advertised it.

Do not, Miss Rye, send any more ladies out Second Class. I shall never forget the passage in my life and when we arrived no one to meet us . . . I daresay I shall not regret the trip when I get back to dear old England again, which I hope to do when I have paid the £20. I like Miss Streeter very much and trust we shall always be friends; her friend Mrs Dillon has been excessively kind to me, nursed me when I came from Goulburn so ill and will have me whenever I am out of a situation, indeed all the people are as kind as they can be out here. The Cricketers will give you an idea of the Australians when they return. I do so wish we could hear of the Mail. And now dear Miss Rye I must not forget to thank you and Miss Lewin for all your kindness in doing all you could for our comfort. I often think of you and hope you are well.

I think first Class Governesses would get on well out here. Excuse all mistakes and bad writing as my head is so bad.

On 28 May, Ellen Ireland wrote from Mrs Dillon's home, regretting her inability to repay any money off her loan:

I only wish it was in my power to send you some money . . . but I have been truly unfortunate in being so ill since my arrival here ... I do not know what I should have done without Mrs Dillon and Miss Streeter, they have indeed been great friends to me. I have been with Mrs Dillon three months and when I am quite strong she is going to get me an engagement, which will be soon I hope.

Her last letter was written more than a year later, on 20 August 1863, from Market Square, Goulburn. She again regretted that she was unable to repay any money to the Society, but hoped to do so soon, since she now had a job with a salary of £35 a year.

This was my first engagement when I came to Goulburn, but the Children were so unmanageable I was obliged to leave. Since then my health has been very bad, and Sydney does not agree with me at all, so I thought as Mrs Butler asked me to come back and told me the children were better, I would return to Goulburn. The climate is much like dear old England and Mr and Mrs Butler* very kind people, so I trust to be able to remain. I have indeed been an unfortunate girl and as soon as I have paid my debts and saved enough money for my passage, I shall come back to dear old England.

O dear Miss Rye I never thought I would feel leaving home so much. I have had trials since I have been in this Colony, but I must pray to God and He will help me, and trust for better days. My dear friend Emily Streeter is as fortunate as I am unfortunate; she has indeed been kind to me, so also has Mrs Dillon. I daresay you will see her when you are in Sydney. I do not know when you will get this letter for you are going about so. The Clergyman and his Wife are the only people here I visit; they are exceedingly kind to me. It is very cold, but I have a fire in my room morning and night, Mrs Butler is so afraid of me having the croup again ...

The letter concluded with a plea that the Society not approach Mrs Corpe, the person who had guaranteed her loan for repayment, but at the same time advising that Mrs Corpe had moved to 114 Upper Brook Street, Manchester. Several other

---

*Ellen Ireland's employers were probably the family who ran one of the earliest stores established in Goulburn — Butler's drapery store, on a site later occupied by the Railways Institute. Another person of that name associated with Goulburn was Edward Butler, QC, a prominent Catholic, who was MLA for Argyle from 1869 to 1877 and Attorney-General in 1872. However, it is improbable that he was Ellen Ireland's employer, since most of the early FMCES governesses, with their letters of introduction to Bishop Barker, obtained positions in Anglican households.

governesses also made similar pleas as the time limit of two years and four months for repayment approached.

Ellen Ireland's life did not improve greatly. There is an indication in a later letter that she was working in Sydney. According to Louisa Dearmer, in a letter dated 14 December 1868, she was receiving £50 a year as a daily governess and could hardly live on the pay, since she had to find her own board.*

The preoccupations of the writers of these letters from the first group of FMCES emigrants are those that recur in the letters from succeeding FMCES emigrants over the next twenty years: the voyage, often a traumatic experience and for most the first long journey away from familiar and family surroundings; first impressions of Australia, sometimes very perceptive but often disappointingly mundane; the lack of welcome from representatives of the Society, which new arrivals continued to expect over the years but which rarely eventuated; the difficulties in obtaining a position when so many governesses and teachers were looking for work; the emigrants' reliance on Anglican contacts, particularly in the early years of the Scheme; and the strong obligation they felt to repay the money lent to them by the Society.

---

*Ellen Ireland died, unmarried, on 6 October 1888 at Prince Alfred Hospital, Camperdown, Sydney, of cerebral apoplexy at the age of fifty years and was buried in the Church of England Cemetery, Rookwood. On her death certificate, her occupation is given as governess. She had been born in London, the daughter of John Ireland, physician.

4 A Mixed Reception

'The Colony is well stocked with Governesses, many not able to find suitable employment.'

Elizabeth Boake, Melbourne, 1868

The emigrant governesses who chose Melbourne as their destination in the early 1860s found a town with a population of about 140,000, considerably larger than Sydney. The wild excitement, feverish upheaval, overcrowding and chaos of the gold-rush era were giving way to evidence of more solid achievements. The muddy thoroughfares were being replaced by paved surfaces, pure water from Yan Yean Reservoir was being piped to houses, gas illuminated the streets and railways radiated from the city to the suburbs of Williamstown, Brighton and Essendon. Illustrating the great confidence in the future that gold had brought to the citizens of Melbourne, substantial public and private buildings were beginning to adorn the main streets. The first stages of the University, the Public Library and Parliament House were already in use, banks and commercial premises were rising in Collins Street and church spires were noticeable on the skyline. Theatres, dance-halls and innumerable hotels flourished.

Nevertheless, despite its air of wealth and advancement, Melbourne, like Sydney, did not provide the employment opportunities the emigrant governesses expected. A few found work in the town, but many had to go to the country, some to the gold-rush towns of Ballarat and Bendigo. Others turned to teaching, some in government schools; others started small schools of their own.

The first governesses to write from Victoria — Caroline Heawood, aged thirty-five, and Maria Barrow, aged twenty-two — arrived in Melbourne on the *Dover Castle* on 28 January 1862. They were accompanied by two sisters named Muskett, neither of whom wrote to the Society, so their movements are known only indirectly through the letters of others. The elder sister, Elizabeth, aged twenty-six, had great difficulty finding a position because she was not able to teach music, something that was to prove a great disadvantage to many other governesses in succeeding years. She apparently was supported by her younger sister, Sarah, aged twenty-four, who obtained work as a saleswoman in a Melbourne drapery firm. This sister appears to be the emigrant later described in an attachment to the FMCES report for 1862–72 as having lost her job through misconduct. Both sisters boarded at 37 Victoria Street. Nothing further is known of them and it is a matter for speculation how they managed to survive.

Maria Barrow was met on arrival by her brother and in the only letter she wrote to the Society, said her relatives did not wish her to take work. From her home with them in the then semi-rural surroundings of South Yarra, she wrote (in a letter addressed 'Dear Madam', but obviously intended for Miss Rye) on 17 February 1862:

> You have been the means of my finding a happy home earlier than I should have done and in this wide earth that is something . . .
>
> I can't quite make up my mind about the Colony whether to like it or not. I know there are some nice people in it, and I may add some *mosquitoes*; they are nasty venomous little things without any conscience and they are just beginning to make acquaintance with me — I am told they are numerous towards the end of summer — the flies too are very troublesome. We have had fine weather ever since I have been here and it is very pleasant, still I miss the freshness of some of our fine days in dear old England, everything is so dried up, and certainly the birds don't sing and the flowers (generally) don't smell.
>
> A friend of ours who has a garden and keeps it in beautiful order has violets, honeysuckle, sweet briars, heartsease, roses, etc. etc., all of which have the proper smell, though not so strong as at home. These flowers always refresh me — they quite look like old friends. The fruit is very fine — such apples and pears and peaches! I can fancy how you would raise your eyebrows at the sight of them!

She then added a few sentences about a gathering of Aborigines she had witnessed: remarkably, Maria Barrow was the only governess to mention Aborigines, although those who went to jobs on outback stations must have had some contact with them. 'A great party of Natives', she wrote, 'had their dinner out under the [?tree], opposite the house and within a stone's throw. They are very ugly and old, the women particularly, and I was rather afraid of them, however, they appear to be quite harmless.'

Caroline Heawood was by far the most professional of the group, although she had had trouble finding a position as a governess in England because she was slightly deaf. In Victoria, she achieved the aims of many of the governesses who emigrated: she obtained a good job soon after arriving where she was happy and then, not very much later, she married. Employed by Mrs James, wife of John F. James, registrar, secretary and librarian at the University of Melbourne, she found the James family 'quiet Christian people and both extremely kind to me'.

Before leaving England, the governesses apparently were asked by the Society to report on the prospects for employment in the countries to which they emigrated. Miss Heawood, in a letter dated 25 March 1862 from Barry Street, near the University of Melbourne, wrote:

> And now dear Miss Rye I know you are anxious to hear what prospect there is for Governesses out here. From what little I know of Australia, or at least this part of it, I do not think there is much encouragement for them. I would not advise any young person to come out unless they have friends to go to on arrival, in the event of their not meeting with an engagement. This in Melbourne is not very easy and to go up the country is very expensive. The salaries in the Bush are higher than in Town; I believe from £80 to £100 (I have £60). Musical Governesses are the most required, in fact, unless they are able to teach Music, which seems to be more thought of than anything else, they are almost sure not to succeed. Female domestic servants seem very much wanted. Good house servants get from £30 to £35 — cooks more — I think Governesses would do better in Sydney.

Caroline Heawood had been disappointed to find that there was no one to meet the group on arrival in Melbourne and she and the Misses Muskett stayed at Cooper's Railway Hotel for two weeks. The group's expectations had been raised by news of those Melbourne correspondents who were prepared to support the work of the Society. These included Mrs Fanny Perry, wife of the Right Reverend Charles Perry, Anglican Bishop of Melbourne, Mrs Laura Jane à Beckett, wife of Thomas Turner à Beckett, lawyer, prominent Anglican layman and member of the Legislative Council, Mrs Gatty Jones and Edward Willis, a pioneer settler at Geelong and a grazier at Koolomurt, near Harrow, where he developed a fine Merino stud.

Miss Heawood and the Misses Muskett called on Mrs Perry and Mrs à Beckett, and also on Mr Franklyn, of F. B. Franklyn & Co., paper and type merchants, publishers of the *Herald* and the *Illustrated Post*, who advertised unsuccessfully for employment on behalf of Elizabeth Muskett. Caroline Heawood also called on Mr Willis at Geelong, but he 'was up the Country so we have neither seen nor heard from him'. In view of the lack of assistance from the Society's Melbourne committee, she offered to help any other governess sent out to Melbourne by the FMCES. This offer was taken up the following year, when she was asked to assist Miss Laing and Miss Wither, but by then she was married to a Mr Löfvén and living in Ballarat.* She enlisted the help of her former employer, Mrs James, who met the two on their arrival on the *Prince of Wales* on 24 August 1863 and who visited all the 'respectable' labour offices on their behalf, but without success. Caroline (Heawood) Löfvén wrote from Ballarat on 24 September 1863:

> Situations are more scarce than ever. Miss Forest, who keeps the most respectable office, told Mrs James that several genteel young people had been long upon her books and would now gladly go as nursemaids in respectable families. I trust Miss Laing and Miss Wither will be more successful and that they will be able to inform you by this Mail that they are comfortably and happily settled.

Neither Miss Laing nor Miss Wither wrote to the Society, although Miss Wither is mentioned in a letter written in the following year by Mrs Laura Jane à Beckett, the Society's representative.

---

*Caroline Maria Heawood was married on 4 June 1863 at St John's Anglican Church, Creswick, to John Robert Löfvén, aged forty-two, a merchant of Ballarat. He had been born in Munkfors, Sweden, son of Matthias Löfvén, a pastor. Caroline Heawood, recorded as aged (?) thirty-two, gave her address as Creswick, but her usual address as Geelong. Apparently she had left the employ of the Barrys at the University some time before her marriage. She was born in London, daughter of John Heawood, a solicitor, and Caroline Tate. John Löfvén is listed in a Ballarat directory as a storekeeper living at Little Bendigo, a small mining settlement in Ballarat.

In mid-1862, another group of eight governesses arrived in Melbourne on the *Result*, on 27 August. They included Isabella McGillivray and her three sisters, who arrived to find that their brother, P. H. McGillivray, M.A., M.R.C.S., who had lived for some years at Williamstown, near Melbourne, recently had been appointed resident surgeon responsible for internal management at Bendigo Hospital.* Dr McGillivray was unable to leave his job for even a day to greet his sisters, but had kept on his house at Williamstown so that they would have a home to go to when they arrived. The sisters settled into the house and the youngest, Margaret, found employment as a governess at St Kilda.

Writing about this in a letter to Miss Rye dated 24 September 1862, Isabella said:

> Salaries are not so high now as they were and many of these Salaries in the Bush are never realised — there seem to be few situations and those persons wishing to employ, beseiged by applicants. We did not hear of another situation at all likely to suit our Maggie but this one and perhaps she owed it to the fact that the Lady's husband (she is a widow for about 8 or 9 months) was a friend of a brother of ours in Edinburgh where both were young men and that she knew our brother here intimately. Maggie applied in answer to an advertisement and was very much surprised to learn who the Lady was . . . She gives only £40, but then we know something of the family and it being so difficult to get situations we thought it better to accept the offer.

Isabella reported that the next youngest sister, Caroline, was unable to take a job because she was still very weak after her illness on the boat trip out.

Isabella McGillivray looked around for a place to open a school and decided on Ballarat, 'a thriving, rising town about 80 miles from this'. She added: 'I would have preferred the neighbourhood of Melbourne and friends here advised it, but that would have required much more capital than we have so, in the circumstances, we think Ballarat the best place for us'.

In her letter, Isabella McGillivray also reported on the fate of several other women sent out by the Society on the *Result*:

---

*Dr McGillivray (the name is spelt variously as Macgilevray, M'Gillveray, etc.) was to remain in this position for eleven years and in 1872 was a member of the first council of the Bendigo School of Mines.

The three Misses Young remained on board Ship till they heard from their friends, who live in a very distant out of the way place, and then set off; poor things they were very lonely, but Mrs Dickinson [the Captain's wife] took them to the Cabin after we left. Miss Crook went to the Wesleyan Home. She was almost engaged to a Lady on board as Nursery Maid for her two little girls. I hope she did get the Situation. She was to go next day or the Lady was to let her know. Miss C. was to come and see us, but has not come — this is about 10 miles from Melbourne and that may be the reason — we should all be glad to hear of her success. Miss Cowan went on Shore with her Sister, who came in a boat for her. She never said what she intended to do; she is a *hard featured Scotch woman,* I mean in character.

Miss Sampson I suppose is still unoccupied, for in today's *Argus* there is an advertisement — 'A Lady recently arrived is anxious to obtain a situation in a respectable Hotel to Sing and play every Evening' — I am certain it is hers. I am afraid she won't do much good here — She is not the person to get on in any hard work or honest employment. She has never been accustomed to employ herself and it is too late to begin and change her habits. I'll say no more of her at present — If you will allow me I will write to you, and let you know how we succeed . . .

Although not approved of by Isabella McGillivray, Miss Sampson's rather adventurous step in advertising for work singing or playing the piano in a hotel may have been a sign of desperation in her attempts to find employment. The advertisement appeared as the first item in the classified section of the Melbourne *Argus,* under the inappropriate heading of 'Tradesmen', on 24 September 1862. The address given for replies was 128 Collins Street East, which was occupied by the Victorian Servants' Institution run by Mrs Forrest.

Isabella McGillivray did not write to the Society again,* but over two years later, on 21 February 1865, her sister Margaret wrote returning the sum of £25 lent to her by the FMCES. She had by this time joined her sisters at their school, for she wrote from Torquay Place, 15 Lyons Street, Ballarat. As the time passed for the repayment of the loan (which would have been due about September 1864), Miss Lewin apparently had written to the guarantor of the loan, the Reverend P. Beaton, Chaplain to the Forces, Hazel-

*At least one of the McGillivray sisters continued to live in Ballarat for some years, but some time during the period 1875–82, they all disappear from the scene.

bank Cottage, Auckland, New Zealand. He forwarded the letter, dated 1 November 1864, to Margaret McGillivray, who wrote:

> My having received it only a few days ago will account for the delay — I have much pleasure in informing you that I have sent as directed a draft (or Bill of Exchange) to Messrs Coutts, Bankers, 59 Strand, London for the sum of £25, payable thirty days after sight, repayment of said sum lent me by the Female Middle Class Emigration Society. This would have been done sooner had it not been for the change of Secretary and the necessary absence of the Revd. P. Beaton from London.

She asked that the promissory deed be sent to the Reverend Beaton. The reference to the change of secretary, apparently refers to Jane Lewin taking over the duties of the office while Maria Rye was overseas.

The difficulty of finding a position as a governess, combined at times with a liking for the more independent life of teaching, led some of the early arrivals in Victoria to start their own schools. One who displayed impressive qualities in this field was Miss Barlow. She may have arrived on 28 January 1862 on the *Dover Castle*, with the first group of emigrants to reach Melbourne. (The Misses Barlow — Nancy, aged twenty-nine, and her sister, Emily, aged twenty-six — are listed as first-class passengers on that ship.) By June of the next year, when she wrote her only letter (the first part of which is missing), Miss Barlow had been running a school at Janefield for six months. Janefield, now submerged in Melbourne suburbia, was then a small village on the west bank of the Plenty River, about twelve miles from Melbourne and connected to it by the Melbourne–Whittlesea coachline through Northcote, Preston and Bundoora. Dairying and agriculture, together with a flour mill on the river, driven by water-power, supported a small population. Miss Barlow wrote, on 24 June 1863:

> My School has prospered beyond my expectations, though I have had many heavy expenses and my remuneration is very small, the fees low even for England, however it is a much more independent life than that of a Governess and I like it. I have taken £60 in the six months I have been here and have paid nearly half that for furniture etc., then I have left my rent and the maintenance of my two Boarders and myself. I have about 13 day Pupils, two Boarders and my five private music pupils, so that I have plenty of teaching

and as I have no servant, the care of the house absorbs all the leisure time I might otherwise have. I should indeed be glad when Mamma comes to render me some assistance in that respect.

I like Bush life very much. I have only twice been into Melbourne since I came, and the Blacksmith and a Storekeeper, who is a very intelligent man, are my nearest neighbours, the latter and his Wife have been truly kind to me since I came.

It is now the depth of winter, a delightful change after the hot winds; my household scrubbing and rubbing used to be rather trying at those times. I am getting quite a Colonial woman, and fear I should not easily fit into English ideas again — can scrub a floor with anyone, and bake my own bread and many other things an English Governess and Schoolmistress would be horrified at.

I must not write you a long letter as it is now past twelve in the night. I have to make all extra employments such as letter writing etc. come out of the night time, and this will I hope be sufficient excuse to my English friends; I have not in the least forgotten them all, but for the last six months I have not had time to write any but imperative letters, all will be changed when Mamma comes, and then I can make up for past neglect. I expect her in about a fortnight . . . I hope to get more Boarders when Mamma comes. At present, without keeping a servant, which would absorb all my profit besides being the most terrible annoyance you can conceive, I could not manage with more inmates. I have great hopes of [my] sister succeeding here in Photography.

From her letter, it would seem that Miss Barlow had made a start towards being one of the success stories of the Society's emigration scheme. Her sister's progress in photography, then in the early stage of its development, is also unknown.

Another governess to start a school was Sarah Webb, who was forty-two years old when she arrived in March 1863 and, at the suggestion of her brother, probably William Webb, a cattle salesman, opened a school at Bendigo for children aged five to eight. She wrote from Sandhurst on 25 April 1863: 'I have 12 children, each pays a Shilling a week. I have the promise of more and hope to increase it to 20. They are all respectable children. It is a small sum, but there are already many [schools] here.' She added:

I cannot say that I like Australia; this part is very barren, the Gold Diggings are on all sides and their white tents scattered over hill and dale. Now the most pleasing thing is the Chinese garden; they bring them to perfection. The Shops in Sandhurst are equal to those in London.

At the end of her letter, Sarah Webb said that Mary Hughes, who had travelled out with her, was about to take a job as an assistant teacher at Beechworth. (Mary Hughes, aged twenty according to the shipping-list, is one of the FMCES emigrants who did not write to the Society.)

The problem of paying back the Society's loan — a comparatively large sum of money — loomed menacingly over the finances of each emigrating governess, unless she had came out to relatives who were prepared to reimburse the Society. All emigrants had to obtain 'securities' in England before they were granted a loan, people who would guarantee to repay the loan if they were unable to do so themselves. In some cases, these were impoverished relatives, who in reality were unable to repay the loan, except at the greatest financial inconvenience. Others who guaranteed securities were prominent people: the Bishop of Chichester, the Right Reverend Ashhurst Turner Gilbert, D.D., was guarantor for Mrs Margaret Allen, who arrived in Melbourne in September 1864; a duchess* was guarantor for Emily Hunt, who emigrated to Wellington in 1874; and many more were people of means and social standing. However, this did not improve the situation, for with their well-developed sense of pride, most governesses shied away from any recourse to their guarantors.

Frequently, a governess unable to repay her loan within the required two years and four months would request: 'Please don't refer to my securities. Give me more time to pay.' The Society usually obliged, particularly where it was obvious some effort had been made to repay the debt. The difficulties the governesses had in doing so are apparent when it is considered that the salaries most received ranged between £40 to £60 a year. Out of this, they often had to spend large sums to travel up country to their place of employment. There was also the expense of buying clothes to outfit themselves for a varying climate and different way of life. Those who commented on clothes showed some surprise at the high standard of dress in the colonies and they therefore considered it necessary to keep up with their employers in style of dress. Marion Hett, who went to New Zealand, was forced to buy a riding outfit and saddlery, since she found that

*The name of the duchess is not disclosed in Emily Hunt's letter of 19 December 1874.

riding a horse was the only way she could get to the outside world from the station where she was employed.

Despite these expenses, most governesses placed a high priority on the repayment of their loans. However, at the slightest sign of any slackness in repayment when the recipient seemed in a position to do so, the Society could be quite severe. Kate Brind, another governess to go to New Zealand, received a rebuke for not repaying her loan more quickly, when she wrote to say she was receiving a salary of £100 a year. She hastened to explain in her next letter that the yearly rate of £100 was for a temporary position, which had lasted only three months.

One who received the full blast of Miss Lewin's displeasure, for her conduct as well as for the inability to repay her loan, was Eliza Walpole, who arrived in Melbourne in August 1863 on the *Result*. (Her letters contain the only instance of a direct quote of Miss Lewin's words.) When Eliza, who appears to have been a rather ineffectual and pathetic young lady, first arrived, she went to her uncle, Henry Walpole, at 'Musk Cottage', Bullarook, near Ballarat.* Her brother was also in Victoria, farther up country, and in her first letter, dated 21 September 1863, in which she gives her postal address as 'c/o Messrs English and Mann's** Branch P. O., Golden Point, Ballarat, she implies that he had agreed to repay her loan. In May the following year, she left her uncle after an argument and went to live in Melbourne with a Mrs Tripp, who ran a Ladies' Seminary at 'East Leigh', Commercial Road, Prahran, where Mrs Tripp employed her in an unpaid capacity. Eliza's uncle must have given his version of the quarrel in a letter to Miss Lewin, for she wrote to Eliza in November 1864 in very strong terms. Eliza replied on 25 January 1865:

I received with much pain and surprise your letter of 18 November 186[4]. With regard to the payment of the £20, I acknowledge that you were quite justified to make all enquiries as to whether it would be returned by me or if you would have to call upon my Uncle and Mr Streeter† for the repayment. This last suggestion was neither

---

*No trace could be found in directories of the period of the Walpole family, either at Ballarat or Bullarook, or in the surrounding areas.

**Samuel Mann was a Ballarat solictor.

†There is no clue to connect this person with Emily Streeter.

my own nor my Brother's intention. My Uncle Henry Walpole undertook the expenses of my voyage from England and perhaps you will remember that when I last saw you I told you this, and also that the money would be refunded immediately on my arrival in this Colony, for my Uncle Henry had promised it should be . . . I therefore blame my Uncle Henry for promising what he did not intend to perform. There is not the least probability of either my uncle or Mr Streeter being called upon for the £20, for my Brother would never allow it. Now that I am aware of the manner my Uncle Henry has written of me I would not accept the money from him. I should hope by the July mail, if not before, to send home the whole amount, so I hope neither my uncle or Mr Streeter will feel at all anxious on this subject. I have also been grieved at the false statements my Uncle Henry and cousin have made regarding my conduct while staying with them and the only way I can account for it is that they wish to cover the unkind and ungentlemanly manner in which my Uncle behaved to me on Sunday 2 May, and not to me only but also to his own daughter and son, who both told me that they would not live with their Father any longer and therefore of course I could not remain after that any longer under his roof so I left Bullarook with my two cousins the following Saturday morning. I had before this been in correspondence with a Lady in Melbourne (who was the friend I made on board ship). She had been interesting herself on my behalf and had advised me to take a daily engagement, and to live with her and her husband, and this my cousin Kate knew, for I had read all my friend's letters to her, so that she knew exactly what my intentions were . . .

I shall now make a quotation from your letter and ask you to inform me on what grounds you lay such an *awful* accusation: 'And then the madness, I can call it no less, of throwing yourself without a protector, into such a City as Melbourne. I tremble to think what might have been your fate! and can only hope that God has been more merciful to you than you deserve — as He is to us all — and has preserved you from the villainy of wicked men and from the consequences of your own folly.'

. . . on receiving your letter I called upon Miss Cope Smith,* as I knew her; she is a great friend of Mrs and the Misses Tripp, also of Mrs Handfield,** a married daughter of Mrs Tripp's and the Wife of one of the leading Clergy of Melbourne, from whom I have received the enclosed letter which I send for *your* perusal, but it is not to be shown or commented upon to any one, but only for you, to show that I am not on the Streets of Melbourne.

---

*Captain Cope Smith lived at Darling Street, South Yarra.

**Wife of the Reverend Henry H. P. Handfield, vicar of St Peter's Church, East Melbourne.

Eliza Walpole concluded: 'I was aware of owing other money besides that owing to the Society, as also was my Brother, and we have been anxious about it for a long time'. She wrote again six months later, on 22 July, to explain that she was unable to send more money that month, having then repaid £5, because she might need what money she had for travelling when she got another engagement. 'I know it is a very sad thing to be in debt, but had you seen the promises that were held out to me of the money for all my expenses being sent home immediately you would not blame me as much as you do.'

Two years later and nearly four years after her arrival in Victoria, Eliza Walpole wrote again, regretting that she was not able to repay any money at that time. Writing on 10 July 1867 and describing herself as 'living in the Bush',* she explained: 'I had saved more than sufficient to pay you, but through the illness and death of my dear brother** it has all gone in necessary expenses'. She said she hoped to save again and repay the money before the end of the year. This was her last letter and she remains an example of the great problems some governesses faced in repaying their loans and the heavy burden imposed on them by the consciousness of their debt.

Misunderstandings about the welcome and assistance emigrant governesses could expect from the Society's Melbourne representatives continued during 1863 and 1864. Jane Kidson, aged twenty-six, wrote to Miss Rye on 23 October 1863, soon after her arrival, from Gertrude Street, Fitzroy, where she lived with her brother James, a stationer:

On my arrival here I was much surprised to find Mrs a Beckett had nothing to do with the Society further than she would be glad to recommend anyone you sent out. I think this should be distinctly told to any Lady before leaving England, for you told me there was a place provided for me until I heard of a situation; supposing I had not had a Brother here, I should have been much disappointed and quite at a loss what to have done. From what I have been told since I came I do not think Governesses are much in request. I am glad to tell you I have a situation; I heard of it through the Wife of the Clergyman of the Church my Brother attends. I called upon Mrs a

*The address on the letter seems to read: 'Hayneer'. No trace of a place of this name, or similar, has been found.

**No record has been found of the death of a male Walpole in Victoria in the years 1864 to 1868 inclusive.

Beckett. She was very kind, but did not know of any Lady wanting a Governess. Thank you very much for your kind interest.

The problem of accommodation for newly arrived emigrants had been broached at a meeting held in Melbourne on 26 February 1863, which received a report from a Ladies' Committee on the possibility of establishing 'The Melbourne Home for Governesses, Needlewomen, Servants and all Classes of Respectable Single Females'. A Melbourne Female Home had existed for about a year during 1857–58 in temporary premises in Smith Street, Collingwood, but had to be abandoned because of lack of funds. The small group of ladies associated with St James's Vestry who ran this home met again in 1862, to consider whether the home should be re-established. This group later was enlarged to comprise a central committee and nine local or suburban committees, with the aim of raising funds. A report produced by the group was the subject of the public meeting in February the following year, presided over by the Governor of Victoria, Sir Henry Barkly, and attended by about 150 people, including many prominent citizens, among them the Honourable T. T. à Beckett, M.L.C. and Mrs à Beckett. In a speech, the Governor summed up some of the problems associated with the establishment of a home intended for such a range of social classes and also expressed some of the prevailing criticism of the immigration of governesses to the colony:

> . . . the ladies' committee judged rightly when they determined to include within their objects all classes of single females, from governesses downwards, because, although it might be preferable, if we had the option, to establish two institutions, there is no doubt that there would be very great difficulty in establishing a second institution. I am almost afraid, from the well-meant, but I must call them ill-judged, efforts which have been made by Miss Rye and others at home to induce highly-educated females to emigrate to Australia, that we may be called upon before very long to make efforts to assist that class of the community if they come out here. It has certainly appeared to me from the first that those efforts have originated in a total misconception as to the nature and requirements of colonial society. (Hear, hear.) In my view, the system of resident governesses is a product of an artificial state of society, in a high state of civilization. I think it almost might be said that it cannot flourish except in the hot-bed of wealth and luxury, where the ordinary maternal duties are so interfered with by other avocations

that it is not practicable for the mother to pay that attention in superintending her daughters' education which she would do in the natural state of things.

By the time of this meeting, only £200 had been raised from public subscriptions against the £1,000 that had been considered the minimum amount required to begin building. Negotiations with the government for a grant of land also had not been satisfactory. Therefore, as an interim measure, a temporary 'Home' was established in the former Prince of Wales Hotel, which was situated on the north side of Flinders Lane, between Swanston and Russell Streets. 'The Home' was described as being for 'governesses, needlewomen, servants, etc.' and as a 'Registry office for the employment of servants, married couples, etc.' It at first was maintained by public subscription, but was intended to become self-supporting. The honorary secretary of the management committee, which comprised twenty-six women and six men, was Mrs Laura Jane à Beckett.

From the description, the Society's 'Home' would not have appealed to many of the governesses and they continued to expect a greater welcome than was forthcoming. Mrs à Beckett attempted to straighten out this problem by writing, in a rather exasperated tone, to the Society on 22 December 1864:

I write by this Mail for the purpose of stating that I receive so much annoyance from the fact of the Ladies sent out by your Society taking it for granted that I should meet them at the Ship, provide accommodation, or get a situation for them, that I wish it to be distinctly understood that I disclaim all responsibility concerning them — the *utmost* I can promise is to give a letter saying I have heard of them from you and that they have their own testimonials upon which they must trust for engagement.

With respect to the testimonials, it is important that your Society should be very particular and not be content with letters from friends and relations only. I am led to make this remark from the very unsatisfactory accounts I hear of Miss Wither. She brought no testimonials with her and it will be a most difficult thing for her, I am afraid, to obtain another situation after the manner in which she has behaved in the one procured for her.

How Miss Wither slipped through the FMCES sponsoring system without testimonials is a mystery. Under the Society's rules, four testimonials were required, two from previous employers and two from personal friends. Although it may have been difficult, or even impossible, for an unemployed governess to obtain a reference from her previous employer, it is hard to believe the Society would sponsor a governess without at least personal references.

Nine governesses emigrated to Australia in 1863, the year of Miss Wither's arrival. The FMCES records on these women read:

No.	*Salary obtained in the Colonies*	*Remarks*
66	—	Went out to a situation, lost it, and married beneath her.
67	£84	Obtained situation two days after landing, and has done well.
68	—	Not highly qualified, health failed, was not very successful.
69		Married within a year.
70		Went to an uncle; experienced great difficulty in obtaining employment.
71		Obtained situation shortly after arrival.
72		Middle-aged woman with broken constitution, unsuccessful.
73	£105	Obtained situation as head mistress of a School.
77		No qualifications as governess, failed entirely in obtaining employment in England, and met with many difficulties in Australia.

If the remarks on emigrant No. 77 refer to Miss Wither, this would account for her lack of work references, at least.

Later, as Mrs à Beckett visited England and Miss Maria Rye visited Melbourne, they may have met and been able to sort out some of the problems stemming from the emigrants' expectations. Members of the Society's Melbourne committee were mostly active citizens, in the forefront of charitable and philanthropic causes, and necessarily would have regarded their responsibilities to the FMCES as only part of their social and community activities. One of Mrs a Beckett's other commitments was as honorary secretary of the Lying-in Hospital, an infirmary for diseases of women and children, and forerunner of the Melbourne Women's Hospital.

Arriving governesses continued to be critical of 'The Home'. On 18 August 1865, Margaret Pyman wrote from Sydney concerning her experiences during a brief stay in Melbourne. Her travelling companion, Louisa Booty, had conducted her to the Home, but, she wrote, 'as it appeared more a place for servants than for ladies I did not wish to go in'. The Matron gave her an introduction to the Rector of St James's, who arranged 'comfortable, cheap and respectable lodgings' for her until her brother arrived.

Her companion, Louisa Booty, went to live at Bendigo with her brother (probably Conrad Booty, a miner). She wrote from Forest Street, Sandhurst, in an undated letter (?August 1865), that she found there were 'very few governesses required here'.

On 9 June 1866, Miss Annie Shaw, an official of the Home, had a crisis on her hands when Omerine Giraud, who had landed by the *Dover Castle* that day, arrived unexpectedly. Letters from the Society announcing Mlle Giraud's arrival, together with her money and teaching certificates, all apparently had been delayed in the mail. This was a common occurrence when the time taken by a sea voyage could vary by months and it was not unknown for one ship that had left England weeks after another, to arrive before the first.

Mlle Giraud arrived not only unannounced, but at seven in the evening of a Saturday, not a time when the Home took in boarders, much less one without money to pay. Fortunately for her, Omérine Giraud had friends in Melbourne, otherwise, as she wrote to Miss Lewin from the Home, Flinders Lane, on 24 June 1866, she 'might have been in great distress, occupation for Governesses being almost as scarce here as it is in London. However I am safe, surrounded with every care and kindness which fill my *heart* with thanks to the Lord for His Goodness to me in giving me such friends in a place where everything was new to me'.

Miss Shaw was so disturbed by Mlle Giraud's plight that she wrote from the Melbourne Home to Miss Rye on 24 June, enclosing Omerine Giraud's letter:

The poor girl is in great perplexity and much want of her money —

The non-arrival of the promised Certificates is very unfortunate for her as it will be very difficult for her to obtain any situation without them. Fortunately she had a few lines with her signed by Miss Lewin or we would not have admitted her into the Home.

There is no indication of what position, if any, Mlle Giraud obtained in Melbourne.

Several governesses were able to get jobs as teachers in Government schools, among them Miss M. A. Kightley. Miss Kightley, who arrived in Melbourne on the *Wellesley* on 9 March 1865 after a 'long and tedious' voyage of over four months from which 'all landed safely', as she reports in her letter dated 24 March, went to live with her brother at Maldon, a gold-mining town near Castlemaine. By the time she wrote on 22 December 1866 from Melbourne, to send £17 owed to the Society, she had a job in a Government school and said:

I am exceedingly obliged to the Society for the privilege of coming to the Colony. I have been tolerably successful and hope to be able to return in a year or two. There are difficulties here as well as at home, but on the whole I think one's prospects are better here to those who are striving to get along uprightly. I have been employed in the Common Schools and have given satisfaction to Inspectors and Committees. I am now going to work for a Certificate, which must be obtained, and hope to be successful.

Miss Kightley said she was unsettled in her movements, so mail should be addressed to her brother, Mr A. Kightley, at the Post Office, Maldon. She said she had seen Miss Rye at the Melbourne Home, but did not know whether she had returned to England.

Elizabeth Boake, who arrived on the *Forest Rights* on 13 January 1867, was another who decided to try teaching in the Government schools, after several jobs as a governess. Her first position was as a daily governess 'with Mrs Greene, who was acquainted with Miss Rye', at a yearly salary of £70, which she obtained while living with her brother, Henry Boake,* a teacher, at 9 Charlotte Street, Richmond. In a letter wrongly dated December 1866, she wrote: 'I have met with

*Elizabeth Boake and her brother Henry were born in Dublin, two of eleven children of Irish Quakers, William and Anne (Capel) Boake. Another brother, Barcroft, was the father of Australian poet and surveyor, Barcroft Henry Thomas Boake (1866–1892).

great kindness everywhere — all my friends here think I have done wisely in coming out to Australia, so I have every reason to be satisfied with what I have done'.

By 26 February 1868, when she wrote again giving the Richmond address, Elizabeth Boake was employed as a governess with the family of a government official (unnamed) at Warrnambool, in south-western Victoria. She asked to be forgiven for not sending money: 'Our present Government is to blame! On account of what is called the "Dead Lock", which no doubt you will have heard of, the Government officials are not receiving their salaries and, as I have been for some time engaged in instructing children of one of these gentlemen, have suffered from the general complaint.' The 'deadlock' she referred to occurred between the two Houses of the Victorian Parliament, when the Legislative Council rejected an Appropriation Bill in November 1867. Parliament was prorogued pending an election in February 1868 and payments suspended. Elizabeth's letter apparently was written over a period of time, for later in it she wrote that she had received her pay and she enclosed £28 for the Society. She said she had no cause to regret emigrating to Victoria, but she added: 'The Colony is well stocked with Governesses, many not able to find suitable employment'.

As she did with other emigrants, when she thought she had an informative correspondent, Miss Lewin kept the correspondence going, asking for opinions of prospects and conditions. In her last letter to the Society, dated 1 January 1869 and again addressed from Richmond, Elizabeth Boake replied to these questions:

I have had very little experience on the whole, so thought my best plan would be to wait and get the opinion of older colonists than myself as I did not feel at all competent to give one on the subject in which you are so kindly interested. I have spoken to many lately and the general opinion seems to be that there are Governesses enough in the Colony. A highly accomplished lady with relatives out here would do well, no doubt, but such people do quite well at home. The average salary seems to be £70 — and my sister gets £80 in Ireland! I never did, but that was my own fault, for I disliked going amongst dignified aristocrats . . .

I would not advise anyone in whom I was interested to come out here as Governess — I have been fortunate, but I have many friends and relatives here, thank God; but unless a lady is very talented and independent she had best stay at home, be that home ever so humble. People pay their Governesses scarcely more than the Cooks here. I heard a lady say, 'I would willingly give my Cook £40 if she would stay'. At the same time the same lady 'could not afford to pay her Governess more than £50' and the poor girl had to do all the needlework for five children, besides housekeeping, teaching and the children were far advanced and very clever. Servants are really badly wanting here.

This may have been Elizabeth Boake's personal experience in her position at Warrnambool, where she was paid £50 and which she had decided to leave because the pay was too low. In the same letter, she wrote concerning her future:

I am not seeking a situation for a while as I have arranged to stay with my sister-in-law (she has a large school), as I intend to study. I am anxious to go for the Examination for Teachers for Government Schools. I shall feel very independent if I succeed in passing. It is hard work, but quite worth the trouble to get a certificate; one is then sure of employment and good pay.

Elizabeth Boake was correct in pointing to the good pay received by teachers in Government schools. A report of a Royal Commission on Public Education, under the chairmanship of George Higinbotham, former Attorney-General and later Chief Justice of Victoria, in 1867, said Victorian teachers were 'handsomely rewarded' compared with teachers in English schools. Teachers were paid partly on the results their students obtained in examinations. The average salary of a headteacher in Melbourne was £275 a year, a suburban teacher £240; a teacher on the goldfields received £218 10s 0d and a teacher in the country, £185. The salaries of assistant teachers on average were £113 a year in Melbourne, £100 5s 0d in the suburbs, £97 10s 0d on the goldfields and £88 in the country.

Despite the relatively high pay, the report found that a large number of teachers employed in the Common (Government) schools fell 'far short in attainments and general qualifications of the standard which the high character of their functions and the liberal remuneration they receive would justify the State in demanding. No fewer than 449 of the teachers are not classified at all.' This was well over half the 771 male and female teachers employed in schools receiving aid from the Board of Education, that is both Government and denominational schools. There were also

507 assistant teachers and 222 pupil teachers. The report recommended that in the future, teachers should be employed only after a strict examination and after receiving a certificate of competency.

The report advised a move towards compulsory and secular education and the establishment of a training school for teachers. It also recommended that the examination of children and part-payment of teachers by results be retained. The inquiry revealed that many children were not receiving an education. Of the 170,000 children in Victoria estimated to be aged between five and fifteen, less than half were attending school. In 1872, an Education Act made education in Victoria free, compulsory and secular.

At this time, teaching jobs in Government schools were advertised in the *Victorian Government Gazette*. An advertisement that appeared on 12 October 1866 read:

> A list of applicants for employment as masters, mistresses and assistant teachers in Common Schools, is kept in the office of the Board of Education.
>
> Teachers desirous of employment are required to furnish copies of their testimonials, names and addresses of employers, if any, during the preceding three years, with the names and roll numbers of the Common Schools in which they have been employed.
>
> Local committees who may desire teachers are requested to state the percentage of school fees and results to be given, and the probable amount of such percentages and whether accommodation is provided, with any other information in their power.

Elizabeth Boake would have had difficulty obtaining a teaching position in a Government school when she first arrived in the colony, for the competition was fierce. Whether she was successful three years later is not recorded in the Society's records.

5 Life with the 'Nouveaux Riches'

'I teach them Music, Singing, French, German and Drawing, for which I receive 80 guineas a year . . .'

Annie Davis, Sydney, 1863

The mixed success achieved by the first groups of governesses to arrive in Australia did not lead to an influx of FMCES emigrants to New South Wales. A restraining influence probably also was provided by Bishop and Mrs Barker, who visited England in 1862 and may have reported on the difficulties of placing more than a very few governesses. In 1863, only two new FMCES emigrants wrote from New South Wales and in 1864 only five. Several of these governesses found situations with prominent families. A few of their letters were written from remote places, but most came from Sydney or its immediate vicinity — from Kissing Point on the Parramatta River or Cook's River, then rural areas.

Mary Richardson, an early arrival, wrote from Willsbro', Rolland's Plains, Port Macquarie, on 13 February 1863, but like some other governesses who found themselves in pioneering settlements, she had little to say about her new life.

I am now between 200 and 300 miles north of Sydney. I am very comfortable but still I find Australian Bush Life very different from dear old England. I have one pupil 15 years of age. Her education had been rather neglected so that she is not too far advanced for me, at the same time she is not at all dull so that I find it very pleasant teaching her. She is very clever at music. I have no one to interfere with me in the least. The family consists of my pupil, her two Brothers (aged 18 and 20) and her Step-father, quite an old Gentleman. I am only afraid I should be quite spoilt here for

holding another situation where I might have more to do.
My Salary is £40, which I consider very small for coming out to Australia for, but I understand that situations are not so plentiful nor Salaries so large as is represented in England and travelling or moving about at all is so dreadfully expensive.

Rolland's Plains was a small township and agricultural district on the Wilson River, about twenty miles north-west of Port Macquarie. Willisboro, consisting of 1,070 acres, was purchased by William H. Freeman and his cousin, William Gorham, in 1837. William Freeman's wife, Emma Gorham, possibly William's sister, was born at Wellsborough, Ashford, Kent, from which the name of the property probably derived.

William Gorham did not marry until late in life. At the age of sixty-two, he married Mrs Jane Sarah Scott, a widow twenty years his junior, who had a family of two sons, William and George, and five daughters Jane, Isabella, Eliza, Mary Ann and Louisa, from her first marriage. Jane Sarah (Scott) Gorham died in October 1860, presumably leaving her children in the care of their step-father. One her daughters would have been Mary Richardson's pupil. William Gorham died in June 1863 and this may have caused Mary Richardson to leave Willisboro after a stay of only six months. She did not write again to the Society.

The other emigrant who wrote to the Society in 1863 was Annie Davis, a more accomplished governess than most and also a better correspondent. She taught the children of some prominent families in Sydney, travelled to one employer's country property and in between experienced some vicissitudes, both at the hands of the *nouveaux riches* and in a clergyman's household.

Almost immediately after she arrived in Sydney, Annie Davis was offered a position as governess to the family of Donald Macintyre,* a squatter, of 'Kayuga House', Pyrmont

---

*Donald Macintyre was a brother of an early settler on the Hunter, Peter Macintyre, after whom the Macintyre River was named by the explorer Allan Cunningham. Donald Macintyre, before emigrating to New South Wales on the *City of Edinburgh* in 1827, had lived in the United States, where he had a property on Cayuga Lake in New York State, after which he named his Hunter Valley property. Born in 1790, he was married first to Georgina McDonald. After her death, during a trip to Scotland in 1846 he married Sarah Robina Todd. They had four children — three girls, including Sarah, born in 1847, and Elizabeth, and a boy, Donald, born in 1849. Donald Macintyre died in 1866. The property has been held in the direct male line since 1827, the present owner, Cr David Macintyre, being president of Scone Shire since 1976.

Road, Glebe. The Macintyres' country property, also named 'Kayuga', was about 160 miles north of Sydney, between Muswellbrook and Aberdeen, at the junction of Dart Brook with the Hunter River.

In September 1863, Annie Davis wrote to Miss Lewin from Sydney:

We landed on Sunday morning; owing to hard winds we arrived too late on Saturday night to land. You were mistaken in supposing my Brothers resided in Sydney, the nearest was a few hundred miles off; neither they nor Mrs Dillon seemed to have found out the arrival of the *Revenue*, so I had no one to meet me. I left my things in the steamer and by dint of inquiry found my way to Macquarie Street. I was just in time to meet Mrs Dillon previous to her setting forth to her Sunday School duties. She was very kind in her reception of me and in all her arrangements. She was fortunately able to get lodgings for me close by at a respectable house — the terms were 30/- a week. I was fortunate enough to meet with a situation at once, the final arrangements were settled two days after my landing. I did not enter on my duties till the end of the week, having taken my lodgings for that time. My Australian experience thus far has been such a singularly happy one that I am rejoiced at having come — I am settled in a most comfortable home, my duties are light. I have five hours work every day, Saturday and Sunday are my own days entirely. I have three pupils, the eldest 16, the next 12, the youngest nine. I teach them Music, Singing, French, German and Drawing, for which I receive 80 guineas a year, including laundry. The family I am with are Scotch, the more I know of them the more I like them. My pupils are singularly free from the usual faults of Colonial girls, viz. pertness and *forwardness*. We are now living in the Town house in the neighbourhood of Sydney; we are to go to the 'Bush' in a few weeks, to remain there till the close of January next. I am looking forward to the change with some interest.

In every question, as regards Governesses coming out here, I must endorse Mrs Dillon's opinion, viz. that they should come as *First* class passengers, they certainly should not go to the 'Home'; from what I have heard of it, it is anything but a fit place for 'Ladies'; also that only for Ladies that can command first class situations are the chances certain of obtaining speedy and well paid employment. There are a great number of Colonial second and third rate Governesses. Certainly an Englishwoman may always compete successfully with an Australian, for English Ladies are very much esteemed — still there are already so many inferior teachers that I should consider it a great risk sending many of them out. Then as regards money, it should be impressed upon every Lady coming out that she should be provided with at least £20 in her pocket when she lands in Australia. It is quite the exception to meet with an engagement at once as I did, indeed my case altogether must be viewed as an exceptional one.

I was quite ignorant of Mrs Dillon's true position until a few days after my landing. It would save Ladies some embarrassment were it made quite clear and plain before they left England — in fact, she is a scholastic agent and makes the same terms as some of the London ones do, i.e. half a guinea as entrance fee and 5 per cent on the first year's salary, therefore I had to pay her nearly £5 at starting — not having calculated on such an expense I might have been placed in a difficulty had I not my Brothers to assist me. My youngest Brother came down to meet me directly he heard of my arrival — we spent some days together in town. He is stationed not far from where I am going in the 'Bush', so that we can meet sometimes, Mrs Macintyre having given him a warm invitation to come to Kayuga Station when he has time. It is very probable that another of my Brothers will settle in Sydney soon, so all things considered I am in a most favourable position as regards everything. I must now thank you for your kind assistance you rendered me. It has been undoubtedly a great advantage to me having come *first* class.

Nine months later, on 17 June 1864, Annie Davis wrote again to Miss Lewin from the Macintyres' Sydney home, 'Kayuga', at Glebe:

I am more than satisfied with the step I took in coming to Australia. I never was so well off before — so little to do with such good remuneration and I should add that my English experience was a singularly happy one . . .

I have not seen Mrs Dillon for some time. At our last interview she seemed to be in dread lest you should sent out those elderly ladies of whom you wrote. Unfortunately nowhere is *youth* more valued than here, I know not why, but so it is: from instances I have heard and from every day conversation it is evident that a moderately qualified young woman would have every advantage over a middle aged one, however accomplished — I would put 35 as the extreme age for anyone intending to cross the ocean for this part of the world. So impressed am I with this fact that I am using all my efforts to be as economical as possible, laying by all I can as a means of support when work is no longer to be had. I am aware there is an idea in England that young and accomplished Governesses soon marry in this land; that is a mistake, at least nowadays; in the early years of the Colony it did happen, for educated women were then very rare. Mrs Dillon tells me she knows of but one instance of a Governess marrying. I however have heard of several, still it should be looked on as the exception not the rule. Music is an indispensable qualification, German is a great necessity, on the strength of which you may expect 80 to 100 guineas per annum . . . Of course it is but few who can expect to find situations in the City, the majority must expect to go to the Country. The Country Ladies have an advantage over the Town ones in one particular, they need very little dress. For my part I am very grateful that a good Providence cast my lot in the City, varied by a few months' visit to the Country, which I enjoy for a short time.

There are many moderate sized Towns where Schools could be opened in which two Ladies with a little Capital might safely embark. According to the statistics, men greatly outnumber women in this land, yet it seems to me the women find it nearly as difficult to get their daily bread here in Sydney as in London; many are the sad tales I have heard of the straits to which educated women have been driven. A new opening for female industry has been opened here in a Cigar Manufactory,* which employs mainly women and children; this is the only new track for female labour that exists at present. Were I in the position of the third or fourth rate Governesses (I was almost going to say second) in England, I would unhesitatingly become a domestic servant in Australia in preference. Here Housemaids have from £25 to £30 a year, good Cooks £35 to £40. It is pitiable to think of young women nominally Governesses yet little more than Nursemaids toiling for perhaps only £10 per year; £20 would be quite a large sum — I have known and still know cases in Wales where respectable decently educated women only earn these sums. I have no doubt it would require some common sense and humility for such a Governess to become a Servant, but she would find herself infinitely better off (salary apart). Servants are more considered, there is more freedom and independence here than at home. If my words could reach some of my toiling sisters at home, I would say: 'Be sensible, undergo a little domestic training and come out here to take your chance with others with a certainty of succeeding withal'.

*Traditional supplies of tobacco were disrupted in the early 1860s by the American Civil War and the price rose to phenomenal heights. Australian growers were quick to recognise the trade potential and by 1863, the Australian colonies were producing the equivalent of nearly two million kilograms of leaf. In the absence of imports, local manufacturers expanded, using local leaf. At least five tobacco and snuff manufacturers operated in Sydney. By 1867, one — the Australian Eagle Tobacco Factory in Bathurst Street, owned by McEncroe and Dalton — was able to advertise itself as the winner of the 'first prize for tobacco at the Melbourne Exhibition'. It is likely that this was the firm that had begun to manufacture cigars.

For respectable well-trained, *Protestant* servants there is always a demand; people are often obliged to take Catholics as they can get no other good servants.

In August, soon after she wrote this letter, Annie Davis had to leave the Macintyres, for they had 'formed new plans'. She accepted a morning engagement, which was not very well paid, but she received enough to pay for the hire of a piano while she waited for a suitable position. By the following January, she had accepted such a position, at eighty guineas a year, with William Durham,* a grazier at Wambo, near Warkworth, in the Patrick's Plains district near the Hunter River, not far south of the Macintyre property. On 20 January 1865, she wrote of her new employers:

My new home will be in the country in the same district where I before resided for three months. I am to have three pupils aged 10, 12 and 14. In my new home I shall make acquaintance with a new class of people — the *nouveaux riches*, but I may consider myself now colonized so it will be only viewing a new phase of life. I was remarkably fortunate in the first engagement I found for it was amongst nice people, a matter of no small consequence when coming fresh from England.

Another governess, Mrs Thomas (not a FMCES emigrant), who worked for the Durhams a few years later (probably about 1871), recorded life there in greater detail than did Annie Davis. Mrs Thomas travelled to the Durhams' home from Sydney, taking a steamer to Newcastle then the train to Singleton. Under the pen name 'Lyth', she wrote:

My destination — a large cattle farm some miles out — was very unlike anything I had hitherto lived at, low and flat; the house, however, was very comfortable and nicely furnished. My own apartments were large, and certainly everything was suitable for our requirements: bookcase and piano for study or amusement.

---

*William Durham, only son of William Durham of Windsor, married Sophia Hill, fifth daughter of the late William Hill of Park Street, Sydney, at St Matthew's Church, Windsor, on 16 December 1847. The ceremony was conducted by the Reverend H. T. Styles. A son, Charles Henry McQuade, was born at Park Street, Sydney, in October 1848; another son, William James Hill, in 1849; and a daughter, Sophie, at Leamington, near Jerry's Plains, in April 1852. Wambo was an original grant to innkeeper James Hale, who when he died in 1857 left it to his stepson William Durham.

My pupil, a girl of 16, decidedly above the average in intelligence, promised to be a pleasant companion. There was originality in her character. Under judicious and wider training she was likely to develop into a clever woman; but with present surroundings I used to think, 'She will grow hard and perhaps sceptical'. Wombo* was a large farm and station for breeding from famous imported cattle. My pupil, the youngest of the family, seemed quite an anomaly there. Though her mother was of good natural ability, a long residence in such an isolated place had to a certain extent dried up the early impressions of a visit to England and life in Sydney.

'Lyth', like Annie Davis before her, left after a short time. She wrote: 'My health being still delicate, I found Wombo too bleak, so after a few months left for Sydney'. Life at the Durhams was not unalleviated bleakness, however. While 'Lyth' was there, the famous orator and politician William Bede Dalley came to visit, together with Mrs Durham's brother. 'Lyth' wrote of this visit:

It was a treat listening to the conversation of these men at dinner in the evening; and afterwards Mr Dalley would come into my sanctum, have a chat, and read to Sophie and me . . . A more courteous gentleman could not be; refined in taste, liberal in views on all subjects, one of Australia's most gifted sons. The fire of eloquence had touched his lips, and his 'silver speech' added beauty to the poems he read to us, which would have given delight to the authors. I had just been reading Longfellow's *Hyperion* and Bulwer's *Pilgrims of the Rhine* to Sophie, from both of which he quoted long passages; then he read several of Tennyson's and Longfellow's . . .**

'Lyth's' description of life with the Durhams gives a rather more balanced view than that of Annie Davis, who merely found the people 'vulgar'. In a letter written from Sydney on 21 February 1867, she reported that her situation with the Durhams had not proved a comfortable one and she had left after five months.

---

*More generally known as Wambo.

**'Lyth' (Mrs Thomas), *The Golden South: Memories of Australian Home Life from 1843 to 1888*, Ward & Downey, London, 1890, pp. 183–4, 185, 186.

Some delightful stories handed down about the Durhams have an appealing ring these days, but illustrate, perhaps, why Annie Davis did not find them congenial. Mrs Durham, apparently a very proud woman, is said to have refused to allow the Duke of Edinburgh to go shooting at Wambo during his visit to Singleton to 1867. She also remarked that there were three inns at Warkworth, should he need accommodation. William Durham was said to have been so fat, there was a table at Wambo so shaped to allow him to reach his food.

From Wambo, Annie Davis then went to Maitland, to superintend a school the Reverend J. R. Thackeray had opened 'for the benefit' of the education of his two daughters, aged fifteen and sixteen. After only a short time, however, she lost this position, without notice, to a Mrs Balfour, the former principal of the Clergy Daughters' School, Nelson Bay Road, Waverley, which the Reverend Thackeray's daughters had attended. Annie Davis tried unsuccessfully to obtain reimbursement for three months' notice, but eventually the Reverend Thackeray agreed to make up the difference in the salary she was receiving at her new post at a nearby school, until the end of the year.

In her letter, Annie Davis also apologised for some comments she had made criticising the FMCES scheme in a letter to a relative in Liverpool. These comments seem to have been publicised by the recipient of the letter, Mrs Robberds.

Taking some interest in the subject of emigration, and as a connection of mine I thought she would be pleased by having some account of my experience and what I might hear from others on my first landing — a month or two after my arrival I wrote to her — in the meantime I had heard a great deal said against Miss Rye's scheme both by the lady with whom I then resided and by others — I, of course, had no experience of its workings in this country further than as it regarded myself, what I stated to Mrs Robberds were mere 'ondits' which I have since found must in some degree have been exaggerations. I regret very much that any words of mine could for a moment either give you pain or do an injury to the Society's working. As regards Mrs Dillon's fees, she told me on my arrival that she had mentioned the matter before, but it is now evident not in the decided way she did after my arrival. Mrs D. I find now makes it almost a rule *not* to meet young Ladies, though she receives them most kindly when they get to her house.

I must most humbly entreat your pardon for the annoyance I caused you personally, as well as the injury done to the Society. Let me assure you dear Miss Lewin that I shall ever remember with gratitude your kindness to me in London — I had not the remotest idea that what I wrote would have been produced as such reliable information. Mrs Dillon has been a kind friend to me. I am sorry to find that she has received some rudeness and annoyance from the late arrivals, many of them I think have behaved very foolishly, for allowing even that Mrs Dillon may have given some little provocation, it is a great mistake to offend the only person they had references to — and though some of them are now in situations, they will not be permanent ones, and in all probability they will have to refer to her again. I have only heard Mrs D's account. I do not know any of the late arrivals, except Miss Maize. I tried to show her some friendly attention, but she met my advances so coldly that I have not visited her much since. She is engaged I think to a family of the name of Allen, very kind people, I know. . . .

By 21 February 1867, the date of her fourth and last letter to the Society, Annie Davis had put these problems behind her and had obtained another engagement in Sydney. This was at 'Lynwood', Ferry Road, Glebe, with the family of George Wigram Allen of Allen, Bowden & Allen, solicitors.* She was very happy with her position with the Allens, which she described as the best she had filled. 'I have a most comfortable home, am with refined, educated people and have duties to perform just suited to my powers. I have a salary of £80, including laundry, and have Saturday and Sunday for my own pleasure.'

She then went on to describe the two FMCES governesses who had held the position before her and who had been unsuccessful. One, Miss Ford, according to Annie Davis, had

*George Wigram Allen (later Sir George), MLA for Glebe from 1869 to 1880, a Minister of the Crown and Speaker of the Legislative Assembly. He held many important posts in education, including Commissioner of National Education (1853–67), trustee of Sydney Grammar School and member of the Senate of the University of Sydney. He was also a prominent Wesleyan and supporter of the Church Missionary Society and the British and Foreign Bible Society. Mrs (later Lady) Allen was a prominent worker for various charities and helped found the Children's Hospital (later the Royal Alexandra Hospital for Children). There were six sons and four daughters in the family.

been 'far *too old** for any situation of this kind, and in every way most unsuited to this family'. She continued:

> I believe her salary here was the same as mine, but during the six months she spent every fraction she earned and ran up bills at two or three Drapers to the sum of £90!! making use of Mr Allen's name. She left here penniless and after some time got a daily engagement, a poor affair. She ran into debt for her lodgings so that she was threatened with jail — however she went on and on, till I heard lately of her being in the 'Home', being placed there in charity for a month by the Emigration Agent. Her time had expired and she was on the point of being turned out, when a kind Providence sent her help — a lady keeping a school proposed to give her board if she gave her services for the afternoon; the following day she made a morning engagement — so she is once again pretty well off.

The other governess employed by the Allens, Miss Maize, was described by Annie Davis as a 'little insane'. She had left Sydney for New Zealand and from there went to Melbourne. 'She never remains long anywhere.' Annie Davis commented:

> Few young women over 30 are suited for Australia, I could almost say 25. I was only a little over the latter figure, and I felt that I had only just come in time; I came with the advantage too of a very youthful appearance. So convinced am I that a teacher cannot expect to do much after *40* that I have already formed my plans for the future. My present plans are to return to England in about four years, when I should be 34 years old nearly, and entering myself in one of the Great Training Hospitals for Nurses; I wish to fit myself for a good sick nurse; I have a great liking for the work and have shown a capability for it — I am laying by all I can now and I trust if all be well to have a small income amassed by the end of four years, for in addition to my savings I have had a small legacy left to me.

---

*It is probable that Eliza Maria Ford died at Woodlands, near Broke, south of Singleton, on 25 September 1874, aged seventy. If this is the case, she was one of the most elderly of the FMCES emigrants. Her death was reported by George Watts, farmer of Woodlands, who may have been her employer. Her death was the subject of a coroner's inquiry, which found that she died from natural causes. She was a clergyman's daughter, born in England, her mother's maiden name being Sarah Fitzgerald. She was buried in the Church of England Cemetery, Broke.

With the exception of Annie Davis, the Allen family must have been disconcerted by the standard of governess they obtained through the FMCES scheme. Eliza Maria Ford, one of the governesses who held a position with the Allens, said in a letter to the Society dated 7 June 1865* that she had obtained the job when, after being unemployed for some time, she had advertised in a 'desperate effort'. Earlier she had worked for a short time for Charles Blaxland, fourth son of the explorer Gregory Blaxland. Charles Blaxland and his wife and eleven children lived at Cleves, Ryde, near Kissing Point, where he was an honorary magistrate and justice of the peace.

Other FMCES governesses to arrive in Sydney in 1864, and who wrote to the Society, were Mrs C. Barton, Fanny Giles, Jane Finch and Caroline Lash.

Mrs Barton had intended going on to New Zealand, but after arriving in Sydney, decided to stay, 'for it is the general opinion that the accounts of New Zealand do not give the idea of a good opening for a first class Ladies' School, that is at Dunedin'. In her letter dated 18 January 1864, she continued: 'I am in the Country about 2½ miles from Sydney and not much more than a mile from Mrs Dillon. The Country around is very beautiful. I am on the Surrey Hills, not unlike our own, if it were not for the fields of Indian corn and the Norfolk Pines; the latter have a very shapely appearance.' Mrs Barton added that she did not know where Miss Rye was 'just now', indicating that she was in New South Wales at that time.

Mrs Barton, with the help of Mrs Dillon, had obtained board with friends of Mrs Dillon's, for which she was paying £1 5s 0d a week. She added: 'The good boarding houses are from two to three guineas weekly and the second rate are not considered *au fait* for an English gentlewoman'. Mrs Barton said she found Mrs Dillon very assiduous in her work. She had advised her to take some good engagements in Sydney, then to 'see what may be done for the future'.

---

*Eliza Ford's letter was written to Mrs Wise, wife of George F. Wise, immigration agent, of Macquarie Street North, whose private residence was at Ocean Street, Woollahra. Apparently, the Wises were friends of Maria Rye's when she was in Australia, for several governesses had introductions to her and a few wrote to her. She must have sent their letters on to London, since they appear in the FMCES letter-books.

In the first half of the year 1865, Mrs Barton went to the Reverend Thackeray's school at Maitland, taking the position later held briefly by Annie Davis. Her subsequent movements are unknown.

Fanny Giles went to Morpeth, a town about ninety miles north of Sydney, on the Hunter River, just east of Maitland. She was paid 'only 60 guineas on account of my deficiency in Music'. In her only letter, dated 10 September 1864, she said: 'The family is one of the oldest and most respected in this Colony and everything about me seems so English that I cannot yet realise being so far from my native land'.

There is no clue to the name of the family for whom Fanny Giles worked. It seems likely, however, to have been that of Mr Edward Close, who lived at 'Morpeth House', described by another governess, Mrs Thomas ('Lyth'), as being one of only two houses of any importance in Morpeth. (The other was the Bishop's.) 'Lyth' worked for the Closes for a year in the 1860s. The family consisted of Mr Edward Close, a retired military man in his seventies, his eldest son, the son's wife and his two daughters, Rosie and Susie, who were 'Lyth's' pupils. She said of the year at 'Morpeth House': 'We lived a quiet uneventful life . . . Mr Edward Close was without exception the most Christian-like man I ever knew'. She described the house as being large, 'standing in extensive paddocks, and surrounded by flower gardens, shrubbery, and orchard'.*

Caroline Lash went to stay with friends at Miller's Point, where, within a few days of her arrival, the family suffered the tragic loss of a small daughter, who took ill in the morning and was dead by five in the afternoon. Caroline was unable to find a job, despite Mrs Dillon having advertised twice on her behalf, but wrote from Miller's Point on 21 September 1864 that she was pleased, nevertheless, 'with all I have seen of Sydney (which is not much). I think the people very hospitable. I have been introduced to the Dean of Sydney and like him very much.'

Jane Finch wrote her first letter to the Society on 21 September 1864, while staying with friends at Redfern. Nineteen months later, she was able to send a repayment of

---

**The Golden South*, op. cit., pp. 131, 130.

£20 by two post office orders, sent independently. This was a practice adopted by some governesses, to avoid the possibility of the money being lost or stolen and increase the likelihood of its arrival. One went further and tore her postal order in two, then posted each part separately. Jane Finch had failed to get a job as a governess, but in a letter from Yass on 20 April 1866, explained her situation: 'When I arrived in the Colony it was in a depressed state and situations very scarce, but am happy to tell you I am in a very comfortable situation and have been for the past 12 months as Bookkeeper in a store up Country 200 miles from Sydney'.*

Eliza Bernard was another governess whose plight apparently was desperate during her first few years in Australia. She travelled first to Brisbane on the *Conway* during 1862, but her first letter was not written until nearly three years later, on 17 December 1865, from Sydney, when she was able to repay some of the amount due for her passage. She wrote from 'Buckhurst', Double Bay, the mansion home of Frederick Tooth, merchant, pastoralist and member of the famous brewing family:

> I regret greatly it has not been in my power to send it to you before; it is only in the last nine months that I have been in a situation; the first two years I was most unfortunate, in fact, suffered the greatest *poverty*. I tell you this that you may dismiss from your mind it was from want of principle I did not send the money before.

Two weeks later she sent a further cheque and on 24 June 1866, in her last letter to the Society, acknowledged a receipt for her payments, and went on:

> I am pleased to tell you that I am much more successful than I have hitherto been and have not the smallest doubt that I shall prosper provided I remain in good health. I am now more adapted for the Colonies than when I first landed; four years of painful experience has wrought a great change.
>
> I trust you will not think that I have or still am regretting leaving my native home; believe me such is not the case, on the contrary I

---

*Jane Finch died, unmarried, on 3 January 1892 at the age of fifty at the Prince Alfred Hospital, Sydney, and was buried in the Wesleyan Cemetery, Rookwood.

am and ever shall feel grateful towards Miss Rye for having been the means of my coming to the Colonies. I am now speaking from the deepest sincerity of my heart.

Mary Bayly, who arrived late in November 1866, stayed first at Newtown with a friend of her brother's, the Reverend Robert Taylor, an Anglican clergyman, and through him obtained a situation as resident governess in what was then the sparsely populated district of Cook's River. Her employer was Robert Hills of 'Marionette', Cook's River Road, Tempe, and Mary Bayly said of him on 22 March 1867: 'Mr Hills is a true gentleman and both he and Mrs Hills are very kind'.

Mary Bayly's salary of £80 a year was higher than most of the governesses received, but for this she had to work very hard. Apparently she was quite accomplished: her testimonials were lost in transit, but are listed in one of her letters — they included one from the Irish Academy of Music and others from persons who appear to be teachers of French and German. Mary's job certainly was demanding: she had to teach six children the subjects of English, French, German, Latin, music and singing. She would have received £100 a year, if she also could have taught drawing, but as she could not, the eldest daughter was sent to a drawing master for lessons and the expense was deducted from the pay Mary otherwise would have received. A fellow governess, Miss Carlow, who came out with her on the *Nourmahal,* was a contender for the position with the Hills' family, but according to Mary Bayly, she had two drawbacks: she did not teach Latin and she had been recommended by Mrs Dillon, and Mrs Hills 'declined to take anyone from her . . . Mrs Dillon's recommendation is not approved in Sydney'. Miss Carlow later tried her luck in Tasmania, but as she did not write to the Society, there is no further indication of her progress.

Although Mary Bayly wrote eight letters, she made few comments on life in Sydney, but she occasionally did comment on the scenery. Like some of the other governesses at this time, Mary addressed her letter to Miss Rye, who for a short time after her return from Australia and New Zealand, seems to have taken a more active part in the administration of the FMCES. On 21 December 1866, she said of the Cook's River district: 'It is the best part of the Country I have yet seen. I think it seems all pretty around Cook's River. I have no great fancy for Sydney (except for the Harbour) and dislike Newtown.' On 22 March 1867, she wrote: 'We had heavy rains the last few days which did much good, for the dry weather had lasted too long that water was very much wanted everywhere. I have as yet seen nothing of Sydney, except to go to Church on Sundays. I am seldom outside the gates. I have been once into George Street in the two months I have been at Cook's River, so I cannot say a great deal about the Country or the City either.'

During that year, Mary Bayly spent a week's vacation at Windsor, on a visit to her brother. On 27 July, she wrote:

> I did not like the town, especially as many of the houses were still in a very dismantled state from the effects of the floods last year. But the view from the elevated spots to the mountains in the distance was really beautiful and when we went towards Kurrajong I could not help wishing I was an artist, and could transfer the scene to canvas. Those mountains and the Harbour are the best things I have seen in Australia.

Mary said she expected to remain with the family until the following May, when Mr and Mrs Hills talked of travelling to France after placing their children at boarding schools 'at home'. She added that the children seemed to take it for granted that she would go with them on the trip, although she did not think it would be worth while, since she then would find herself back in England without a job. She added:

> I have not much fear of finding a difficulty in procuring another engagement, for I have been told of more than one since I have been here. I am very busy, having six pupils, all of them learning music and singing, so that until late in the evening I have no time to myself. I rarely see any of my friends, except in the holidays, and my usual amount of walking in the week is to Church on Sunday. In the vacation I went to Woollahra to see my kind friends Mr and Mrs Wise, who treat me almost as if I were a relative; they could not be kinder to me. I spent a day also with Mrs Alex Gordon,* whom I like extremely, but it is only when vacation

---

*Mrs Gordon, the wife of Alexander Gordon, a barrister, seems to have been another friend of Miss Rye's when she was in Sydney. Their home was in Cleveland Street, Redfern. Mrs Gordon was also one of the Society's Sydney representatives.

returns I can pay a few visits. I hardly think that when I change, I need be afraid of meeting with a more arduous situation than my present one. Will you kindly, dear Miss Rye, when you have a spare moment, write me a line, and I shall gladly receive any advice you may give, trusting to your better judgment.

On 29 April 1868, Mary Bayly wrote again of the scenery: 'The beauty of the Australian sky was not exaggerated to me, I never saw so beautiful a blue . . . As to the Harbour and the views over the sea, they can never to me lose their charming freshness and attractiveness. I often wish I had the brush of an artist to transfer to canvas this fascinating scene for after study when deprived of the original.'

At this time, Mary Bayly was still working for the Hills' family. Her pay had been increased to £85 a year, since she now had another pupil for music, but she wrote: 'It is almost more than my health can stand working from morning to night without even time for a walk'. In this and a short letter dated 21 April 1868, she repaid £25 to the Society. She sent what she described as a 'First of Exchange' via Marseilles and a 'Second of Exchange' via Panama, hoping that, in that way, she would ensure the safe arrival of the money.

There are no further letters from Mary Bayly after April 1868. As the Hills family left Cook's River Road about this time, she may have accompanied them overseas.*

Isabella Rodgerson, who arrived on 30 January 1867 on the *William Duthie*, also had an introduction to Mrs Alex Gordon from Miss Rye. She went to a position at Douglas Park, about forty-five miles south of Sydney, in the Camden district, one of the earliest settled parts of New South Wales and site of the Camden Estate, where John Macarthur made his

---

*Mary Frances Bayly of Windsor was married on 27 June 1872 to Francis Henry Hole, gentleman, also of Windsor. The ceremony was performed in St Matthew's Church, Windsor, by Anglican clergyman Chas. F. Barnsey. Apparently Mary Bayly had kept up her acquaintance with the Hills family, for one of the witnesses was Annie L. Hills. The other was W. Henry Bayly, who may have been her brother who lived at Church Street, Windsor. The Holes had a number of children, including Mary Elizabeth, born in 1873, William Francis, in 1875, Reginald T., in 1876, Harold C., in 1878 and Walter H., in 1882. Harold died in 1895 and another child, Herbert G. M., whose year of birth is not known, died in 1887. On the birth certificate of the eldest child, Francis Hole is described as a teacher, aged twenty-six, of Parramatta. Mary was then thirty-two and had been born in Dublin.

first experiments in breeding merino sheep. Her employer was R. L. Jenkins of 'Nepean Towers', a well-known breeder of Shorthorn bulls. Miss Rodgerson, in the first of her three letters to the Society, dated 15 July 1867, said nothing of her life at 'Nepean Towers', except that she was 'happy and comfortable'. In this letter to Miss Lewin, she repaid £8 to the Society. On 16 October, when she sent a further £8 10s 0d, she complained that she had not been well and had had to spend 'a great deal on medicines'. However, on 5 July of the following year, she paid the final instalment on the sum of £30, which was the amount she had borrowed from the Society. She asked that a receipt be forwarded to her mother at No. 6 Clyde Terrace, Brockley Road, New Cross, and said she would inform Dr Pye Smith, her guarantor, that his responsibilities were ended.

A far more communicative correspondent was Louisa Dearmer, who arrived in Sydney on the *City of Melbourne* on 23 May 1868. She landed penniless, having been unable to pay her fare from Melbourne and expecting to be able to draw on money that had been forwarded to a bank in Sydney. To her dismay, she found that there were 'eight different Banking Houses'. She had an introduction to Bishop Barker, but as he was away, she was directed to the Dean of Sydney, the Reverend W. M. Cowper. He and Mrs Cowper accompanied Louisa to all the banks without locating the missing remittance, so they lent her some money. The next day, she called again at all the banks, eventually locating her money at the Bank of Australasia. Less serious setbacks had distressed other FMCES governesses, but Louisa Dearmer was a very confident woman. Of the Dean and Mrs Cowper, she wrote in a letter dated 1 June 1868 but added to on 16 June: 'Words fail to express the gratitude I feel towards them for their kind Christian conduct towards me'.

Through the Dean, Louisa Dearmer was offered a position in a private school, where she 'would be received in the best society', but preferred to take a teaching job in a Government school, offered to her by the Committee of the Council of Education. The Council had been established under the Public Schools Act of 1866 to control all schools receiving Government funds; these included Government schools and certified denominational schools, of which about half were Anglican, one-third Catholic and the remainder Presbyterian and

Methodist. Teachers in the denominational schools, as well as those in Government schools, were employed by the Council of Education. The Council ran a training school for pupil-teachers and untrained teachers, gradually extending the course from three' to twelve months' duration. The classification, salary and promotion of teachers were determined by written examinations and by marks for teaching skill given by inspectors, mainly based on the pupils' success in reaching the Standards of Proficiency laid down by the Council.

Only a few weeks after her arrival, Louisa Dearmer started work as a teacher employed by the Council of Education at a salary of £150 a year, with the prospect of a rise to £250. She wrote: 'I have caused great dissatisfaction among the teachers — there are Natives who have been waiting a very long time for an appointment. They do not like that I should be appointed and in charge in less than three weeks after my arrival.'

Miss Dearmer found that there were many governesses out of work, thirty of whom were on the books of the Governesses' and Servants' Home waiting for positions. She stayed at the Home, which was situated at 98 Elizabeth Street and was under the control of a matron, Mrs Stephen Clarke. Louisa Dearmer said of these governesses:

> Most of them are so incompetent. It is useless for anyone to come here as Governesses who cannot play the Piano; even with that acquirement Governesses in private families get badly paid. Thirty they think fair for a Governess when they give the General Servant Twenty-five. The National School Mistresses get from £108 up to near £300 with the advantage of taking private pupils for accomplishments and they have such a mania for music, there is no difficulty to get pupils for that. I have been very much amused to hear the tones of a really tolerable Piano issuing from a little cottage, one could wonder where they could find room for it. Passing through the streets in the evening music seems to come from every house, and every Public House has its band of music. I don't know what the colonists can do when they come home. I must add that in many cases it is a libel to call it music, but I think they are not very particular as long as it is a noise.

Following the arrival of this letter, Miss Lewin wrote from London asking for more information about the prospects for governesses and for teachers in Government schools. In a reply dated 14 December 1868, Louisa Dearmer said:

You say the Bishop thinks it useless to send more Governesses out — I am sorry to say the whole Colony set their faces against all new arrivals, they are dreadfully narrow-minded in this respect. Do not think me uncharitable, but they are so intent on getting money for themselves that they overlook the welfare of the Colony.

There are plenty of inefficient Governesses, but I am sure that efficient people of all classes would work their way very well, but a Governess who does not understand music has no chance. There is a great want of Protestant servants here; a servant girl gets from 10/- to 14/- per week and they are the most insolent, independent creatures imaginable. The people in Victoria laugh at the New South Wales people and call them 'money grubbers'; it is but too true, there is so little enterprise, it is sad to see a Country with such resources so neglected.

The vine grows so plentifully, yet they will not take the trouble to cultivate it; the extravagance is pitiable. Meat being so cheap it is only the best parts are eaten, and the dress of all classes is absurd. Although the people profess to be as good as one another, it amuses me to see the ridiculous pride so visible on the face of their equality: labouring people, who would be unpretending people at home, assume such airs here, they call each other Mr and Mrs so and so and speak of each other as ladies and gentlemen, the children call their parents papa and mamma. They are very fond of making themselves out to be descended from good families and take the greatest pleasure in bringing down those they feel to be superior.

You are aware I dare say that the Colony is in a financially bad state just now, which, of course, affects all classes.

You ask if there is any opening for National School teachers — I will tell you the exact state of things and leave you to draw your own conclusions. There are at present nearly 400 pupil teachers who assist in schools and after serving their apprenticeship are trained in a College. There are 150 that have just completed their training and are now waiting for schools. There is a very jealous feeling towards anyone getting an appointment. I have myself suffered some of it. The Secretary of the Council of Education told me it was a thing they never did to appoint anyone to a School without passing the Training School; it was a piece of good fortune for me, but it was entirely the Dean's influence that obtained it for me.

I have enquired about private Governesses, Mrs Clarke at the Home told me that a Miss [Ellen] Ireland who came from England with letters to the Bishop, receives £50 per annum and does not live in the house, so, expensive as things are, she can scarcely live on it. Another, a Mrs Shangster and her daughter, have been four months out of employ; they are fearfully in debt, the daughter, a fine pianist, has just obtained a situation up country at £40 per annum. I know of one who receives £70, another £100, but they are with rich people; the average is from £40 to £50 per annum, but I am sure anyone who is persevering may in time do well. The climate is incomparable and the scenery about Sydney charming. Of course all people cannot live in Sydney and a Bush Town or squatters' house, which are isolated in the Bush, you could have no idea of. I have been several times in the Bush and was once for about ten minutes lost. There seems one interminable growth of the tea tree with here and there a large Gum or Iron Bark tree, all of a dingy brown green colour.

If you turn a yard out of your road you are lost, it is all so alike and the intense solitude is most oppressive. At home in the woods one hears the birds sing and chirp, and a buzz of insect life, but here there is not a sound, excepting towards evening when the locusts make a noise like letting off of steam from a railway engine, and the buzz of mosquitoes. I am told the mad house is constantly full of people who go mad from the intense solitude of the Bush; they come into the town and rush into its excitement, which from the great contrast they cannot bear. You will perhaps think I am giving a very decided opinion having been here so short a time, but when I will tell you that I dine at the Dean's house every Sunday and teach in his Sunday School, visit once a week at the Refuge for fallen women, also at the Benevolent Institutions and sometimes go to read to the patients at the Infirmary, I hear all that is going on at the Home and I am obliged to live at a First Class Boarding House where I constantly see a great variety of people. The children in my school are of all classes from professionals downwards. As I have occasion now and then to visit them I have an opportunity of seeing all classes, and nothing transpires but what I do hear.

The Home is a very comfortable place. They charge Governesses 11/6 per week and Servants 10/6. Mrs Clarke, the Matron, when one knows her is a kindhearted woman and has everything clean and comfortable, but until one does know her, she is a most forbidding woman to speak to and so excessively proud. She treats poor Governesses with the most supreme contempt, but she is exceedingly kind to those in distress. It is really a great boon to Servants and Governesses to have such a place of refuge; she is a most conscientious woman. I am sorry to say I could not submit to be put down by her, a woman. I felt I was at any rate her equal, but now we understand each other we are the best of friends. She is one who strongly opposes fresh people coming out.

There is one sad thing I feel bound to mention: so many of the girls sent out, particularly in English vessels, but in others as well, get ruined on board ship; when they arrive here they have no character and go on the town. A sad case in point, the *Devonport*, which arrived a few months ago, no one would engage servants from her so bad was the report and an action was entered against the Doctor for breach of trust. The Captain and Matron were fully acquitted. Many of the poor girls died.* Morality is at a sadly low rate here; it is a common thing to see girls from 13 to 20 confirmed drunkards. Indeed it is the curse of all classes. If you will tell me the names of those you have sent out I will make enquiry about them and let you know . . .

I am afraid you will think I have sent you a very gossiping letter; you must kindly excuse me, I cannot help noting everything around me.**

---

*The *Devonport* arrived in Sydney on 31 July 1868 after a ninety-day voyage from Portsmouth. According to the Report of the Immigration Board later presented to Parliament, four emigrants died from pulmonary complaints during the voyage. The remaining 438 emigrants were placed in quarantine, where a further four died, and another at the Sydney Infirmary. At a subsequent inquiry, the reasons for the great amount of sickness on board were said to be the bad weather and the consequent wet state between decks caused by the violent rolling of the ship, for which the cargo of iron and cement was partly responsible.

Charges of dereliction of duty were made to the Immigration Board by Matron Mary Ann Hancox and some of the single women emigrants against the Surgeon Superintendent, Dr J. C. Sanger, and also against two of the officers, for associating with the female emigrants. The charges were investigated at six sittings of the Government Immigration Board, during which the Matron and many of the emigrants gave evidence. In its findings, the Board recommended that Dr Sanger 'should not be employed again in the Immigration Service', although its recommendations were later rejected as being too severe. The Board also described the matron as being 'wanting in tact and temper'. (Archives Office of New South Wales. NSW Colonial Secretary, 'Letters Received', CSIL 68/5504, and enclosures in 4/636.)

**Unfortunately, records reveal that Louisa Dearmer's promising career ended prematurely. She died on 10 March 1870, at the age of thirty years, after eighteen days of continued fever. On the death certificate, her address was given as 9 Bligh Street, which was probably a boarding-house. Apart from listing her birthplace as England, the certificate discloses no other details about her background. The Reverend W. M. Cowper officiated at her funeral at Balmain.

6 *Station Life*

'... "bush life" is a strange mixture of roughing and refinement'.

Louisa Geoghegan, Neuarpurr, Vic., 1867

The first governess to write about life on an isolated station property was Louisa Agnes Geoghegan, who arrived in Melbourne on 20 December 1866. She travelled out on the *Swiftsure* with Mr and Mrs Francis P. Hines* and their two children (and like them travelled first class) and apparently had been engaged in England or Ireland as governess for the children. The Hines family were returning to their property, Neuarpurr, which was situated in the Wimmera district in western Victoria, close to the South Australian border and just south of the Little Desert.

Although she went to work for an established and wealthy squatting family, Louisa Geoghegan's shock at the loneliness, isolation, hardships and tragedies of life in the outback stands out starkly in her letters. She began her one-week journey to Neuarpurr on Christmas Day 1866, and described this and the first weeks with her employers in a letter dated 19 February 1867. The more usual way to reach Apsley, the small border township, which was a centre for the isolated properties, was

*Francis Hines, a member of an Irish family who had settled in Tasmania, had followed his brother-in-law, Hugh Lawrence McLeod, to Victoria in the early 1850s. Both men were among a number of adventurous squatters who, having arrived late in the colony and found the eastern parts of the Wimmera already settled, pushed on farther west into drier country. Hugh McLeod had taken up Benyeo Station, near Apsley, on the South Australian border, in 1846. Francis Hines purchased the adjoining property, Neuarpurr, which was regarded as the best grazing land in the district, from the original settler, Stephen Rowe. The properties between them had a carrying capacity of some 30,000 sheep.

by rail to Geelong, steamer or coach to Portland, then another coach through Hamilton to Apsley, about fifty miles to the north-west. Louisa Geoghegan, however, went through Ballarat by the recently opened railway. She wrote:

On Christmas Day we began our journey up the Country — went by rail to Ballarat, there Mr Hines's brother-in-law met us; we made all one party and were twelve in number. We drove 260 miles — used to start very early in the morning, rest in the heat of the day and make another start in the evening — the weather was very hot, more so than has been felt for the last four years. We had all kinds of adventures in the shape of kicking horses and broken poles, but we reached Benyeo (the residence of Mr McLeod — brother-in-law to Mr Hines) on the following Sunday.

It is 14 miles distant from this place [Neuarpurr]. Mrs Hines and I were over here for a day or two, made all right for the children to come, but when we returned to Benyeo for them Mrs Hines took measles and from that day, which was not a week after we reached Benyeo, up to the present there has been nothing but sickness. Just as Mrs Hines was over the worst of the measles, the eldest girl was taken ill, the day after her 12th birthday. She was affected very strangely and though a doctor was sent for at once it was 48 hours before one arrived, then Bessie was dangerously ill with inflammation of the lungs — about 10 days after she was first attacked, measles came out on her slightly. The Doctors (for now there were two), thought she might now get better, but her strength was all gone and she gradually sank and died at Benyeo last Saturday, exactly the day month of her birthday when she appeared in her usual health. Her death has cast a great gloom on everything; she was a gentle, companionable, intellectual child liked by everyone who knew her — the second girl misses her sadly. Bessie was laid beside a brother in a small burying place, adjoining the garden on Sunday and on Monday we all came here for good. Everyone who had not had measles before had them during the six weeks we were there — 15 cases in all, fortunately I had had them and was able to look after some of the invalids.

I like the people I have met in Australia much better than I like what I have yet seen of the country, but it is too soon to judge — I have experienced nothing but kindness from Mr and Mrs Hines all through, but particularly lately. We have done nothing yet with lessons — they brought out a beautiful piano, the only thing poor Mrs Hines now cares about. She idolized her eldest child.

As soon as I receive any money I will remit it to you.

Louisa Geoghegan wrote again later that year, on 18 October, when she returned some of the money lent to her by the

Society. She also sent a contribution to the work of the Society, but like many other governesses, she disliked publicity and asked that her donation be listed as anonymous. She continued:

I am very glad I came to Australia, but I cannot say I like it very much, it is such an out-of-the-world place and so monotonous, but as far as kind treatment goes I could not meet with or desire kinder. With no one in this neighbourhood have I seen the social distinction made with Governesses that there is at home.

I have very little work here in comparison with London — I do not think £80 here as much as £60 at home, dress is very expensive and the people are dressy. You will be glad to hear that my pupil has made great progress in her studies, but particularly in music, which pleases Mrs Hines very much. They brought out a very nice piano, in fact, 'bush life' is a strange mixture of roughing and refinement. In this district there are two distinct sets, one gentry and one *would-be* gentry — there are more of the latter. In the former I think an unfinished, unladylike Governess would be unwelcome. Literature is much more brought forward than at home because there are no new daily topics — the standing one is sheep — in which ladies take no part — of course, this is only my experience, which is not very extended.

Her next letter, dated 17 May 1868, is in reply to one from Miss Lewin:

I thank you for your kind letter and offer of getting me a box sent out free of expense; it would be a consideration as the overland part is both expensive and slow. I am getting a box out now, it is travelling since the beginning of January. I am now so reconciled to Australia that I was surprised to see by your letter that I had apparently been disappointed at first. At times I feel it is rather dull work never to go beyond the garden or Croquet ground, but then I remember I can rake or hoe in the garden as I please and the freedom to please oneself more than compensates for monotony. Occasionally we have a good deal of riding, and I have a nice horse for my own use — then, if Mr Hines is busy we are sometimes weeks without going outside the gates.

Latterly there has been a great deal of gaiety for this place — one Public Ball and two private ones — one of the private ones here. The style is to dance until daylight, because it is impossible to ride or drive in the dark, so those who must go, dance until it is light enough to start and the rest take thankfully anything they can get in the shape of a bed — when it comes to provide for 30 you cannot be very particular.

I felt the heat much more this summer than last — but it was much more continued and unusually severe — this part is nearly as hot as Adelaide. I hope this Christmas to be able to take a trip to my brother and sister; travelling there is very expensive and last year I felt economical.

Louisa's brother Charles and sister Jane lived at Sale, in eastern Victoria, a distance of about 400 miles from Apsley.*

Her next letter was written on 12 August, also in reply to one from Miss Lewin, who following her usual custom, assiduously cultivated correspondence with any of the emigrants who wrote letters descriptive of life overseas. She asked Miss Geoghegan about the prospects for governesses and teachers in Victoria, but she did not receive an encouraging reply. Victoria, in fact the whole of Australia, was in a depressed economic state in the latter part of the 1860s. There were adverse seasonal conditions throughout the country, with little interruption, from the early 1860s to 1872, combined with a severe drought in the mid-1860s. In 1866, there was a financial crisis in England, which affected the colonies, and there was widespread industrial and commercial depression with many unemployed in Sydney and Melbourne. Unemployment continued to be very bad throughout 1867 and in 1868 Louisa Geoghegan wrote that the Melbourne papers carried accounts of a Society for Educated People in Indigent Circumstances, with teachers of both sexes figuring largely in the lists.

Louisa Geoghegan continued to be an acute, if class-conscious, observer of country life:

In this district for three gentlemen there are six mushrooms,** I suppose you would call them, the former I have heard say, would like thoroughly good Lady Governesses from Home if they had anyone there conscientiously to select them — the mushroom class pay largely but expect rather queer things, viz. that the Governess

---

*Charles Robert Geoghegan was Town Clerk and Surveyor of the Borough of Sale, capital of Gippsland. The first Town Clerk, G. R. Coulson, was appointed in 1863, but died soon after. Charles Geoghegan, his successor, then held the post until about 1903. Regarded as one of the chief designers of Sale, he was president of the Gippsland Hospital Committee for many years and a leading Mason. He died at Sale on 2 April 1909, at the age of seventy-three. Jane Geoghegan died at Sale on 3 December 1921 at the age of eighty-one.

**Mushroom = upstart, parvenu, *nouveau riche*; i.e. 'sprung up overnight'.

should light the schoolroom fire and similar things; they have been accustomed themselves to manual exertions and don't understand not keeping it up. In my short experience I have known of two cases where *ladies* got with these people and very soon had to separate. In *nearly* every instance you are looked on as the Intellectual Member of the Establishment; you are the constant companion of and associate of the Lady, considered, I might say indulged, in every way and your only difficulty is to civilize the children, which you are supposed to do through example, as they are uncontrolled to a degree, and the parents object to anything else.

I believe in Adelaide salaries are much lower than in Victoria — I think that capable women have a better chance here than at home — but I think a few of a good class not *long* accustomed to home scrubbing and drudgery would be a better importation than a larger number of the common run of governesses.

Louisa reported that besides paying off her debts, she also had been able to send £25 home. Her next and last letter to the Society was not written until two years later. On 10 August 1870, she wrote to Miss Lewin:

I have gone on steadily here for three years and a half, and have managed to scrape together money enough to buy a piano and otherwise enable me to go to live with my brother in Sale, Gippsland, and enter into partnership with my sister, who already has a pretty good school.*

I do not leave Mrs Hines until Christmas. She is sending home for a Governess, or rather she is getting me to do so for her, as she knew no one whom she could depend on — I am writing by this Mail to Miss McBean, Priory Road (26), Kilburn — I was with her in London and I have given her all particulars — Mrs Hines will not pay the passage for any one and, as I do not think there are many Governesses willing or able to embark the necessary sum, I have mentioned you to Miss McBean as helping through your Society deserving persons in such a dilemma — I also told her that I thought, if she could not undertake the trouble of selecting a suitable person, that perhaps you would. I hope you will not consider I have taken a liberty, but I feel I would stretch a point to oblige Mrs Hines . . .

You will perhaps wonder that when Mrs Hines had so much difficulty in the matter, she should send home — but she came to

*There is no mention of Jane Geoghegan's school in a list of nine schools that advertised in the *Gippsland Times* (published in Sale) during the years 1862 to 1894.

this decision from her observation of Governesses in this district who have come from Melbourne and, as a class, they are not much to be admired. Mrs Hines and Mr Hines and the children are very much to be liked, but no convent life could be more monotonous than life here is. The routine is teaching from 8 o'clock to dinner, [?12] o'clock, again from 2 to 3 o'clock, after which you are your own Mistress, but your resources are limited solely to intellectual amusements. Walking, owing to the heat and wet, is only possible a short time through the year and you must be brave enough to go by yourself for here they think it laborious. Driving is inconvenient there being no roads, only tracks, and as Mr Hines is now overseer, he seldom has time to take us out riding as he used to do and a book, the piano, or fancy and plain work occupy you until bed time. No one comes and there is no place to go. I have never been unhappy here and though I am sorry to part from Mrs Hines I am not sorry to leave the Bush.

I hope your unselfish efforts for the good of others meet with satisfactory returns. Believe me, always yours gratefully, Louisa Agnes Geoghegan.

A radical change occurred in Louisa Geoghegan's life during the next six months. She abandoned the idea of going to live with her brother and sister at Sale and instead married in April the following year, information that is contained in a letter from her successor.*

Louisa Geoghegan was followed by Miss M. A. Oliver, formerly a governess to a family in France, who arrived in Melbourne, probably on the *Sussex* on 21 March 1871, and left about the end of the month to travel to Neuarpurr, arriving on 6 April. Miss Oliver was not nearly as tolerant as Louisa Geoghegan had been of life in the bush; she wrote only once to the Society, on 2 October 1871, giving every indication that her stay in the Wimmera would be short:

I did not write immediately on arrival thinking it better to give myself time to form an opinion of Colonial or rather bush life. Of my voyage I have nothing to say. It was prosperous and very

*On 6 April 1871, at Neuarpurr, Apsley, Louisa Agnes Geoghegan, aged twenty-eight, born in Co. Kildare, Ireland (daughter of William Pace Geoghegan, doctor, and Elizabeth Evatt), married Frederick Vaughan, aged thirty-two, born in Wales (son of A. Henry Frederick Vaughan, gentleman, and Mary Anne Caroline Williams). Frederick Vaughan, a sheep-farmer of Biscuit Flat, Robe, S.A., was a widower with no children. The ceremony was performed by the Reverend R. R. Collins, Church of England minister, and the witnesses were F. P. Hines and H. L. McLeod.

disinteresting, the passengers few and not very agreeable. I landed under a curious circumstance, being met not by anyone from Mr Hines but by a brother-in-law of a friend of mine in France. Fortunately I had written that I was coming out to this gentleman's wife and they kindly took me to their house. By a very curious coincidence she knew a Mrs Hines living in the same neighbourhood, on whom I called, hoping she might be a relation able to give me information how to act for my journey up the country. Happily for me she was the right person to apply to, having been requested by her nephew, Mr F. Hines, to meet me, but owing to Miss McBean forgetting to mention my name and there being some error about the ship, she did not know what to do. As it was all came right in the end and I started for my 300 miles up the country. Such *travelling* in a vehicle one can only call a covered cart, across miles of uncultivated flat country, diversified only by ugly dark pine trees, heath and swamps, not a person to be seen, every 20 or 30 miles a station or small township. In my opinion it is very disagreeable for a lady alone, travelling in this style, especially in a country where society is so united, and it is impossible to say who may be your fellow-passengers.

I have now had nearly six months' experience and without hesitation I can say it is not a life I should like to try long, notwithstanding the nice people I am with. There are perhaps few families as intellectual and well educated as this, at all events in Victoria. Still had I known the very isolated life I was to lead I do not think I should have been induced to come out. This is not the only drawback. One could cheerfully bear it two or three years if there were any advantages to be gained in the end, but I must candidly confess from what I have heard and seen, there is no better chance of getting on out here than at home, the expenses are far greater, and the salaries are not in proportion. Consequently £100 is not more than £60 in England, that is taking travelling expenses into consideration.

The bush life is a perfect exile; there are about three estimable families near. If a Governess has friends in Melbourne it is something like £20 if she takes a holiday, the transportation of luggage is fearful, only small portmanteaus are allowed and, if there is anything extra, it is heavily charged. I am perhaps putting things in their worst light, but home ideas of this Country are very false. A Lady, unless she be a musician, either vocal or instrumental, will not succeed very well for music is very much cultivated. As to dress, although much is not necessary, still everything must come from Melbourne and there is either postage or mail parcel to pay.

I do not know if you have heard of Miss Geoghegan since she left; she married the day I arrived here and is living about 100 miles away. The greatest amusement we have is riding, but even too much of that becomes monotonous, with no object in view. As to scenery there is none; it is certainly the ugliest country I have ever seen, reminding one of the North of France. I only wonder the sheep thrive on such poor land. Of course mutton forms the principal dish; the living is simple enough; there are times when we cannot get butter. I have not yet experienced the hot weather; the winter is over now, although not the cold of home, still I think I felt it quite as much, perhaps this was owing to the house being only of one storey, and the rooms all leading into the garden so that it is almost like living in the open air. The garden is looking nice, but nothing to equal the flowers at home, the soil is bad, and the heat with hot winds will dry up everything. If you want any more information that you think I can give, I should be very glad to do it. All I can say is that I do not like Australia and would rather be in England or the Continent with £50 than here. With regard to the £30 due to you, I hope that will be settled shortly.

By the time this letter was written in 1871, the prosperity of the earlier years, when open houses and generous hospitality were the rule, was over. The prolonged drought, the expiration of leases, changes in the land laws, particularly the passing of the Land Act of 1869, which allowed free selection, all contributed to the changes that were becoming apparent in Louisa Geoghegan's letters. Earlier there had been balls, to which people came from long distances, but later there was only monotony; earlier Francis Hines had found time to take the women riding, but in later years, as his duties as overseer, as well as his responsibilities as owner and manager, increased, he could do so no longer. When Neuarpurr was thrown open for selection in the 1870s, Francis Hines secured part of the freehold at the upset price of £1 an acre. He later sold out and went to New South Wales, where in the 1880s he is listed as a squatter at Merri Merrigal, west of Lake Cargellico, in the Hillston district.

Another governess to go to a station in the Wimmera was Rosa Phayne. Although she arrived with the best of credentials, including a letter of introduction from Miss Maria Rye to Mrs Thomas Learmonth, wife of one of the pioneer squatters in the Buninyong—Ballarat district, she was unhappy from the moment she arrived and spent three miserable years, during which she seldom managed to rise above a state of general depression.

Her first letter was written on 13 August 1869, addressed from the Melbourne Home for Governesses and Servants, then being built on the south side of Little Lonsdale Street, between Queen and William Streets:

I had a very long letter written to you soon after my arrival in this Colony. Perhaps it is as well it was never sent. Reading it over I find it was written in such wretchedness of spirit it would have done no good and now I am glad you never received it . . .

I landed in Melbourne weary in mind and body. I had great difficulty in finding the 'Home' and felt rather frightened not knowing where I was. Mrs Roe, the Matron, is an extremely nice lady-like woman. I knew some of her connections at home, she being sister to the present Bishop of Peterborough.* I found the Melbourne Home most comfortable and desirable more particularly to ladies landing in a strange country. It is still in an unfinished state being only in progress of building, but when all is completed it will be a great boon to Governesses.

My impressions of Melbourne and the Colony are *thoroughly* unfavourable. I was not one hour in it when I regretted deeply the step I had taken; had I possessed the money I would have returned in the next ship, but all things considered it was just as well I had not money. I do not use too strong a language when I say *no one* with the tastes, habits or feelings of a lady should ever come out to Australia. It may do for mediocre Governesses who can put up with roughness — or I should say vulgarity of mind, a great want of intellect, but I never would advise a lady to try it. I hate Australia and the Australians, I shall [be] with them but never of them. I would rather have £15 per annum in London than £50 here.

Mrs Tom Learmonth to whom Miss Rye kindly gave me a letter of introduction was most kind to me — on my writing up to her and enclosing my letter she at once invited me up to Ercildoun, Ballaarat, her house, at the same time telling me of a situation in the Bush with a Mrs Scott. I accepted the situation, the salary is £40 per annum; all said it was far too low a salary, but situations are *most* difficult to obtain; it is a great mistake to think they are easy to get. Finishing Governesses are better off in that respect than any other class. I did not visit Ercildoun but hope to spend my holidays there; the Learmonths are amongst the *nicest* of the Colonists, of course I don't class them or a *very few others* under the head of disagreeables in Australia.

Australia is by no means the Eldorado it is supposed to be or perhaps once was. There is a vast amount of wretchedness and poverty in the Country and men of talent and ability find it most difficult to obtain employment; even I lately come to the Colony, know instances. How much more then for a Governess?

---

*William Connor Magee, Bishop of Peterborough, 1869–91.

As to the town of Melbourne it is beyond anything abominable in every respect. I was more than thankful and glad to leave it. I was quite sorry to find by a letter I had from Mrs Roe another Lady Governess was coming out in the *Highflyer;** I think it is a great pity. There has not been one Governess to whom I have spoken on the subject but has not, like me, deeply regretted coming out and who would return to England could they afford it and so very, very many have gone back hating place and people. You have no idea of it.

I am quite satisfied with my present abode. I leave the word happiness out of the question. I only feel as though all the rightness has gone out of my life. I am very sorry I did not think of India or Rio, unprejudiced and unbiassedly. With no feeling of actual home sickness do I write, only weary disappointment. Now that I am here I should be ashamed to return without feeling I had made some effort for good. On all sides do I hear sad tales of the struggles for our daily bread, and the last few years and seasons have been so bad. There is, of course, much wealth in some instances, but it is confined to the few. I would recommend no one, unless indeed servants, to emigrate to Australia.

The climate is trying also, so many sudden changes. This winter has been very severe. You will say perhaps I am writing one-sidedly; not so, I am and have been most fortunate in getting my present situation and have by no means seen or felt the worst side of the picture, but I hear a great deal and cannot help judging accordingly. One thing I do know: I never, never shall like or be happy in Australia and would leave it tomorrow if I could. I just try not to think, or else I would die, but there are times when I must think, and I am weary of life and everything and everyone. Mrs Scott, the lady in whose family I am, said to me on hearing I was writing home: 'Tell your friends, Miss Phayne, we are both, Mr Scott and myself, very pleased with you, you are so attentive to the children and so bright!' She does not know my heart is nearly breaking sometimes. I knew they were satisfied with me and I with them.

Dear Miss Lewin this is a different letter perhaps from what you expected from me, but I cannot write otherwise, it would be untruthful. Will you write to me? How much I wish you would, it would give me such pleasure and happiness. Address to the Melbourne Home.

Rosa Phayne was by this time employed by Thomas King Scott and his wife on their station, Rich Avon West, on the west bank of the Avon River, about sixteen miles from

---

*Annie Hunt, who arrived in September 1869.

St Arnaud in the Wimmera, north-west of Melbourne. The nearest townships were St Arnaud to the east and Glenorchy to the south-west. Travel from Melbourne was by train to Ballarat, then coach from Ballarat to Glenorchy on the Ballarat—Horsham road. An example of the isolation that affected Rosa Phayne, used to life in closely settled urban England, was the mail service, which ran once a week, starting from 'Four Posts', the original name of Glenorchy, a small township of about 180 people, and travelled north to Corack by pack-horse, serving stations including Rich Avon. All supplies came by bullock-wagons and drays from Ballarat or via the coast.

Rich Avon was originally a 120,000-acre cattle-station, established in an area discovered by explorer Thomas Mitchell after he crossed the Murray River at Swan Hill. It was taken up in 1845 and, in the early days, was one of the few properties to be fenced. It originally covered both sides of the Avon River, but in 1858 was divided into east and west. In 1865, when Thomas King Scott of Warracknabeal bought Rich Avon West, it was a sheep-station of some 50,000 acres with a grazing capacity of 30,000 sheep.

Following the 1869 Land Act, a rush of selectors to the area coincided with the worst drought the Wimmera had experienced since settlement. No rain fell from the South Australian border to the eastern extent of the Wimmera for many months, following years of poor seasons. During the drought, water had to be carted to Rich Avon from Scott's Crossing on the Avon River near Burrereo. This water, with the stagnant stream at low level, was frequently muddy and full of debris and animal remains. Epsom salts and lime were added to clear the liquid mud of sediment and clay, and make it fit for use. This was the setting for Rosa Rhayne's life at Rich Avon West, Avons Plains, by Glenorchy, from where she wrote to Miss Lewin on 25 March 1870:

I am now satisfied I must have written my letter to you in great bitterness of spirit and in utter disgust to and of the Colony. Now I shall endeavour to modify and moderate my feelings and give a juster and unprejudiced view of things. My lines are now cast in pleasant places, strange as it may seem to you. It just feels here as though it were my groove in life. The Scotts are pleasant, educated, kindly people. My duties are not laborious and what they are I like greatly. In Bush Life there is a great charm; lonely perhaps, some people would find it. I never have done so. I have seen more of life, of the springs of action in people, their ways and peculiarities than I ever did in my life before and I have travelled and seen much; perhaps it is because there is less reserve, less stiffness, less of the conventionalities of life, I like it. I am very happy with all this; I feel I am in the Colony, simply not of the people or with them beyond our own household.

I had the pleasure of staying at Mrs Somerville Learmonth's* about six weeks ago. She is very nice and I liked her greatly, so like home she is. She regretted not having seen you and spoke so highly of Miss Rye at the same time. She quite agreed with me that it is a mistake sending Governesses out to Australia. There are quite sufficient to suit the requirements of the Colonists and, in so many cases, utter misery to the ladies who do come out. I never would advise a sister of my own to act as I have done, particularly now the Colony seems to have reached a culminating point of difficulty and embarrassment. There is nothing doing in business. This is quite universal. Many settlers (squatters) have failed, many have abandoned their runs. If rains do not come soon I don't know what will be done, for the sheep are dying for want of food, literally there is not one blade of grass.

You ask me why do I hate Australia and Australians. I expressed myself rather strongly then; now I shall just say I do not like the place or people nor *never* shall, but as I have made it my home I shall put up with it and all its shortcomings. Place and people, with few exceptions, are verily the Antipodes of home, selfish, mortally, and so unsympathizing. I think I have said all I have to and I wonder what you will say on reading this production. Thanking you once more for your kind letter and hoping when you have leisure you will sometimes bestow a thought on me.

Rosa Phayne's period of grudging acceptance of her life at Rich Avon West, however, did not last. On 18 May 1871, she

---

*Miss Phayne stayed with the Learmonths at Ercildoun, a homestead built in the Scottish baronial style. Thomas and Somerville Learmonth, pioneer pastoralists at Port Phillip, arrived from Van Diemen's Land in 1838. From Geelong, they went to the Ballarat district, where they established a station at Buninyong and from there took up a larger run at Burrumbeet.

In 1856, Thomas Learmonth married Louisa, youngest daughter of Sir Thomas Valiant. After she died in 1878, he married the fourth daughter of Lestock Reid, an uncle of his brother John's wife. Reid's second daughter had married Somerville Learmonth in 1860.

Thomas and Somerville Learmonth, who were noted for their wool production, also pioneered an educational venture when in 1848 they started a bush boarding-school at Buninyong for the children of workers on their properties. Unfortunately, it proved to be more costly than they had anticipated. A matron and three servants had to be employed, apart from the teachers, and the Learmonths found they had to charge substantial fees to cover costs. Other squatters, observing their problems, were deterred from following the Learmonths' example.

wrote again to Miss Lewin, telling her that she could stay no longer in Australia and asking for help in finding a position when she returned to London:

You may possibly be surprised at hearing from me again, but the fact is that do my very best, I cannot like the Colony or people. More and more do I dislike both. I am exceedingly unhappy and heartily weary of it. I have been in my present situation ever since my arrival, which will be two years next month, and during that time have had more to contend with than I ever before had in my Governess experience. Mrs Scott and I have *never* got on well, be the fault where it may. One thing, she has not one feeling like a lady, although one ostensibly, and I cannot conscientiously approve of children having their own way in all things. It has been and is a very difficult situation to fill. I should long ere this have left it, but the difficulty of obtaining another situation in this country is extreme and the *remuneration* not adequate to the disadvantages! I tried in many quarters and made many an inquiry about another situation, but to all my applications there was the invariable reply, any number of applicants on the same errand and no chance of their being supplied, nothing to be got.

Into the details of Bush life I shall not enter much. Its advantages and disadvantages — of the former, the principal one is one does not spend too much money, which is desirable as things are very dear in this Country; of the latter, the place feels like a prison to me, only without the ignominy, no books, no Society, *nothing improving*, everything retrograde, conversation, scandal and gossip, things I hate and have never been accustomed to. You may say perhaps I am overdrawing the picture because I am prejudiced against; not so, I would not wilfully or willing do it, it is the case.

Now I am quite determined to return home and I have saved sufficiently for the purpose and want to ask could you assist me in obtaining a situation in England on my landing. I would rather have £25 there than £100 here. My own cannot help me, they find it quite enough to do to aid themselves. I must bear my own burden, but it would be no burden were I out of this land. Can you and if so, will you help me in this? I would not care how much I had to do, preferring an active life to my present desultory one. I know all you would say of over-population, and number of applicants for situations, but in extenuation of returning home, my plea is I so dislike the Country and everything in connection with it and I am satisfied I shall not regret taking a step homeward. If quite possible or convenient, would you kindly answer me by return of post. I shall D.V.* remain here a few months longer,

***Deo volente*: God willing.

I mean at Rich Avon; it will suit all parties. I doubt if I am suited for the climate or the people or an Australian life at all. I should very much like to be in or near London, having an intense admiration, if not love, for the Metropolis of the world. Will you kindly give me your candid opinion and advice in this matter? If I mistake not, you have copies of my Testimonials and I am sure Mrs Scott will give me a good one.

Rosa Phayne was still in Australia a year later and she wrote for the last time to Miss Lewin from the Melbourne Home, Little Lonsdale Street, in June 1872, as she was about to board a ship to take her back to England. She again appealed for help, apparently having received a refusal from Miss Lewin to her previous request, not a surprising response, since the Society had such a number of women wanting to leave England to get jobs overseas but was unable to assist more than a handful. Miss Lewin also would have been conscious of the valiant efforts by many other governesses to adjust to situations more difficult than that confronting Rosa Phayne.

Rosa Phayne began:

At the risk of again incurring your anger I write once more to you. When this reaches you, I shall have sailed (D.V.) for England, and I do not think even you would blame me under the circumstances; did you know what life in Australia for a Governess is — its sense of intense loneliness and unprotectedness, utter friendlessness. All whom I have met in the same position reiterate what I write. I have saved sufficient money to take me back second class; would have had more but sent money home. I would most willingly go as a Nursery Governess, children or teaching are no trouble to me — I do teach French and Music. I enclose a testimonial from Mrs Scott; it is a favourable one and, without boasting, she could not have done less, but my life there was a difficult one in every respect. How deeply grieved have I been in having left England, the intense selfishness of all, the great want of intellect, and in many cases the utter want of truth, straightforwardness and frankness, is most trying. The great expense of everything, travelling especially, often hundreds of miles by coach, constitution and purse suffer alike. Will my appeal be in vain this time, or will you still say you will not help me. I am so unhappy for my family are very poor and I am wretched out here alone. Granted that I should have weighed all this before leaving home, still I could not foresee much that has occurred and was sanguine, thinking that I would battle against everything. If you would kindly help me! and you have so much influence! May I ask if it were possible for me to obtain employment in London, in the City,

I don't care where; it has always been to me such a wonderful place.
I have been, since I left the Scotts, in a school in Tasmania, into the details of which I will not enter. The Principal (Lady), as is usual with Bush Ladies, no mind or thought, and in consequence is fast losing her pupils. Hoping you will kindly think me over, and not too severely.

If Miss Lewin did assist Rosa Phayne to find work on her return to the 'Metropolis of the world', the details are not recorded in the Society's files.

7 Hard Times in Depressed Years

'I have suffered more hardship *and* want *than I thought possible . . .'*

Susan Penrose, Melbourne, 1869

Compared with other governesses who arrived in Melbourne in the latter part of the 1860s and early 1870s, Louisa Geoghegan and Rosa Phayne were very fortunate. Miss Lewin's rebukes to Rosa Phayne for wanting to return to London are understandable, for at the same time she was receiving desperate letters from other FMCES emigrants unable to get any kind of work. Unemployment was widespread and some teachers and governesses were reduced to offering to work for no pay, just to put a roof over their heads.

On 2 July 1868, the Melbourne *Argus* ran the following advertisements:

A Lady, with highest references, would be glad to TEACH ENGLISH, Music, French and Drawing in respectable family, for board and residence . . .

Governess — a lady experienced in tuition, is desirous of a RE-ENGAGEMENT in a gentleman's family. Acquirements — English, music, singing and French (acquired in Paris) . . .

Lady, with best references, able to teach English, French and music, wants a comfortable HOME and very moderate salary . . .

Lady as Governess, can teach English, French, music. Salary no object . . .

These were only a few of one day's pleas from the unemployed.

Laura Jones and Susan Penrose were two FMCES emigrants who faced the daunting prospect of finding a job in this overcrowded marketplace when they arrived in Melbourne on 8 October 1867 on the *Swiftsure*. In an undated letter from the Melbourne Home, 73 Russell Street (another temporary address for the Home before a permanent building was built in Little Lonsdale Street), Susan Penrose wrote:

> We have neither of us obtained situations — everyone appears suspicious of engaging new arrivals. I hope to get something soon — I saw Mrs a Beckett last week and gave her your letter.
> Miss Jones is quite in despair, her English Certificates are not of the slightest value here, in fact could she obtain a situation, she must go through an examination before she could obtain a Certificate. They all seem to prefer Colonists. Everything is dull at present and applicants for situations as numerous as in England. I hope to get a situation soon and will repay my passage money as soon as possible.

Susan Penrose did find a situation in the bush, but left it soon after when she became ill. She wrote again, on 7 December 1869, to say that she still was unable to send any money for her passage. 'I have earned very little since March. I was ill and left the Station, but I am sorry now as it is very difficult to get another.' She had been living at the Melbourne Home for Governesses and Servants since 2 August and said she was 'very thankful to get Needlework to help me. I hope after Christmas to get a situation in the Bush, which I prefer to living in Melbourne, and will send you the money as soon as possible.'

Laura Jones also fared badly. She tried at first to get a job as a teacher and must have had some temporary employment, for she sent £5 towards the repayment of her loan on 22 May 1868, giving the Melbourne Home as her address. On 7 November, however, she wrote: 'I have been very unfortunate in the Colony, my English Certificate being no good and my letters of introduction did me no service'. This letter was written from Waranga, a mining and agricultural village on the Goulburn goldfields, near Rushworth, in northern Victoria, where she had eventually succeeded in getting a position as an assistant teacher at a school. The letter included a further repayment of £5.

Laura Jones was treated very harshly at Waranga and

wrote about her experiences there after she returned to Melbourne. The letter, dated 13 August 1869, included £5 towards the repayment of her loan.

> I am sorry you have had to wait so long, but I have been totally unable to send it any sooner, not having prospered in the Colony, indeed, I have suffered more *hardship* and *want* than I thought possible I could suffer. Some weeks after I landed I went up the Bush to a school as assistant, where I had to live in a hut about six feet square, and I soon discovered that everyone connected with the school were dissenters and objected to me on account of my religious principles. I couldn't and wouldn't go to their chapel, until at last I was obliged to give up my situation. For five months following I existed by doing needlework for the diggers' wives, when I managed to get money enough to come to Town. I am now teaching English at a boarding school and getting along a great deal better.
>
> I have not written to any of my friends at home as I disliked telling them of my circumstances, but I will write soon now and may I ask a favour: that you will not answer any enquiries that may be made respecting me — I will write and tell them as much as I wish them to know.
>
> Servants do better here than Governesses. Scores of the latter are always wanting situations and the salaries are not above a servant's, sometimes less. Our Cook has £10 more than I do and I hold an English Certificate, [which] is as much value as waste paper here.
>
> Dear Miss Lewin don't think I am discontented. I am giving you a plain unvarnished state of the case and I do not wish others to be misled by misrepresentations in the old country. I have fought my battles and come off victorious. I most sincerely beg of you not to communicate with my securities if I am a week or two behind my time. Indeed I have done my best and I hope that my letter will come safely to hand. You will receive the next before I can possibly hear, but will you please send me an acknowledgement and let me know whether *any enquiries* have been made concerning me.

Laura Jones wrote again, on 2 October 1869, giving her address as 'The Castle', Sandhurst (Bendigo), and enclosing £7 to cover the remainder of her debt to the Society, making a total repayment of £22 over two years — a remarkable achievement, considering her spasmodic employment. She again asked Miss Lewin to let her know whether any enquiries had been made about her and by whom. As did some of the other governesses, she appeared to have an obsessional fear that details of her circumstances would be made known. She added: 'I think it advisable not to sign my full name in case my letter may fall into other hands than your own'.

Clara Stone was another emigrant who had difficulty obtaining a situation. She wrote from Clych Cottages, Northumberland Street, Collingwood, on 28 January 1868:

> I think I might have waited a very long time had I been dependent on the help of the 'Melbourne Home', for each time I called there was not a single engagement on their books for Governesses. I saw two of the Ladies of the Committee who assured me there was not sufficient demand here for Governesses and that they could not recommend ladies to come to this Colony unless they had influential friends who could advance their interests; they said they had given Miss Rye that information by letter, they would be glad if I would mention it again. From what I can gather, needlewomen and good dressmakers would make a fortune in an inconceivably short time. The salary I am to receive is at the rate of £70 per annum, but I go on approbation for a quarter. I think people here are somewhat shy of newcomers; they prefer those who have had some colonial experience.
>
> I do not regret however that I have come to this country now, but some weeks back I was anything but sanguine of success; indeed I thought I should have been obliged to have turned my attention to other ways of obtaining a livelihood.

Clara Stone mentioned that her sister Ellen had just arrived in Natal and had obtained an engagement twelve days after landing (Ellen Stone was a FMCES emigrant who did not write to the Society) and that she had three sisters teaching in England, but she would not advise them to emigrate to Australia.

Another who arrived in the late 1860s, Annie Hunt, one of the few FMCES emigrants to Australia who was not a governess, coped with some seemingly overwhelming problems. She emigrated to Melbourne to join her fiance, only to find he had died. She suffered serious ill-health, found there was no opening for the law copying, which following Miss Rye's London example, she had intended doing as a means of earning her living, and met many setbacks before finding secure employment as a seamstress.

Annie Hunt wrote to Miss Rye from the Melbourne Home on 11 October 1869, soon after her arrival:

I hope you have returned safely from your American trip and that your Gutter Children's work is prospering as you could wish.*

I do not think Law Copying will be accepted here very quickly as there are so many men with nothing to do. The Ladies of the [FMCES] Committee also think it will take more time, so I mean to look for other things in the meantime. Fortunately I am not bound to this one means of getting a living and have already found employment with my needle — this, however, will have its disadvantages because if I follow this for a living I could not stay in the Home on my present footing and I would not mix with the Dressmakers and Needlewomen here . . .

The *cause* of my journey here, I am grieved to say, journeyed to that Land from whence no traveller returns, so besides being alone in a strange land, I am quite a Widow at heart, but still, hard though it is, I strive to say God's Will be done and bow to this chastisement and to others. Of course time will soften my sorrow, but at present I am feeling quite broken-hearted, for who could help, to come all this way to find this melancholy news awaiting them.

The following year, on 9 May 1870, Annie Hunt wrote to thank Miss Lewin for a letter of condolence on the death of her fiancé. Miss Lewin's letter, written on 22 December 1869, was delayed in reaching her, since she had moved to Wangaratta, a town in northern Victoria with a population at that time of about 650, to take a job. Annie Hunt's letter is an example of the strong religious feelings and resignation to 'God's Will' that motivated many of the governesses and, to a marked degree, Miss Lewin herself.

---

*'Gutter children' was a term in common use to describe poor children, many of whom were homeless. The Melbourne *Age* of 31 January 1873, in an article on the working of the Education Act 1872, stated that there were few instances of the children for whom the Act was passed benefitting from it. None of the gutter children had taken advantage of the free and compulsory education offered. The *Age* added, in an éditorial: 'The comparatively rich have taken possession of the free schools and the poor are told they must keep away till gutter schools are built for them . . . the gutter children should be brought in . . . The more ragged and dirty a child is the stronger are his claims on the State . . .'

About 1865, Miss Rye began to devote her energies to the emigration of destitute and neglected or 'gutter' children. She, her sister, Miss B. Rye, and her friend and secretary, Miss Still, took small girls from workhouses and slums to Avenue House, Peckham, where they were taught housework and given a rudimentary education. When a party of thirty or forty was ready, Miss Rye herself, or a matron, escorted the children to Canada, to a house purchased by Miss Rye at Niagara and where she lived at various times, once for a period of six years. From here, the children were placed in Canadian homes. Over twenty-five years, 4,000 children were taken to Canada under this scheme, which later was known as the Waifs and Strays Society.

I thank you heartily for your sympathy with my heavy affliction and all other good wishes your letter conveys and, as you say, doubtless my Heavenly Father saw I needed this chastisement. I must admit that many times on reflection I found I was placing far too high a value on the affections and things of this world, even though I was not neglecting entirely that higher and more lasting affection of the world to come; so, feeling assured my Heavenly Father will never leave or forsake and will only chastise in love, I strive hard to say 'Thy Will, O God, not mine be done' and when I think how bountifully He has provided for me in this strange land, I am sure no thanks I can give by words can suffice and I would not even for a moment allow my heart to murmur at His decree, for I am fully persuaded God doeth all things well.

You will be glad to hear I am getting on very well indeed. I have taken a situation as Milliner, Dressmaker, Machinist etc. up country, 186 miles from Melbourne. I am in receipt of £100 per annum, and, although not very comfortable owing to the Family being Papists, still I have been here three months and think of staying to complete my engagement, which terminates in August, and probably longer, for I dislike changing and, go where I will, I think I must find something disagreeable and, as the journey is a terrible one, indeed, I may as well stay here as chance faring worse elsewhere, for I know it is only ignorance that makes them lead such a life as they do.

Annie Hunt told Miss Lewin that the prospects for shop and tradeswomen were very good in Melbourne, provided they were of 'good character and address' and willing to persevere and resist temptations, which were 'very great in the City but, of course, not in up country places'. She said salaries were far higher than in England, and added:

I am very glad to say I am now getting quite well and strong, although my life was despaired of a month since. I like Australia very, very much indeed and I fear I shall never like to live [or work] in England again, although I do not mean to be long before I visit it. It is just 10 months to the day since I sailed and God alone knows how much I have endured since then.

Before she posted this letter, Annie Hunt suffered a further jolt when she was dismissed from her job, apparently because of a slump in her employer's trade. On 17 May 1870, she wrote that she was taking legal proceedings to recover her salary and an allowance for board, since she had a six-month contract.

. . . everyone here well knows what the people are I lived with and even the Mayor of the Town* says I cannot possibly lose. The people here have undertaken to give me work to support me till the trial comes off on August 11 and a Barrister resident here has so kindly offered to fight the case for his own credit, even to the Court at Melbourne. The inhabitants have offered to lend me a Sewing Machine and I think, on the whole, I should be better off for my misfortunes.

The outcome of the court case, if she proceeded with it, is not disclosed in the correspondence. (Her next letter does not seem to have reached the Society.) At the time of her final letter, written on 3 December 1871, Annie Hunt was back in Melbourne and living at 85 Gore Street, Fitzroy. She had been ill since the previous February, but her health had started to improve following the arrival of her brother, Edward. She had been about to leave for a job at Bendigo, when 'after all were asleep, I had a slight [?paralytic] stroke. It has settled in my back and I cannot move my arms or legs, neither can I bear to be moved, and to write this puts me in fearful torture.' She added:

I could not earn a shilling from February to August. Then I took a small cottage and several people who know me have kept me constantly supplied with work ever since. I took a partner, but I lost so much by her bad work that I had to dissolve that and now, or up to last Saturday week, I had kept from five to seven girls employed and paid a person 15/- a week to superintend them. Up till this time the business has cleared off the debt I incurred during the first part of my illness.

Despite her partial paralysis, Annie Hunt remained confident of recovery and of being able to accept one of the two situations offered her by the clothing warehouse firms of McNaughton, Love & Company and McArthur, Sherrard & Copeland.

Often I think it very strange, some girls here can hardly get a situation for any price, and yet no sooner am I able to work, than I can often take pick of three or four. Oh! How I do wish I could only get strong enough to earn what I owe you! You may depend I will pay it with 10% interest as soon as I can.

---

*J. Dixon was Mayor of Wangaratta in 1869–70.

Nothing more was heard from Annie Hunt.

The combined effect of the negative responses received from its correspondents eventually must have decided the Society not to encourage further emigration to Victoria. From early in 1870, when Sarah Hammett wrote from the Melbourne Home on 28 February to announce her safe arrival, and throughout the 1870s, very few FMCES governesses arrived in the colony. One who did come out in 1873 was Mrs Lucy Phillips, aged twenty-nine, who landed about the middle of the year with her seven-year-old son, Josey. However, possibly because of the long break between arrivals, the Society's representatives in Melbourne seem to have disbanded and Mrs Phillips was unable to find out who they were or anything about them. On 12 August, she wrote from South Yarra asking for their names and a copy of the Society's rules: 'No one I come across seems to know anything about the Society, which seems to me so strange . . .'

Mrs Phillips received another blow when she found that she 'could not possibly be admitted into the Home with my dear little Josey. It was quite against the rules; so I had to do as every one else does on first landing here, that is go into a boarding house until I met with some engagement. This I did for 28/- a week.' She soon obtained a temporary job in South Yarra as a visiting governess, teaching three pupils, aged ten to fifteen, at a salary of £100 a year. Her employer, Mrs Payne, however, was 'a very peculiar woman, *not a lady* by *any* means and she is never satisfied with her Governesses'. She added:

She wants more *superficial* teaching than I can *conscientiously* give when I find there is no foundation whatever to work *upon* and so she means to try somebody else after the 7th prox. I am told, however, not to be disheartened by this freak of hers, it appears it is the usual way with many of the colonial families, there being a sort of jealousy between them and *English* people.

I have been told to try and open a preparatory school at Hawthorn,* a sweetly pretty suburb of Melbourne. It appears the demand is *great* for a really nice School of the kind, as there are many families in that part with little Boys. If I can secure a few of them, I am strongly advised out here to avail myself of the opening

---

*A Mrs Phillips is listed as running a school at Prahran at about this time, so she may have chosen that suburb rather than Hawthorn for her school.

and then I shall be able to keep my dear little Boy under my own eye . . . If I only had a *few pounds* to start it with, it would be such a relief; however, as it is I must struggle at first the best I can in hopes of brighter days.

Mrs Phillips had enrolled her son as a day boarder at twenty guineas a year at 'an excellent Preparatory school close to here, strongly recommended to me by Mrs Roe'. Her plans were upset when scarletina broke out among the students and her son had to stay away from the school. This lent urgency to her move towards starting her own school.

Lizzie Cooleu wrote her only letter to the Society in August 1873, from King William Street, Fitzroy. It was a short letter asking by what method she should repay her loan, suggesting that she may have emigrated perhaps two years earlier.

The next FMCES emigrants to write from Melbourne were Edith Jadis and Cécile Nagelle, who arrived together on the *Anglesey* in December 1873. They seem to have been well-qualified ladies and both soon had jobs. Mademoiselle Nagelle was engaged almost immediately, to teach German and the piano at a girls' school in Adelaide run by a Miss Senner, to whom she was introduced by Mrs Roe, matron of the Melbourne Governesses' and Servants' Home. Her pay was £60 a year, with laundry and travelling expenses, and Miss Senner paid her board in Melbourne until she was required in Adelaide towards the end of January. She wrote on 31 December 1873:

I am told that Salaries are not so high, nor situations so easily obtained as they were formerly, owing to the many Colonial young ladies who go out as Governesses, yet those who are competent in what they undertake meet with pretty good success. The chances for schools are greater than for families of which there are very few nice ones. As I don't care to go to the Bush, I am very well satisfied to go where I am bound for . . . Mrs Roe thinks I am extremely lucky, and I have great reason to be thankful for what a very nice kind person she is, I do like her so much, and indeed it is a great advantage to Governesses on arriving in Melbourne to be able to come to such a nice Home, as this proves to be.

Edith Jadis, whose family lived in Kent, was engaged by the Broughams, a Riverina family, who were then living at 'Clairville', in Alma Road, East St Kilda. In a letter written early in 1874, she described herself as fortunate 'in securing a most comfortable situation in a squatter's family'.* She continued:

They are all so kind to me, I have been here since January 25th and like them more every day. I think we shall not go up to the Bush this year, it is too late in the season, when we do it will be 700 miles away. I much look forward to bush life; Mrs Brougham says I may ride as much as I like.

I am very fortunate to have obtained this situation. They are very scarce and the place overrun with governesses. I believe it is the same in Sydney; salaries also are much misrepresented at home, £100 per annum being very rare. I am to have £80 first and £100 after, but I am told that only few give that.

Edith Jadis was another governess who was extremely concerned to preserve her privacy. She asked that her name should not appear in the Society's report, only her initials, and those to be reversed as J. E.

She next wrote to the Society nearly two years later, on 11 December 1875,** from Wanganella, north of Deniliquin, in the Riverina district of New South Wales. Her letter was entirely concerned with the mechanics of returning the £25 she owed to the FMCES and contained no comments on life on an outback station. She apparently had had a reminder letter from Miss Lewin, for she declined an offer to repay by instalments. Her repayment was sent to her sister Bessie Jadis, 31 Bromley College, Kent, who was to pass it on to Miss Lewin.

---

*The education of their children and the ever-present fear of serious illness posed many problems for the families of the early squatters in the Riverina and most established second homes in Melbourne, which was more accessible and closer than Sydney. Patrick Brougham, Edith's employer, was a nephew of Henry Brougham, created first Baron Brougham and Vaux, an eminent British statesman, who was one of the founding fathers of the FMCES. Patrick and his brother John held leases on many large pastoral properties in the south and south-west of New South Wales. Both brothers married daughters of John Kennedy of Gunning, another early squatter in the Deniliquin district. In 1865, Patrick Brougham was chosen as a member of a delegation sent to London, in an effort to have the Riverina made a separate colony. However, events intervened and he did not go. In later life, he moved to Gunnedah.

**Eighteen months later, on 13 June 1877, Edith Jadis married Edward Fredericks Augustus Young Lautour at the Parsonage, Narrabri, in north-western New South Wales, according to the rites of the Church of England. At the time, they were both living at Molly, a station between Wee Waa and Narrabri, Edith Jadis' occupation being given as governess and Edward Lautour being described as a gentleman. By 1881, they were living at 418 Castlereagh Street, Sydney, where Edward Lautour was employed as a guard on the tramway. On 30 January 1881, a son, Percival J. D., was born, two other sons having been born previously, of whom one survived. At this time, Edward Lautour, who had been born in Scotland, was twenty-eight and Edith, who was born in Yorkshire, was aged thirty.

8 *Disappointments and Difficulties*

'Schools abound and Governesses are not wanted.'

Maria Atherton, Brisbane, 1862

As a place of employment for governesses in the mid-1860s, Brisbane seems to have been a worse choice than either Sydney or Melbourne. The Queensland economy, dependent on the pastoral industry, began to approach a financial crisis from 1865 with the onslaught of a severe drought. At the same time, migrants, lured by the land-order system, were flooding into the colony. The development of public works, particularly a railways system, proceeded at great speed, financed by unrestrained government borrowing. The crisis came in July 1866, when Agra and Masterman's Bank, which had floated a loan to finance the railways construction, failed. The Premier and Vice-President of the Executive Council, Arthur Macalister, advised the Governor, Sir George Bowen, on 14 July: 'The Government account at the bank is largely overdrawn; our credit is stopped, and the Government cheques dishonoured. We are landing thousands of immigrants upon our shores without the means of paying for landing them from the ships, or of supporting them for a single hour.' Railways construction, the building of a new Parliament House and all public works were suspended, and the unemployed and hungry migrants were close to riot. It was not until the discovery of gold at Gympie in 1867 that the Queensland economy began to recover.

In the early 1860s, Brisbane was a small town with a population of about 6,000 living in three settlements, at north and south Brisbane and Kangaroo Point. With rapid migration, the population had grown to about 25,000 by the end of the decade. North and south Brisbane were joined in 1865 when a temporary wooden bridge over the Brisbane River was opened for traffic, but it was swept away in the floods of 1869. It was replaced by the Victoria Bridge, containing a swinging span for the passage of vessels, which was completed in 1874.

When Queensland became an independent colony in 1859, it inherited the dual educational system of New South Wales, both National (Government) and denominational schools being supported by the government. It was the first of the colonies to modify this system with the passing of the Primary Education Act in 1860 (similar to the Victorian Common Schools Act of 1862 and the New South Wales Primary Schools Act of 1866), which encouraged the development of a comprehensive government system of primary education. By 1862, the first FMCES emigrant to Brisbane was remarking on the proliferation of schools. As in the other colonies, some of these would have been denominational schools and others small private institutions.

The earliest arrival in Brisbane to write to the Society was Maria Atherton. In her letter, dated August and 2 September 1862, from South Brisbane, Miss Atherton said she had had no success in finding a job. She appears to have been one of the older women sent out under the Scheme, who always were regarded as hard to place. She had travelled from London with her sister, who had some prospect of a job in the country, and with Jane Smith, who had obtained a job, which she said she liked, with Mrs Green of the South Brisbane Church School.*

There are several references in Maria Atherton's letter to the land-order system. Under the 1860 Queensland Land Act, orders entitling the holder to purchase any available Crown land to the value of £18 were given to emigrants who arrived in the colony at their own expense and to any person who paid for the passage of an immigrant. A regulation introduced in 1862 limited the orders to men under forty and women under thirty-five, in good health. A further land grant worth £12 was made if the immigrant stayed two years. There was also a system providing free passages for agricultural labourers and domestics.

---

*This school continued to operate for many years in Hope Street, South Brisbane.

Generally, the operation of the land-order system was not successful, for migrants readily sold their orders for cash. Among the eager buyers were land-hungry squatters and the British shipping company, the Black Ball Line, which accepted the orders as payment towards the migrants' passages. Henry Jordan, a former and again later a member of the Legislative Assembly, the Government Agent appointed to administer the land-order system in Britain, had arranged for the company to have a monopoly on the carriage of migrants and by 1864, it held land orders worth £40,000. A government inquiry in 1863 led to some tightening in the operation of the system.

The number of Irish in Brisbane, remarked on by Maria Atherton, was also related to the land-order system. In 1861, the Catholic Bishop of Brisbane, James Quinn, established the Queensland Colonization Society, to take advantage of the system by financing the passage of Irish migrants. About 3,900 had arrived by 1863, until complaints by Protestants led to the cessation of the scheme.

In her letter, Maria Atherton reported to Miss Rye:

I am sorry to say that there appears no opening for educated women in Brisbane. Schools abound and Governesses are not wanted.

We have got cheap lodging and living is not so expensive as we expected, but in the meantime we see no prospect of employment and are consequently anxious and harassed with doubts and fearing that our means may be exhausted before we can meet with any supply.

Brisbane is a lovely place as regards scenery, but dull in other respects. The Citizens are an uneducated Class and Irish mostly abound; of course, there are many exceptions.

The Revd. Mr Bliss* and Mrs Bliss have called to see us and have promised to do their best for us and the Revd. T. Jones** of

---

*Reverend John Bliss, M. A. (Oxon.) was born in London on 25 April 1828. After holding positions as a curate in Norfolk and London (Pimlico), he arrived in Brisbane in 1860 and was minister at St John's, Brisbane, until 1870, when he returned to England. He was vicar of South Tawton, Devon, until his death on 29 February 1880. His wife, Jane Harriet, died on 25 October 1903.

**Canon Thomas ('Tommy') Jones was the pioneer Anglican clergyman (1861–64) in Rockhampton, then the furthest outpost of the Church. He was rector of All Saints, Wickham Terrace, 1865–77, then after a trip to England, briefly acted as Dean of St David's Cathedral, Hobart. In 1881, he was appointed to St James's Church, Toowoomba, where he remained until 1889, before making another trip to England. In 1894, he was appointed rector of St Andrews, Indooroopilly, where he remained until his death in August 1918.

Rockhampton has also written us a very kind letter offering to serve us if possible and also giving us a caution which we *ought* to have learnt on board ship, namely, '*to be very careful* whom we *knew*'. I am sorry to say that the bad *element* appears to predominate. Drunkenness and vice show themselves openly on every side . . .

Many of the labouring classes are still out of employ and blaming Mr Jordan very bitterly for misrepresentation. I think the free Emigrants appear to be more fortunate in gaining situations than those who go out on their own account . . .

My sister has got her land order and I find that others, older than I, have done the same, but being above the age *specified* I did not, of course, attempt it. My sister has written about a situation up the Country; the Salaries are not above £50 or £60 per annum, but I hope she may be successful. I should be glad to follow her there if any opening appears as there is so little to be done in Brisbane. We have made many inquiries here and exerted ourselves to the utmost, but hitherto in vain . . .

I am ready to take Needlework or anything else as a temporary resource, but find there is little doing at Brisbane at this season, excepting always at the Public Houses! . . . Five or six Emigrant ships have arrived lately and the Brisbane people say they will soon be overstocked in Queensland. What they want are Capitalists. Many Governesses have also come up from Sydney and Melbourne during the last twelve months . . .

I am sorry I cannot give you a more favourable account of this place, but the people here are totally indifferent to education and the terms they offer to accomplished Governesses are from £20 to £40 per annum . . . We are going to remove to North Brisbane tomorrow, hoping to be more successful there than we have been in South Brisbane.

Miss Atherton's movements following this letter are unknown, but about the end of 1872, a Miss Atherton is mentioned in an undated letter written from New York to the Society by Mrs M. Carruthers.

The second of the three correspondents from Brisbane was Agnes Macqueen. Two years after her arrival, she wrote to Miss Lewin saying she was 'indeed exceedingly grieved' to be unable to repay the sum advanced to her by the Society. Her letter, dated 18 November 1865, continued:

On our arrival here we underwent great hardships and for many months were unable to find employment and the greatest part of last summer and winter I suffered from extreme ill health, which entirely prevented me from employing myself in any way. In consequence of this I am unable to return the sum advanced, although aware the time will have expired before you receive this. I must therefore beg for your indulgence and, in granting me a few months longer, you would do me a very great favour. Should this not be in your power I would ask that under any circumstances you will not apply to Mr Edward Green and also that the matter may be kept *private* as it might interfere with the prospect of my brother, who has every chance of getting on well in this Colony. He holds a moderately good appointment* and I have been living with him for some time past.

Five months later, on 18 April 1866, she wrote again, asking for further time to pay, again emphasising how anxious she was that her securities should not be applied to for the money, 'especially not Mr Green'. Agnes Macqueen was then keeping house for her brother Arthur, who was being paid £300 a year in his job at the Treasury Department and had promised to pay off her debt. She explained the difficulties of getting employment in Brisbane:

For months after my arrival here no employment could be obtained, while respectable board and lodging were not less than 30/- per week. Fortunately I obtained a few small sums by my drawings. Subsequently I held at intervals two situations, but for short periods only. In each case my services were highly appreciated and I left solely on account of the children being sent to school.

There are several good schools in Brisbane and as a rule parents have their children educated in that way in preference to employing Governesses. In fact employment in that capacity is very precarious indeed and not at all to be relied on as a source of livelihood. I have known instances of females coming out as Governesses and being compelled to take situations in shops at a better rate of pay.

Latterly I have been unemployed and during the summer months my health has suffered so severely from the excessive heat that I have been obliged to be under medical care and consequently totally unfit for the task of tuition . . .

Respecting the general aspect of affairs, Queensland appears to be an excellent Colony for people possessed of Capital and for the labouring classes. The latter thrive well and obtain high wages and cheap land. Female servants are in request and command, especially for experienced hands, £20 to £25 per year. Shopwomen with a knowledge of business can always find employment, but for

---

*Arthur Macqueen's appointment as a Fourth Class Officer in the Treasury was notified in the *Queensland Government Gazette* of 2 September 1865. In another notice in the *Gazette* of 30 December, he was promoted to a Third Class Officer of the Civil Service in the Treasury Department, to take effect from 1 January 1866.

(*above*) A scene the FMCES governesses endeavoured to avoid: on arrival, they preferred to be met by prominent citizens, representatives of the Society.

Rex Nan Kivell Collection (NK11231), National Library of Australia

(*below*) Immigration Depot, Brisbane. Many governesses objected to staying at homes established for immigrants, which they regarded as being for the 'lower' classes.

Photograph album 256, National Library of Australia

(*above*) Some FMCES governesses ventured even further afield in their efforts to obtain work; one travelled widely in Russia in the 1870s. 'Governess arriving at a merchant's house in St Petersburg', painting by V. Perov.
Tretyakovsky State Gallery, Moscow

(*below*) Mr A. Manning's home in the Brisbane suburb of Milton in 1868, typical of those houses owned by prominent colonial families who gave employment to emigrant governesses.
Photograph album 257c, National Library of Australia

Governesses there is little encouragement — few situations to be had — remuneration not particularly good and much required with regard to tuition.

The only other Brisbane correspondent was Mrs Hannah Wilson, who arrived with her daughter to join her husband and son late in 1864 or early 1865. She wrote three times to the Society, mainly about her inability to repay her debt. With her last letter, dated 22 March 1872, more than seven years after her arrival, she was able to send her first repayment, even then a sum of only £2. Her first letter was written from 'Parkside', Gregory Terrace, on 18 February 1867, at a time when the Queensland economy was still depressed following the crisis of 1866.

I regret that I will be unable to repay you the money advanced for my passage to Brisbane and I am afraid it will be some time before I can do so, unless we should be fortunate as to get a good purchaser for the land when the deeds are given up to us in March, but I think that is scarcely likely as things are in such a dreadful state here. If the land had been given up to us on our arrival there is no doubt but we could then have sold it to advantage as everything was then in a more prosperous state.

We should not have trusted to the land if Mr Wilson* had had any employment, but unfortunately he has not had any for the last two years and my daughter's school** has fallen off considerably through the present distress in the Colony.

When no payment had been received from Mrs Wilson after she had been in Brisbane over six years, Miss Lewin wrote to her concerning repayment. Mrs Wilson's reply, dated 13 May 1871, was written from 'Ballantyne Cottage', Wickham Terrace.

I am truly sorry that before this I have not been able to pay off at least a portion of the passage money that you wrote about, but affairs have not prospered as I could have wished.

---

*Fletcher Wilson is listed as living in Gregory Terrace in 1868.

**A Miss Wilson is listed as a teacher at Boundary Street, Brisbane, in 1868. A school run by a Miss Wilson is listed at Wickham Terrace in the 1880s. Another daughter may have been Mary C. Wilson, who emigrated to Wellington, New Zealand, in 1870. (There is an unexplained cross-reference from Mrs Hannah Wilson's letter of 22 March 1872 to Mary Wilson's first letter from New Zealand dated 25 September 1871.)

After my son's marriage nearly three years ago we had little else beside the school to depend upon, and that is not so remunerative as when Miss Rye was here.

My husband has at last got a situation with a small salary and plenty of hard work, but we have hitherto been unable to lay by a penny, although we do not employ a servant but do all our own household work, so that you can see it is not through idleness that we have been unable to repay but from sheer inability, but if Mr Wilson should be spared to keep his situation a few months longer, I trust I should be able to send something shortly. Please give our regards to Miss Rye* and thank her for her kind interest in us. My daughters often think and speak of her.

Only two governesses wrote from South Australia: Mrs Margaret Allen and Mlle Cécile Nagelle. Mrs Allen was one of the few married women to emigrate under the Scheme and was probably a widow. When she arrived in Melbourne aboard the *Dover Castle* on 30 September 1864, she had a son living in the country and a sister in Melbourne. Although highly connected, she was unable to find a job for over a year, despite the endeavours of Mrs Fanny Perry, who together with Bishop Perry had returned to Melbourne on the same ship as Mrs Allen. She then accepted an offer of a situation at Mount Gambier, which required a steamer journey to Port MacDonnell, only because of the necessity to make money to repay her loan. Soon after her arrival in Melbourne, she wrote from 36 Queensberry Street, Hotham (North Melbourne), on 21 October 1864 of her difficulties:

I took your letter to Mrs à Beckett; her first exclamation was one of dismay, she has in fact not power to obtain any respectable employment for persons of education, few apply at the Home for Governesses. She registered my name on payment of 2/6, but on calling this week they had not heard of anything. I am with my sister, so will remain a little longer to try, and if nothing offers, go to some country village near my son and open a school.

Melbourne is too full, hundreds are in the greatest distress . . . House rent is very high and many other things . . . since I landed I have wished myself in England again, but trust I will get reconciled when settled near my Boy.

Mrs Allen's employer at Mount Gambier was Charles G.

---

*Miss Rye was in Australia between 1863 and 1865 and visited Brisbane, among other places.

Doughty, a justice of the peace, commission agent and resident magistrate. From his residence, on 16 January 1866, Mrs Allen sent £7 of the £15 advanced to her for her passage and wrote:

> I have been here just three months and have the care and education of two nice little children of the ages five and eight years who have lost their Mother. Mrs Perry recommended me; she has been very kind and tried to get me a comfortable situation for a long time. All employers here require Music to be taught and there are few exceptions where the Governess is not required to take the entire charge, wash and dress them, or as one Lady who wished to engage me expressed it, never to let them out of your sight or mind. She had six; I thought that too much to promise and indeed would not have taken this, so far from my son, and an expensive and dangerous voyage by steamboat, but as the time drew near for repaying you I had no choice.

The other South Australian correspondent, Mlle Cécile Nagelle, who had arrived in Melbourne at the end of 1873 with Edith Jadis, had been engaged to teach at Miss Senner's Ladies' School, Palm Place, Hackney, in Adelaide, for twelve months. Although she was later a prolific correspondent, she did not write while teaching at the school and does not mention it in subsequent letters. Her first letter was written soon after her arrival in Melbourne and her second from Gawler, a wheat and wine-growing centre, twenty-six miles north of Adelaide, where she was teaching music nearly two years later. A great part of Mlle Nagelle's numerous letters from South Australia are taken up with problems about repaying her loan. Unlike many other governesses, at one stage she asked her securities to repay some of the loan for her, but eventually managed to do so herself. After sending a payment of £12 10s 0d covering half her loan, Cécile Nagelle wrote on 26 February 1876 from Gawler:

> I am happy to say it is not from a case of dishonesty that I will not be able to pay the other half, for some time to come, but merely that I would really not know where to take the money from at present. No one is to blame for this neglect but myself — which occurred by some mismanagement of my own. I feel terribly sorry for it and that I should have been obliged to apply to my securities for help, but under the present circumstances, I would not know any other way to help myself; as painful as it is for me to say, it is nevertheless a fact that I have really never been so badly off since I

had to earn my own living. It makes me fearfully fretful and no wonder, for I have nothing but difficulties to contend with; I wish I could see my way.

When I came to Gawler I had every reason to hope that I would get on, but what can I do with only seven pupils — it adds greatly to my disadvantage that there are others that teach Music here, although I am the only professional in the place and well known too, as I have several times played in public in Gawler. The Colony begins to be overrun with Teachers of all kinds — Colonial girls and those who have means too but know comparatively nothing, actually turn to teaching and you may think are rather in the way of those who do understand their profession and need support. But such is the way of the world. In Adelaide Masters, no matter how bad a teacher he may be, are much preferred to a lady, just because he is a man; I don't wonder if you feel amused at my saying so but it is quite true. I have joined a young Lady who started a School last month, but really I can't say if it will answer as there are many other Schools, although I consider she can give a far superior English Education than any other Teacher in Gawler.

There were numerous private schools in Gawler, among them those conducted by Mrs Murphy, Mrs Helmore, the Misses Lewis, Misses Phillipson and Misses Finch. The passing of the State Education Act in 1875, making education compulsory, and the expansion of the public school system that followed were to have a drastic effect on private schools in South Australia and resulted in the closure of many.

By the time she wrote again, on 14 June 1876, Cécile Nagelle had moved to Angaston, about fifty miles north of Adelaide. She explained: 'In Gawler there was too much competition to contend with, whereas here I have none to battle with, being the only Teacher in the place to instruct the accomplishments required. It is thought I should succeed in time, and I myself think so too.' She described Angaston as 'such a pretty country place surrounded by beautiful hills, which are now covered with pasture of a deep rich green in colour'.

Later that year, she wrote again from Angaston on 3 November:

I am happy to say I have come to the right place at last. I mean Angaston where I have some chance of getting on. I am already beginning to gain ground, still past experiences have taught me the lesson not to rely on anything for certain. I have met with so many disappointments and difficulties in my professional life, still I cannot but hope for the best and leave the rest to God. He has taken care of me hitherto and I feel sure He will continue to do so.

We have had a terribly dry season, the Crops are very backward in the North. Sheep and cattle are dying fast for the want of food and water. I fear it will be a very dear year in every respect. We had some splendid rain last week, but it is all over. The sun shines again and hotter than ever. The fields and hills begin already to look quite brown.

Mlle Nagelle was the only governess to write at any length about the seasons, the effect of drought and the problems faced by farmers in the country around her. Her last two letters also were written from Angaston, where she was teaching music, singing and languages in a private school* and gave piano lessons at her home. On 26 January 1877, when repaying the final £12 10s 0d of her loan, she wrote: 'We have had very hot weather and [it] is so still. Everybody is crying out for Rain, a great blessing if it would come on, but there is no appearance of such a change as yet.'

On 14 May 1877, when she had been in Australia for three and a half years, she wrote enclosing a view of the Bank of Australasia in Adelaide: 'It will give you an idea of the kind of buildings Adelaide may boast of . . . since I have been in the Colony I see a vast improvement that has taken place in Adelaide'. She added:

The Farmers are quite pleased with the splendid season, we have Rain and fair both alternately — sufficient of the former to make the Fields fit for the plough . . .

Angaston looks so pretty now surrounded by its green hills — although the trees and shrubs begin to be deprived of their foliage yet the Country looks splendid — I only wish you could get if only a glimpse of it. This is the time for the Flowers. Fruit has not been very abundant, except Apples and Pears, but very small in size — I am sorry the grapes are all gone, I did enjoy them so much.

I fear I have not been explicit enough in my last letter, for evidently from what you say in Reference to my School, makes me think that I made you to understand that I kept a School. If I did so,

*In 1877, a considerable number of private schools were operating in Angaston and it has not been possible to identify the one with which Mlle Nagelle was associated. Among them were those run by Mrs Todd (at German Pass), Mrs Evans, Miss Loutit's Caithness Girls' School and Miss H. Tucker's Girls' Grammar School. The Angaston State School, which was built in 1878 and opened with 160 pupils, probably caused the demise of most of these schools, as did the opening of the Gawler State School in Gawler early in the same year.

I must contradict myself this time, as I do not keep any School of my own but I am living with an old lady who keeps a School — the pupils of which I instruct in Music, Singing and Languages — I don't think it a school that will keep up very well long on account of the old lady not being able to get a good English Teacher for the small salary she gives, as at present a daughter of the resident Dr in Angaston assists, but I don't think she will assist much longer because she is wanted at home. The school is kept in the old Baptist Chapel about ¼ of an hour or less from the house — I never go up as the Piano stands in the house and there is only one for languages . . .

Florence Allen, the only governess known to have gone to Perth under the FMCES scheme, did not arrive until 1880. She travelled out to join her sister at Bishop's College in Perth. Landing at Albany, she travelled overland. On 10 March 1880, she wrote:

I landed in Australia on Thursday January 22nd, but that was not the end of my journey for 256 miles lay between Albany and Perth. We came overland instead of waiting a week for a steamer and I enjoyed the bush journey very much. It was all so entirely different from anything I had ever experienced. We started on the morning of Friday 23rd and reached Perth that day week, the 30th. The school did not open until the 1st of March so I had a pleasant holiday with my sister, staying with different friends of hers, who have all been very kind and friendly to me.

We began school with 38 pupils and the numbers have swelled to 46, which is a good many as my sister and I teach almost everything. We have 18 boarders. The Lady Principal is, strange to say, a Mrs Allen and her husband is the Bishop's Chaplain.* I am thoroughly happy and contented in my work and out of school hours we are like one large family.

Perth is on the banks of the Swan River, over which there is

---

*The Reverend James Allen, husband of the principal of Bishop's College, was chaplain and bursar of the school, 1878–88, and Chaplain to the Bishop of Perth, 1888–1902. In 1888, he was appointed curate of St George's Cathedral, Perth; in 1893, rector of Pinjarrah; and in 1896, Canon of Perth, a position he held until 1902.

Mrs Allen was born Catherine Maria Barlee in 1828 and was educated in Suffolk, London and France. She lived for many years in Canada and in the United States, where in 1861, she married James Allen, son of a Norfolk clergyman, who was ordained in 1869 in Iowa. They arrived in Western Australia in 1876. She died there in 1900 and he in 1908. They had one daughter, Mary (Mrs Law), whose descendants still live in Western Australia. Mrs Allen was a sister of Sir Frederick Barlee, Colonial Secretary of Western Australia, 1855–75.

a very pretty view but the country around is very sandy and uninteresting.

The school was located in the Cloisters at the western end of St George's Terrace. Built about 1854 as a private residence, the Cloisters was acquired by the Church of England and used successively as a boys' school (Bishop Hale's School), as Bishop's Girls' College and later as a theological college and a university hostel. A contemporary advertisement for the school indicates that Miss Allen and her sister had a considerable workload:

Bishop's Girls' College,
Perth, W. A.

Established 1879.

PRESIDENT:
The Right Rev. The Lord Bishop of Perth.

Resident Chaplain — Rev. J. Allen.
Lady Principal — Mrs Allen.

TEACHERS:

Miss Allen*	*Head Teacher*
Miss F. C. Allen	*Second Teacher*
Miss S. Hancock (Fremantle)	*Third Teacher*
Miss Ethel Clifton	*Fourth Teacher*
Mrs. Broadhurst	*Music Mistress*
Miss F. C. Allen	*Dancing and Ass. Music Mistress*
Miss Hancock (Melbourne)	*Singing Mistress*
Miss Allen	*Drawing, French, German Teacher*
——	*Wardrobe Keeper*
Sergeant Latimer	*Drill Master*

The ordinary School course embraces all the higher branches of English Education, French, Plain and Fancy Needle-work. Extra charges are made for Latin, German, Music, Drawing, Painting, and Dancing. . . .**

*Jessie Allen, sister of Florence, died in January 1886 from consumption. She was born in March 1853, the second daughter of Edwin Allen, surgeon, of Eynsham, Oxfordshire. Educated at Denbeigh, at a training school for daughters of medical men, she later became a pupil-teacher there. Before emigrating to Perth, she was governess to a family on the Continent.

**The school did not prove successful and closed in 1888.

9 *The Last Emigrants*

'You meet with as much cool hauteur in a Melbourne drawing room as you ever would in an English one.'

Caroline Haselton, Melbourne, 1879

The discouraging reports reaching the Society from Australia during the depressed years of the late 1860s slowed FMCES arrivals over the next decade. This was probably fortunate, for although the economies of the Australian colonies began to improve in the 1870s, culminating in the extraordinary boom conditions of the 1880s, another problem now beset aspiring emigrant governesses. In all the colonies, the government system of education was expanding. This eroded the role of governesses, who increasingly were needed only in isolated country areas — not a popular destination for many of those accustomed to urban living. The small private schools to which they had turned before when positions were not available, also began to close.

All the colonies, mainly during the 1860s, passed legislation that resulted in education in Government schools being made available to more children. In New South Wales, under the Public Schools Act of 1866, for example, the minimum attendance for public schools was lowered to twenty-five pupils and, in small communities, provisional and 'half-time' schools were established in privately-owned buildings. In the 'half-time' schools, teachers divided their time between two schools, travelling between one school and the other either during the lunch-hour or on alternate days.

The number of Government schools increased rapidly and by 1872, there were about 700 in New South Wales, including 300 provisional and half-time schools in the sparsely settled districts. Nearly 90,000 children were enrolled in elementary schools, an increase of one-third in five years, and education now was available to almost all the children in the colony. However, this did not mean that all children were receiving an elementary education: many were enrolled for brief periods only and many others attended only spasmodically. Nevertheless, the extension of schooling to most country areas limited the need for governesses.

The 1866 Act also affected the small denominational and private schools in which some governesses taught, which began to go out of existence. Government assistance was available only to certified denominational schools, which were subject to inspection and were required to have a minimum attendance of thirty pupils. The teachers in these schools also were required to be of a certain standard, since they were employed by the government-appointed Council of Education. Thus another avenue of employment was closed to untrained governesses unable to meet these rigorous teaching standards.

The passing of the 'free, compulsory and secular' Education Acts in the various colonies in the 1870s and 1880s accentuated the drift away from education in the home, until only a few teaching outlets remained for governesses, mainly in the outback. Most FMCES emigrants who arrived in Australia in the late 1870s went to jobs in the country, where either because of their isolation or their dissatisfaction with government-controlled education, the parents preferred a more personal approach to education.

Ellen Ollard, who arrived in Melbourne on 1 November 1874 on the *Shannon*, had great difficulty in finding work, and those jobs she did get, for one reason or another, did not last long, so that after nearly two years in Victoria she had earned altogether only about £13 and was dependent on the charity of a cousin to give her a home. She was quite unable to repay her loan to the Society. The story of her search for employment is a catalogue of disasters, partly due to her apparent lack of qualifications and, perhaps, to an element of bad luck.

A short time after she arrived, she obtained a situation at Boggy Creek, near Kyneton, about fifty miles north-west of Melbourne. There, as she described in a letter written on 4 August 1876:

I took the measles from the children and the unfeeling woman sent me home, when I had been there only five days and I had them very severely. My cousin kindly had me at her house and nursed me herself. The doctor said I might have lost my life. I had to have my hair cut short like a boy and it has not grown yet.

After I had got quite well I got another situation through an Advertisement, which was supposed to be as companion to a young Lady, but when I arrived there I found that there was no servant kept and the man was a travelling hawker and I was requested to help his daughter make fancy articles for sale and do all the housework besides, so I did not stay there very long.

After that I went to Wangaratta and when I had been there a little over two months they gave me notice to leave and I think they were in difficulties. After I left I did not get employment for a very long time and what I should have done without my cousin I really do not know, for I should have wanted for food, and clothes too, but for her.

Mrs Roe at the Melbourne Home is one of the most kind and motherly persons I have met, but she is quite powerless to assist anyone who cannot pay their way and the ladies of the Committee have passed a law that nobody shall stay there who cannot pay 17/- weekly in advance, so that really I do not know what benefit is to be derived from being there, excepting of course that if one stays there 'tis a guarantee (to the employers) as to their respectability.

From what you told me and judging from the report (the little book I mean), I quite thought there would be someone to meet me at the vessel and also that some little interest would be taken in you by some members of the Committee, but I soon found that I was mistaken. Of course, if any one comes to the Home requiring a Governess or Nursery Governess, as the case may be, if you are suitable you have a chance of getting the situation; but if you are staying elsewhere and you see the Advertisement you stand just as good a chance of getting it, if you answer it in time. Now I should very much like to know if you have received the £15. I think that was the sum borrowed. When I left England my Father told me not to trouble myself at all about [it] as he intended paying it within a month or two, but as he has not sent me any money or even written to me, I much fear that he must have been in difficulties and I do not think my Uncle or Mr Dalton would be very pleased at having to pay it. I should indeed be very thankful if I had the means of sending it to you, but when I tell you that since I have been in the Colony I have only earned about thirteen pounds, you will know that I have not got it to send, especially when I had nothing to start with. I never thought that I should live to be in the unhappy position that I am in now.

The very first day that I went to the 'Home' I was told that I should never get on here without music, for the very commonest people have a piano and have their children taught to play it. There are very few respectable situations to be got where music is not required. I was in a nice family in St Kilda for a time where I used to do all the needlework and attend to the younger children, but I was not very well while I was there and the lady told me she was sorry to part with me but she required someone who was very strong. She had only been married a month when I went there, to a widower with a family of five and, as she was very delicate, I had to leave, so it seems as if misfortune attends me wherever I go.

My Cousin (whom I had never seen till I arrived here) is very good indeed to me and never allows me to want for anything and always gives me a home when I'm out of a situation, still I cannot help feeling that I've got no right to be living upon her and her husband, although they are both kind enough to tell me not to worry about it. I had no idea that Melbourne was such a large place as it is or I should never have come to it. The people here are very different to what they are in England; *gold* is their God and it does not matter to them how ignorant a person is if they have money, but if they have not they are not considered worthy of notice.

My Cousin lives a very quiet life and does not visit anyone or receive any visitors so I do not see any chance of getting into society where I might be likely to meet with any nice situation, where I should be kindly treated.

Several people in England promised to give me letters of introduction to friends or acquaintances of theirs out here; but I had not time to go for them and my Father promised to send them and so I have not had them. I wish my Father had sent me to learn a business, Millinery or something of the kind; he always used to tell me never to marry for a home and that at his death I was provided for, but now I find that I am entirely at the mercy of the world.

Sometimes I think of working my way back to England, I mean with a family, but perhaps I should not find it any easier to get employment there. I know a lady much older than I am who is far worse off, for she has no relative here, and she is now giving her services for board and residence and she has not a penny in the world. 'Tis all very well for people to say 'Take a situation as a housemaid or nursemaid.' Employers require thorough hard-working servants who fully understand their duties, and I am sure I could not do the work they require.

I fear you will consider this a most miserable letter and I am almost ashamed to send one so badly written for I have left it so many times, but I have not time to write it again as the 'Mail' goes tomorrow.

Eleanor Tindall, who arrived on board the *Chimborazo* on 12 March 1878, began her new life with greater advantages than the unfortunate Ellen Ollard. She travelled out first class with the help of a friend in England and, through the influence of friends in Melbourne, soon obtained a situation with Mrs Bell, the wife of Robert Lewis Bell, at their cattle-station at Mount Mercer, in the Buninyong district, near Ballarat. On 20 May 1878, she wrote:

> I am very comfortable here and I think I shall get on for they seem so glad to have someone straight from England. I get £50 a year and have not at all hard work; five hours teaching a day, except Saturday, and the rest of the time, as well as Saturday, is all my own.

Nearly two years later, on 15 March 1880, she wrote to Mrs Sunter, giving her address as care of E. E. Morris, Esq., Church of England Grammar School, South Yarra, enclosing £15 of the money lent to her in two separate postal orders and expressing the hope that her surety would advance the remaining £7, which she would repay in a few months. She had just left the Bells and was about to go to another job 'up the country' to a Mrs Mack, where she was to receive £80 a year. Apparently she continued to make use of influential friends, for she asked that any letters be addressed to her care of George Higinbotham, former Attorney-General and soon to be made a Supreme Court judge, at North Brighton. Eleanor Tindall gave no further details about Mrs Mack* and she did not write to the Society again.

In her only letter to the Society, Pauline Jordan wrote on 14 September 1877 from the Melbourne 'Home' that she was getting on well.

The last of the governesses to write to the Society from Victoria was Caroline Haselton, who arrived in September 1879. The FMCES previously had assisted her to emigrate to South Africa, where she taught at Graaff-Reinet. She was unhappy there, became ill and received further assistance from the Society to emigrate to Melbourne. This assistance appears to have been confined to advice, however, since Caroline Haselton seems to have been financially secure. While in South Africa, she sent a donation to the Society and

---

*She may have gone to work for Mrs Joseph Mack (née Helen Dodds) at Berry Bank, near Cressy, between Ballarat and Colac. Mrs Mack was married in 1869 and eventually had a family of five girls and six boys. This family's records survive and although Eleanor Tindall is not mentioned in them, they do indicate that the family employed governesses. An entry in a diary kept by Joseph Mack records that on 24 March 1882, 'Miss Jane B. Walker, governess, died this morning' and he added the note that she 'was buried at Lismore 25 March'. Generally, Joseph Mack did not mention the names of female staff, presumably because they were under the control of his wife. Alternatively, Eleanor Tindall may have been employed by one of Joseph Mack's brothers, Austin or Albert, both of whom were farming in north-western Victoria. Detailed records of these families do not exist.

in her letter there is no mention of repayment of a loan.

Melbourne did not come up to Caroline's expectations and in her only letter to the Society from Australia she talks of moving again. She wrote from Melbourne in November 1879, after obtaining a temporary job teaching English at a boarding-school:

> It was a matter of surprise my getting an Engagement the same week I came, *teaching is not plentiful here* as we are led to believe in England; salaries are not high; there are *numbers* of unmarried ladies; I think it is high time the *fables* about Australia were ended. I am getting £70 here, while in Africa I had £80 and £100 offered me; I feel inclined to return to Africa only that I feel *well* here, but the hospitality and friendliness *there* are charming to remember; people are cautious in Australia and the kind-heartedness one had heard and read of is certainly wanting *now*. You meet with as much cool hauteur in a Melbourne drawing room as you ever would in an English one. For a Governess who is strong enough for African life, there is certainly a better opening than in Australia. I have corresponded with Miss Herbert [the Society's agent] and shall perhaps proceed to New Zealand if teaching is advisable there. I hear there are no 'State Schools', while *here* they abound and perhaps are a great cause of the difficulty in getting private teaching and the low salaries . . . Do you know anything of teaching in India? or South America? I have been advised to go to the latter, but have no addresses to either place.

Caroline Haselton's remark about the proliferation of State schools in Victoria reflects the early start made there in introducing 'free, compulsory and secular' education. The Victorian Act establishing a State system of education was passed in 1872 and was followed by Queensland in 1875, South Australia in 1878, New South Wales in 1880, and Tasmania and Western Australia in 1893. Typical of those in other colonies, the aim of the New South Wales Public Instruction Act of 1880 was to provide 'the best primary education to all children without sectarian or class distinction'. In the first three years of its operation, enrolment in Government schools increased by 60 per cent to 177,000. Many new public schools, including the provisional and part-time schools in the country, were opened and itinerant teachers were employed to instruct the children of isolated families. In the face of these educational developments, the employment of governesses, except in the outback, became almost an idiosyncrasy.

While some emigrants were dispatched to Victoria in the

1870s, the emigration of FMCES-sponsored governesses to New South Wales virtually ceased. Between Louisa Dearmer's last letter in December 1868 and April 1881, only one letter was written to the Society from New South Wales. The exception was Emilie Carttar, who arrived in the early part of 1876 with her sister, the sister's poor health being one of the reasons for their emigration. Later, the sister recovered and went to a situation in Queensland. Emilie Carttar wrote on 31 March 1876 from 'Gledswood', the home of James K. Chisholm, J. P., of Narellan, in the Camden district south of Sydney, reporting that 'we have all been very successful'.*

The next New South Wales correspondent was Mrs Ida White, who wrote only one letter but a very newsy one, perhaps the brightest ever written to the Society. Mrs White and her husband landed at Melbourne on 6 October 1880, aboard the steamship *Aconcagua*. The same day, the Melbourne *Argus* published a sixteen-page supplement on the Melbourne International Exhibition. The Whites visited the Exhibition and stayed some months in Victoria, but Mr White was unable to find a suitable job on the land, so they moved north to Burradoo Park.

Bowral, of which Burradoo is a part, was a boom-town in the 1880s. Because of its reputation for having a healthy climate, several private schools were opened in the area, most of which did not last long. On 27 April 1881, Mrs White wrote to the Society from Mrs Sullivan's Ladies College** at Burradoo Park, Bowral, south of Sydney:

---

*Emilie Ann Carttar of George's River was married on 29 August 1882 at Christ Church, Sydney, to John Dodds, a sailor. She had been born in England, a daughter of Charles Joseph Carttar, a solicitor, and Clara Waite. John Dodds had been born in Ireland, a son of Samuel Dodds, a carter, and Margaret Smith.

**The college was run by Mrs Mary Matilda Sullivan, wife of Captain Daniel Henry Sullivan of Burradoo Park, a hero of the Crimean War and the Indian Mutiny. He was appointed a Justice of the Peace in Bowral in 1883 and, after a long illness, died on 11 September 1886 at the age of fifty-six. Mrs Mary Matilda Sullivan died on 26 July 1895, also aged fifty-six. There was also a Miss Sullivan, but it is not clear if she was a sister or a daughter of Captain Sullivan. On 3 April 1886, Captain Sullivan advertised the sale of a carriage and pair of grey ponies, a ladies' hack and a saddle horse, owing to the departure of Miss Sullivan for England early in April. In the same year, the rector of St Jude's, Bowral, Mr Debenham, made mention of the fact that the pupils of Mrs Sullivan had been withdrawn from his Bible classes. A history of the district states that Miss (?Mrs) Sullivan established a boarding-school at Burradoo with a Mrs West in 1882. (Mrs Sullivan's Ladies College was operating in 1881.) This Mrs West predates the more famous educationist Winifred M. West, who arrived in Australia in 1907 and in 1913, with Miss Phyllis A. H. Clubbe, founded the famous Frensham School (now Winifred West Schools Ltd) at Mittagong.

We had taken our passages to Tasmania, but on reaching Melbourne we were so delighted with it that we took the advice of the colonists we met on the ship and resolved to remain on the Continent. It would be impossible to describe our first sensations on landing in Australia. We were simply delighted, and were and are now quite sure, that if the people of England had any adequate idea of it, they would want to come here in a body. I think what struck us most on landing was the beauty and tasteful dress of the Melbourne Ladies: such a contrast to those of Manchester. [Melbourne] is a most beautiful town, but not at all English, quite American. Never in my life [have I] beheld such a wealth of flowers, roses and geraniums everywhere, the latter forming hedges, higher than the one-storeyed verandahed houses. Then the air, so pure, and clear, one could see for 30 miles and Melbourne is *innocent* of *smoke*. Meat was from 4d to 2d a 1b, butter 6d and everything else proportionately cheap; delicious grapes at 3d a 1b, fine apples 4d each, white bananas, locquats, peaches and strawberries were in the greatest abundance.

We went to a nice Hotel where we paid a £1 a week each, which charge included a private sitting room and separate meals, the landlady declining payment for any friend who might like to take a meal with us.

As Mr White wanted to go up the country, after remaining a fortnight in Melbourne seeing the Exhibition and all the sights, I went to stay with a nice family in the suburbs where for £1 a week I had a most luxurious home and every comfort and met the best people in Melbourne, making numerous pleasant friends and acquaintances.

Mr White, after seeing me settled, departed for the Western District where he hoped to get on a Station, as he wished to have 12 months Colonial experience before settling. He went from squatter to squatter, being most hospitably entertained by all and, had that been the kind of experience he desired, might have had 12 months without any difficulty. He, however, wanted *practical* experience of Australian Sheep Farming, but found it impossible to get on a Station in any other capacity than as a guest, everyone declining to employ him in a menial capacity and there being nothing between, for a new chum, as he did not know the ways.

Meanwhile I was trying for three months to obtain a situation in Victoria. Owing to the State Schools, to which as in America the better classes send their children, I could not obtain any, except one which required residence, which I declined to take.

Mr White joined me at Xmas, which festival appeared very strange to us as on Xmas Day the Thermometer marked 103 in the shade and we all in white dresses breakfasted on the Verandah among the roses and oleanders, everyone assuring Mr White that it would be madness for him to try sheep farming on his own account without Colonial experience.

He resolved to get it his own way, so dispensing with the ever-ready letters of introduction, which invariably resulted in an invitation to pay a visit, he took the train for the Riverina, New South Wales, and then tramped through the bush in a shabby suit and a Colonial Hat. He was not long before he fell in with two young fellows, Australian born, who had just taken up a run, and engaged him as general assistant at £1 a week, he living with them, first in a tent, and afterwards in a hut they raised themselves and all working hard at fencing, mustering cattle and bullock driving. Their arrangements were most primitive. Mr White did his own washing in a pail, and learned to make damper and fry chops. However, he liked the life immensely, especially as the work was varied by Kangaroo and Turkey shooting.

Shortly after Xmas I obtained a situation in a country boarding school in New South Wales. I teach French, Drawing and Painting. I only asked £90, which I obtained readily, and since I have been here have been offered £140 for a school in Queensland. The difference between New South Wales and Victoria is truly wonderful. The people of New South Wales are as thoroughly English as the Victorians are American, [and] decline to patronize the State schools, consequently governesses are in greater demand. If you know a lady who is a really good Musician, Artist or linguist, her prospects here are infinitely better than at home — She could readily obtain £100 a year on a Station, and more in a School with a good home and the kindest treatment. This refers only to *first class finishing* governesses, mediocrity must be content with a less Salary, from £40 to £60. As for nursery, and the various stages of incompetency, it would be a mistake to send them out, the place being overstocked already. Pretty, lady-like girls who go on distant stations, especially in *Queensland* — are certain to marry well. The Australian men seem to have quite a fancy for marrying governesses, and it is not at all usual to look for money with a wife . . .

Through the efforts of my employer, Mrs Sullivan, Mr White has now obtained, under the Colonial Sugar Co., the appointment of Manager of their plantations in Fiji, for which place he sailed a month time since.* Owing to the want of suitable accommodation,

*Mrs White's intimation of her husband's appointment to a job in Fiji is confirmed by CSR Ltd's records. He was appointed Cane Inspector at Fiji in April 1881. This was shortly after the Colonial Sugar Refining Co. decided not to depend entirely on purchasing cane, but to grow a proportion for their mill on company estates in Fiji. The company's general manager, Mr E. W. Knox, inspected the plantations in 1881 and said he hoped good-quality cane would be grown. Results at first were not as satisfactory as had been hoped, since Nausori, the area chosen, was a very wet part of Fiji and the cane grown was not as sweet as that grown in New South

(*above*) Governesses were expected to be able to teach children of all ages a wide range of subjects. 'An object lesson at the kindergarten', *Australasian Sketcher*, 8 August 1881.
National Library of Australia

(*below*) Governesses were required to be able to impart to their charges the rudiments of such refined accomplishments as painting and music. Those who could not had difficulty in obtaining positions. A painting class, *c.* 1860; pencil drawing by Betsey (Wright-Curtis) Nairn.
Alexander Turnbull Library, Wellington, NZ

Clara Evans, later Mrs Meredith, who emigrated to South Africa in March 1879 under the FMCES scheme to join her sister Sophia, also a FMCES emigrant. Clara obtained a position as governess on a farm south of Graaff-Reinet. Her descendants still live in Graaff-Reinet.

Mrs R. B. Kingwill, Craaff-Reinet

it will be some months before I can join him, but in the meantime, I have a most comfortable home here, on the slopes of the Blue Mountains, where the climate is simply perfection, and scenery most lovely — I go out riding nearly every day, and am happy with the girls (who are all boarders, of from 15 to 20 and very nice), 23 cats and 3 Newfoundland dogs. I don't think you would know me, I am so stout and strong. I am only sorry our lot is not to be cast in Australia, to which, and its kind-hearted people, no description of mine can do justice. Everywhere we have met with the greatest possible kindness and most certainly have every reason to be thankful we came out, Mr White's prospects being exceptionally good.

One word in conclusion, I don't think men who have been used to a town life, or indoor employment, should come here, unless they have exceptional physique, and can cope with the country as Mr White did and if needs be, do *a hard day's work*. Many come here and hang about the towns, trying for genteel employment, which is almost as difficult to find as at home, until they have spent their last shilling, then become hopelessly shabby, they lose self-respect and take to drinking . . .

. . . let no one choose Victoria, it is *quite overdrawn* in *every way*, New South Wales is the place and Queensland is better still; though the climate is hot, you don't feel it, as you do in England. Mr White has *worked* with the glass 100° in the shade, and I have gone out walking at 103°, feeling no more than a hot day at home.

The letters from Australia end with two that are the last to appear in the FMCES letter-books, one from Miss M. Crowley and the other from Miss J. Oberman. Although they are undated, they appear from internal evidence to have been written earlier than some of the other letters, probably about mid-1881.

Miss Crowley wrote from Illabo, between Junee and Cootamundra, where she was employed by Matthew Hamilton, a sheep-farmer and a widower. She had three pupils, aged seven, ten and thirteen, and wrote of them: 'My pupils are attentive and obedient, which makes my work

---

Wales. Cane also was damaged by floods on the Rewa River. After another visit in 1883, however, E. W. Knox said that the planting of the cane nurseries and the erection of labour houses was being pushed ahead.

Mr Adam White, who had continued as Cane Inspector for two years, was appointed manager at Naitasiri, one of the company's plantations, on 1 April 1883. He resigned from CSR on 13 October of that year.

pleasant and interesting'. She apparently had not intended to come to Australia, for she added:

I was dreadfully cut up at not getting to China, but when I found that the money I had would bring me here and a sure promise of work, I took it as an *open* door and looking back can now see the leading of the Lord.

Miss Oberman, like Mrs Ida White, landed first at Melbourne, but despite the 1880s boom in 'Marvellous Melbourne', was unable to obtain a situation there so moved to Sydney, where she was employed by Mrs John Woods of 'Fairlight', Manly, near the North Head of Sydney Harbour. 'Fairlight', a large sandstone house standing above a small beach facing Sydney Heads, had been built in the 1850s for H. G. Smith, an early Manly pioneer, and named after a village near Hastings in England. The property was bought by John Woods, a contractor and later Mayor of Sydney, who added a tower, porch and other buildings before selling the property in 1885.

Miss Oberman wrote from Manly:

The family leave for a visit to Europe next Xmas and I then hope to do better as my present salary is only £50, but I am very comfortable and kindly treated and have no reason to regret coming to Australia.

10 Following Miss Rye to New Zealand

'. . . there is plenty of work here for women who know how to do it . . .'

Maria Rye, New Zealand, 1863

For those governesses who were not attracted to Australia, New Zealand was an alternative and popular destination. It had been well publicised as a result of a visit by Maria Rye, who as part of her interest in the broader field of migration for women of all classes, arrived at Dunedin in the South Island in February 1863 with one hundred female emigrants. The women, mainly servants, but including some governesses, had been offered assisted passages by the Otago Provincial Government, provided Miss Rye came with them in charge of the party. She accepted and took the opportunity to see for herself the difficulties and trials the emigrants faced.

Miss Rye successfully placed all of the large group of women she had escorted. This fact became widely known following publication in the London *Times* on 29 May 1863 of a letter she wrote from New Zealand, in which she said: 'With the exception of about three or four servants (who will probably be placed in a few days), all my girls and governesses have found suitable employment, the latter at salaries of from £60 to £40, the former at wages of from £40 to £20 per annum'. The letter concluded: 'I repeat my assertion that there is plenty of work here for women who know how to do it; that for women who can take care of themselves, and intend to walk uprightly, it is a place where they must get on in the long run'.

The arrival of these women at Dunedin coincided with

the discovery of gold at Lake Wakatipu, about 90 miles to the north-west, and an influx of miners (more than 6,000) arrived in the first six weeks of 1863. A ship carrying another one thousand miners from Melbourne passed Miss Rye's group at Port Chalmers and these men were on the jetty at Dunedin when she arrived. In another letter to the *Times*, published on 14 April 1863, Miss Rye described them as 'a fine navvie lot of looking men' and she was 'favourably impressed with their appearance'.

The heartening news of the discovery of gold and the availability of jobs started a flow of FMCES governesses to New Zealand, where they found, as others had in Australia, that there was only a very limited demand for their services. Those who did find work, were paid generally low salaries. Conditions often were fairly primitive and several mention the small houses and makeshift furniture. They also reported that governesses often were expected to help out with household tasks.

Some arrivals also were confronted by the effects of a downturn in agriculture, which had repercussions on the economy of the entire country, so much so that one governess reported that the settlement of New Zealand was regarded by many as a mistake. In later years, the Society had the advantage of advice from Harriet Herbert, a member of a well-known Hawke's Bay family and a prominent figure in New Zealand education. She at first encouraged the sending of more governesses, but later, in a dramatic letter to Miss Lewin, she wrote saying: 'Hold!'

The first two FMCES governesses to come to New Zealand arrived at a disturbing time: in the middle of the Maori Wars. In 1840, by the Treaty of Waitangi, the Maori chiefs ceded all their rights and powers of sovereignty to Queen Victoria and in return were promised undisturbed possession of their lands. The treaty proved unworkable in the face of wholesale European migration and led to much hostility. With the population increase, the settlers' demand for land increased. Many Maoris refused to sell their land, but in 1859 an offer to sell from a subchief was accepted by the government, which ignored the veto on land sales by the paramount chief, Kingi. Early in 1860, troops were used to dislodge Kingi from his land, 'the Waitara block', and war between the Maoris and the colonial forces broke out. In 1861, Governor Grey, fearing Auckland was menaced, took measures that were interpreted as acts of aggression and the hostilities spread from Taranaki to Waikato. Imperial troops and the colonial militia did not have an easy task fighting the Maoris, but by the mid-1860s, Maori resistance had ended, although guerrilla warfare flared again in the latter part of the decade.

The first governess to write from New Zealand, Miss J. Merritt, mentions her fears that the Maori war will involve her brother. Her letter is dated 31 July 1863, soon after her arrival in Auckland:

> the war here has struck such a panic everywhere that if it assumes a much more serious aspect than it already does I shall not feel disposed to run the risk of remaining here, in which case I think Sydney will probably be my destination . . . I am so charmed by the beauties of this exquisite country that I should quite grieve to leave and as to returning to England, I would not on any account. From the little I have seen of this place I do not consider Governesses are a class of persons wanted here. Salaries are very low, £40 is the highest anyone will give, indeed Mrs Abraham* offered a Lady who applied to her before me £25, but I would rather take a Servants' situation than *that*.
>
> Most of the residents here are educated people, of far more refined manners than one would expect in such a comparatively young Colony . . .
>
> My brother is in the Bush and likes the life very much. I hope he will remain there as they are taking every available man above 16 for the war and I should dread his going. You will probably see by the papers the fearful murders these cowardly Maoris are committing daily.

Miss Merritt mentioned in her letter the possibility of a job at the Reverend Lloyd's St Paul's School, and a later correspondent, I. M. Cary, said in a letter dated 18 October 1863 that she was teaching at Mr Lloyd's school.**

Miss I. M. Cary, from Belfast, who arrived on the *Telegraph* in July, was the only other FMCES arrival in New Zealand in 1863. She went first to Auckland, where like Miss Merritt, she found panic because of the Maori Wars. On 18 October, she wrote from 'Manor Lodge', Dunedin: 'When

---

*Mrs Abraham was a cousin of Bishop Charles John Abraham, first Bishop of Wellington, 1858–70.

**Reverend John Frederick Lloyd, senior vicar of St Paul's, Auckland from 1858 to 1865. The first Diocesan Synod of New Zealand was held in 1859 in St Paul's School. The school is believed to have had a relatively short history.

we arrived in Auckland our first news was that the war had broken out on 4th July and when the Pilot came on board, he told us the Natives intended to sweep us all into the sea.' She found no opening in Auckland and wrote:

From all I could see and learn of Auckland I found there was little use in my remaining there; teaching is badly paid, worse than at home, and you are expected to work as a Servant and not be paid better. The person* you sent by the other Ship called upon me; she is of the Class that suits.

Over the next four years, Miss Cary tried her luck at Dunedin, Wellington and Wanganui, but with only spasmodic success. At first, she obtained a position in a Ladies' School in Dunedin, where she had letters to people of influence. She was to be paid £100 a year, but seemed dubious about whether she actually would receive this amount, for she had heard the people were not good at paying. In her letter of 18 October, she went on:

this Island is not a good place for Governesses to come to; the most anyone can get is £40, hard work and cold, wet climate, very little comfort. Miss Rye has written a letter in the *Times* which has given great offence to the people here, and my friends at home are in a state about me from having seen it . . . My advice is do not send first class Governesses here, they will not be paid, there is no inducement. I may not be able to send you the £20 for a year, but I trust I may before that time, for if not paid in this situation, I do not expect to get a good salary anywhere.

The letter to *The Times*, referred to by Miss Cary, was that published on 29 May, in which Miss Rye announced the successful placement of most of her emigrants. In addition to this news, the letter (which was very long) included some overly emotive sections on the hazards facing female emigrants. Miss Rye wrote of 'fearful tales' of 'immoralities' on emigrant ships, intoxication, particularly on ships carrying brandy and wines, and male and female emigrants, and even more alarming accounts of the Dunedin Immigration Barracks, where female emigrants were given temporary accommodation. These included charges that the barracks was filthy, that a contingent of constabulary was crammed into

*Apparently a reference to Miss J. Merritt.

the building with the female emigrants, that illegitimate children and their mothers were living in the barracks and that the top floor was inhabited by 'disreputable' women.

It is not surprising that Miss Cary's family and friends, reading these charges on the other side of the world, should have become alarmed. They may have been less worried after publication in *The Times* on 25 June of a letter from James R. Allan of Scarborough, brother of the Immigration Agent in Otago, who had instructed him to refute the charges. This he did and concluded by alleging that Miss Rye had interfered with the running of the barracks and had been interested only in getting the best accommodation for her emigrants. Her charges, he said, were for the most part 'founded on the evidence of hearsay'.

Later, Miss Cary ran a girls' school of her own in Dunedin, but had to pay a yearly rent of £200 for the premises. On 15 September 1864, she commented:

> Oh! I have suffered much since I parted from you in England. I shall not tell you all one has to bear up against in this place — all I will say is, that it is a sad mistake for a *Lady* to come here as a teacher, the place is full of schools, but no one can get a situation as Governess, the houses are too small, you must keep a School or be a Servant, the latter I have not the strength for . . . P.S. Oh tell the young women to work hard and remain there.

Miss Cary asked for an extension of time in which to repay her loan of £20 and also asked that her securities should not be applied to for repayment.

She wrote next from 'Elliselin House', Dunedin, on 17 August 1865, to say she was unable to repay her debt because 'the sudden crash in trade' had caused her school enrolment to be reduced to three. Later she lost all her pupils, suffered a breakdown in health and after getting behind in paying her rent, lost everything she possessed.

After conducting a school for nearly a year in Wellington, Miss Cary wrote finally on 2 October 1867, from Wanganui:

> Mine has been a life of trial and much suffering since I came to this Colony . . . Believe me it is a hard struggle for a Lady to succeed in this country, the lower classes as well — but it is no use for a well-educated Lady over 30 years of age to come out — what the settlers like is a young strong middle class sort of person that can be helpful to them and teach their children to read and write — there

are now a great many in New Zealand of this class. I only get the same terms I did in the home country and the expense of living is three times what it was in Belfast. . . .

It is a great mistake to fancy that an unprotected woman can make money in a Colony — men can do it — they know how to rough it, and it is land that turns in money . . . A great many girls are left unmarried; the men who come out are the younger sons of poor families, *many* are very much addicted to drink, just such men as no nice girls would marry — I fancy about five years back all the eligible men were picked out by the servant girls; however, their day has passed — there are young ladies enough now.

The next FMCES arrivals in New Zealand were Fanny Thomas and Lizzie Braddell, who both went to the South Island. Fanny Thomas obtained a teaching situation with Mr Ord, a Scots widower at Puerua, an agricultural and farming district in South Molyneaux, near Dunedin, where her charge was a thirteen-year-old girl. She wrote from 'Cheviot House' on 12 July 1864: 'I did not at first like the idea of coming here when I heard there was no Lady living in the house as I dreaded having disagreeable remarks passed; as soon as I saw Mr Ord I felt I had nothing to fear'. Lizzie Braddell took a job at £50 a year, teaching the two small sons of Charles F. Blake, at first at Anderson's Bay and then at Omakau Station, Manuherikia, Otago, about 130 miles inland from Dunedin. In a letter to Miss Lewin dated 12 September 1864, she said she liked it better than Dunedin. She had a horse to ride whenever she liked and every comfort and luxury and a fine climate.

Two sisters, Georgina and Augusta McNeill, also arrived in 1864 and went to Christchurch, on the South Island. They showed in a succession of letters an almost obsessive compulsion to repay their loans, despite (for Augusta at least) very brief spells of employment. Georgina found a job at £40 a year, working for Robert Rhodes* (who had an income of £10,000 a year, according to her), at first living at Rhodes Bay, Lyttleton, and later at Hawkesbury, Canterbury. Over the next two years, she regularly remitted small sums to the Society. Her sister Augusta repaid £7 on 4 April 1865,

*Robert Rhodes and his brothers William and George secured land where Lyttleton now stands and later exchanged their property with the Canterbury Association for land at Timaru.

although she was then out of a job, since the family she had worked for was returning to England. In a letter addressed from Riccarton Mills,* she wrote:

Governesses here have no very enviable position: they are Governess, Nurse and Sempstress all in one; they are expected to be highly accomplished and to make first rate Scholars out of wild, petted, vulgar, passionate, ungovernable children, but all this might be done if it were not that the foolish Mothers almost invariably stand in the way of the Governess's authority and do what they can to render all her heartbreaking efforts useless.

Salaries vary from £30 to £40 — a good Cook gets as much. A Governess is expected to slave from 6 a.m. until 10 p.m. and if any of the children be ill she must remain up two or three nights in succession without even being desired to make a cup of tea for herself. This has been my last six months' experience. I trust I may get among kinder people next time or I shall break down.

Augusta's next job, on the Waimakariri River, inland from Christchurch, proved to be no improvement on the first. On 8 October 1865, she wrote to Miss Lewin, when returning £5 of her loan:

Oh! I was treated in a cold, cruel and unkind manner by Mrs Kesteven and some of her grown-up daughters . . . after driving two long days in a Bullock-dray heaped with all kinds of rubbish I arrived (much fatigued) at my journey's end. Almost all the road had been trackless and treeless; the house was a small, miserable looking, broken down thing situated on the river bed of the Waimakariri, everything about the house and its environs was wretched and comfortless to a degree. I was received by Mrs Kesteven, a large, coarse, cross-looking woman. She introduced me to my six pupils, the eldest sixteen years old; they were like wild, untamed colts, but as pupils none could be better, they were most anxious to learn and got on amazingly. Mrs Kesteven frequently told me that she thought they were making rapid progress but notwithstanding this Mrs Kesteven was dreadfully rude, unkind, yes, even downright cruel to me, especially if she saw me looking ill . . . I was only engaged to teach five hours a day but I found I was expected to teach eight and a half hours and, although there were six daughters above twelve years of age, I was expected to clean out the School hut, also to fetch sticks and light the fire etc. I had to scrub floors, wipe up dishes, etc. etc. and do all kinds of

---

*Riccarton Roller Flour Mill, near Christchurch, founded by W. D. Wood and operated by Wood Bros. until 1895.

menial work and after all I was accused of not doing enough and not sewing sufficiently for the family . . . every evening was spent in playing the piano from 6.30 to 9.30 for the amusement of the children or Mr Kesteven and every moment stolen from that time was spent in fancy work for Mrs Kesteven.

Even allowing for some exaggeration in Augusta McNeill's report, this was a particularly arduous situation and she soon left. Later, while unemployed, she wrote from Diamond Harbour, on 12 December 1865: 'The country is actually teeming with unemployed Governesses, every ship brings several, and many are working like Slaves for £20 per annum and for the most part treated with great indignity and almost always with coldness and neglect . . . most suffer as I have done; it is the custom of the Colony to do so'. She later found a position teaching three children at Governor's Bay, a holiday resort on Lyttleton Harbour, and said her employer* was 'kind and considerate and friendly'.

Arabella James arrived in Auckland, on the North Island, on 31 October 1864 with her sister, to join her father, two sisters and a brother. She wrote on 4 November 1864 that she was about to take a position with Dr Arthur Guyon Purchas, a surgeon and clergyman, who was, from 1853 to 1875, in charge of St Peter's, Onehunga, now a suburban borough of Auckland. Two years later, in a letter dated 12 October 1866, from Drury, near Auckland, after her marriage to Mr Brown, she wrote to explain that she was unable to repay her loan to the Society, since her husband had been unfortunate financially, owing to the 'hard times in New Zealand'. She was thinking, she said, of opening a school at Otahuhu, also near Auckland.

Many of the governesses mention the economic conditions in New Zealand at the time. In the early and middle 1860s, economic growth on the North Island was retarded by the Maori wars, but the South Island, particularly Canterbury and Otago, prospered with the expansion of the pastoral industry. Also on the South Island, the discovery of gold, first at Otago and then on the West Coast, led to a sudden boom in trade. The European population increased rapidly as diggers poured in and economic life quickened as gold brought prosperity, less so to the diggers than to the bankers,

---

*Written in the letter-book as both Mrs Mills and Mrs Miles.

merchants, land-dealers and farmers who supplied provisions.

Attempts by other provinces to emulate the economic development in Canterbury and Otago ended in failure because of unwise borrowing and in 1867, the central government banned overseas borrowing by the provincial governments. About this time, depression struck the greater part of the country, especially the South Island, where the first of the alluvial gold had been worked out. In 1870, the Colonial Treasurer, Julius Vogel, introduced a development policy by borrowing overseas capital for public works and by promoting assisted migration. An investment boom followed in the mid-1870s.

The only evidence that the Society received requests to find governesses for specific positions is contained in a letter from Dr Henry T. Spratt of Greytown, one of the oldest towns in the Wairarapa Valley, north-east of Wellington. On 10 July 1864, he wrote to Miss Lewin, having been advised to do so by Miss Rye while she was in New Zealand:

> I want a middle aged lady to educate my four girls, of whom the eldest is eighteen and the youngest eight; the accomplishments are simply plain English, plain sewing with a little piano and singing. Of course when I offer £50 a year, which is certainly much higher than many obtain here, I fully trust you will make a careful selection, for I hope to get one gentle and ladylike in her manners and accustomed to teach. She will have no household work of a menial kind, but I wish my daughters to have no companion who thinks it derogatory to be domesticated.

He asked that Miss Lewin refer her choice to his mother, Mrs S. Spratt, wife of Dr Spratt, of Margaret Street/Regent Street, London.

Martha Wyett was selected by the Society for this position, but arrangements must have been prolonged, for eighteen months elapsed before she arrived in New Zealand. On 10 February 1866, she wrote: 'You had prepared me to expect something very rough, but my imagination fell far short of the reality, but I have no doubt (excepting in one particular) that I shall soon cease to miss the comforts of our English homes'. Miss Wyett reported that situations were not plentiful in New Zealand, one governess having advertised twenty-one times without result.

In a letter written on 10 May 1867, Martha Wyett gave an account of what had happened to her first year's salary:

'Advance by Dr Spratt spent in England £10; sent as a present to Mamma £27; payments to the Society two of £2 each; unaccountably lost £12-10-0, a total of £53-10-0. I offer you this account that you may not think I have been enjoying myself on the money.' Apart from the loss, which is not explained further, the account is indicative of the obligation many governesses had towards families in England, often in worse financial straits than they were themselves and dependent on the fortunate one receiving a salary in the colonies. Miss Wyett's gift to her mother was half of her year's salary.

In her last letter, dated 7 December 1868 and addressed to Miss Lewin, Martha Wyett apologised for not having had the money to refund her loan previously. 'I have been most anxious on my friends' account, knowing Mamma was not in a position to pay the money without great inconvenience to herself, should you apply to her for it', she wrote. She said her salary from Dr Spratt had been reduced, since one of her pupils had left and another, who was nearly twenty, would leave in three months.

Another governess to go to the provincial district of Wellington was Miss M. E. Smith, who after three months without work, during which she stayed with Captain Andrew Hamilton Russell and his wife at Redclyffe, their property near Napier, found a job teaching Mr and Mrs Charles Bidwill's* five children at a salary of £50 a year. The Bidwills lived at Pihautea on the western shore of Lake Wairarapa. On 22 March 1867, Miss Smith wrote to Miss Rye:

> [Governesses] are not required in the Colony at present; good servants are what families want in the way of assistance . . . everyone is hoping that the servants who are coming out will be of a better class than those who have preceded them; they certainly are perfect torments and behave shamefully.

Lucy Scott, who went to Christchurch, reported that things were the same on the South Island. Late in 1867, she wrote:

> [it is a] dire mistake which people fall into at home of fancying that more governesses are required in the Colonies. New Zealand is over-stocked with them already, indeed they are quite at a discount;

---

*Charles Robert Bidwill was the first settler to take sheep into the Wairarapa Valley. His wool was sent by packhorse to Te Kopi on Palliser Bay and then by small ships to Wellington. He also kept cattle and thoroughbred horses.

many have latterly been compelled to become nursemaids, the salaries they receive in nine cases out of ten do not exceed £35, the same sum is given to common housemaids.

There is only one letter from Barbara Starky, who found the first situation she obtained, with Mrs Newton, teaching 'five great boys', too much for her and took another with Mrs Elizabeth Crosse, wife of Charles Grant Crosse, on their station, eighty miles from Napier, on the North Island, and about seven miles south-west of what was to become the township of Porangahau, to which she had to travel by bullock-dray.

Mrs Crosse was a fluent speaker of Maori and was for a time the only white woman living in the Porangahau district. In 1855, when she first travelled to the station, it was a journey of 120 miles by Maori tracks. Leaving Napier, she and her husband walked for one day, then travelled a further two days by canoe to Patangata, where they stopped while Elizabeth bore her first child, a son, Thomas. When she was fit to travel, they went on to the coast and walked along the beach, at one stage having to wait for low tide to cross a five-mile stretch of rocks, then paddled up the Porangahau River to the site of the present Porangahau township, where while they camped during the night, an unexpected flood washed away their belongings. Maoris accommodated them until their own hut could be built at Mangamaire from poles cut from the bush. Charles and Elizabeth Crosse had ten children and Elizabeth lived to the age of 103.

Barbara Starky was of very different physique. Her letter contains ominous references to her health: the continual coughing, the doses of cod-liver oil and the doctor's opinion that her left lung was in a bad state. Nevertheless, she asked Miss Rye, to whom her letter was addressed, not to tell her family, for it would make them unhappy. She wrote on 24 December 1868: 'I should of course go into one of the hospitals were I to get worse and know that I should not recover'.

Two sisters who arrived in 1868 found work around Dunedin, Eliza Brook as a governess a hundred miles up country at £55 a year, and Mary Brook as a milliner at £2 5s 0d a week. Both married during the following year and on 18 December 1869, Eliza (now Mrs MacDonnell) wrote:

We think ourselves fortunate to have met with gentlemen who belong to good families at home . . . Oh! Miss Rye it is women of our class who need your assistance, and when you helped us you were the cause of our present happiness and comfort . . . you may have forgotten the two sisters who once came to ask your assistance and counsel. I however have not forgotten your kindness and encouragement in persuading us to carry out the scheme of leaving England for New Zealand and I shall always feel grateful for the interest you manifested towards us and the help you rendered us. From the time of our landing we have been wonderfully fortunate.

Later, Eliza MacDonnell was asked to assist a new FMCES emigrant, Mary Wilson, but on 27 July 1870, she wrote to Miss Lewin, explaining her inability to help and replying to Miss Lewin's request for information:

There has been for some months past a great depression in Dunedin, consequently trade is very dull and I should imagine business people little wanted. I do not think experience so much a requisite as at home; at the same time a thoroughly competent business woman would command a far higher salary than one unaccustomed to its details . . .

Most though not all of the wealthy people here have risen from nothing and I daresay you can imagine the feelings of importance they indulge in and those who have once been poor and common would be little likely to treat with consideration a lady unfortunately circumstanced. There are many, many such here and I feel bound to say their conduct is invariably such as one ever finds in people of that class.

I have from the first observed how dreadfully exaggerated all accounts of daily life in New Zealand are at home; most of the situations are up country, long hours in general and in the families of runholders.

By the time she wrote this letter, Eliza had a four-month-old daughter, Muriel, and her sister had a son.

Mary Wilson, who, according to a cryptic note in the FMCES letter-book, may have been a relation of Mrs Hannah Wilson of Brisbane, and who travelled out on the *Bouverie*, wrote only once to the Society. The letter was addressed from Matahiwi, about six miles from Masterton, in the Wairarapa Valley, and dated 25 September 1871. She said she had had no help from Mrs MacDonnell (née Brook). Her first position had been in a station-holder's family and she had been in her present position for six months. She had obtained it through a lady to whom she had a letter of introduction from friends in Scotland and was receiving £40 per year.

Marion Hett, who arrived at Christchurch on the *Ramsey* on 23 June 1870, was remarkable, even among such a class-conscious group as the FMCES emigrants, for her upper-class sensitivities. She was employed first at Napier, on the eastern coast of the North Island, by a storekeeper's wife, Mrs F. Sutton,* who herself had emigrated as a servant. Miss Hett was engaged to teach the three girls in the family at £40 a year. On 28 July 1870, she wrote: 'I should never like Colonial life sufficiently well to wish to become a settler — it seems to me that even the most affluent of the population have no sort of comfort in their lives'. She left the position after only five months, because her employer was 'not a *Lady*, and in going to her, I placed myself in a false position, and that you know never answers'. She said in a letter to Miss Lewin dated 16 June 1871:

> From the very first she was extremely rude and overbearing, but I resolved to stay a year with her if possible . . . However it was not to be. One day, at the end of six weeks, I had occasion to administer a *very mild* chastisement to one of the children for bad behaviour and disobedience, but in the evening she rated me so soundly for it in the presence of the children and the little maid, that I gave her notice on the spot as, of course, that sort of conduct could not be submitted to for a moment. . . . During the next three months her insolence was excessive . . .

Marion Hett's next job was on a different social stratum, at Major Marshall's station, Tutu Totara, near Marton, north-west of Wellington. She took a steamer from Napier to Wellington, then travelled by coach on a journey of one-and-a-half days to Marton, about 120 miles north, then rode a horse another eight miles, the last three along a bridle-path. She found the house comfortable, was admitted to the family circle and thought Mrs Marshall's outlook compatible. 'The present Mrs Marshall dislikes the ways of the Colony quite as much as I do and strives to make everything about her house

---

*Frederick Sutton arrived in New Zealand in 1857 and settled in Napier, where he started a business. In 1867, he was elected a member of the Provincial Council, a position he held until 1877, when he was elected the member for Napier in the General Assembly. He died in 1906, leaving a widow and one son and six daughters.

as English as possible so our views in these matters coincide very nicely.' She added, in her letter to Miss Lewin of 16 June 1871:

In New Zealand things are dreadfully bad — the settlers are nearly all ruined and the only people who are tolerably well off are the Agents and shopkeepers — both these classes know they are necessary and fleece the settlers shamefully.

Major Marshall* is very poor, but he is only like his neighbours . . . I am inclined to think that New Zealand is a decided mistake . . . More than one Lady has told me if their husbands had never seen this Colony, they would be far better off . . .

I am grievously disappointed about my salary . . . (£40), but really at the present prices of produce employers cannot afford to give more . . . The population is not sufficiently numerous to create a demand and the country is so sadly governed, or rather misgoverned, that things do not seem likely to improve. The taxes are very heavy. Major Marshall said the other day that this is the most expensive country in the world.

Marion Hett also had an interesting comment to make on the small houses and lack of furniture. She thought that lack of room was one reason that forced people in Napier to send their children to 'very inferior schools' rather than employ governesses.

Most of these wooden houses are so small that accommodation is very limited indeed, it is some time before a newcomer can reconcile him or herself to keeping all their things in boxes instead of drawers, which boxes even must stand one upon another if you wish to have room to turn in.

---

*Major John Williams Marshall had served with the 65th Regiment, in the Canadian rebellion (1837–38), in England (1841) and in New South Wales (1846). He arrived in New Zealand in 1846 and took part in the campaigns at Hutt and Pahahautanui. In 1858, the regiment moved to Auckland and in 1860 to Taranaki, where Major Marshall took part in the Maori War. In 1853, he had acquired Tutu Totara, a large block of heavily bushed land nine miles north of Marton, as a 'Queen's Grant' and began farming the land, which later grew into a successful fattening and cropping property.

Major Marshall was responsible for the safety of what was then the Upper Rangitikei district. His home was the most northern outpost of the district. From Tutu Totara to what is now Taihape was unbroken forest, and the only access north was by the Maori track to Taupo or by canoe on the Rangitikei River. A photograph taken in 1870 shows the homestead he built was a large two-winged, shingle-roofed bungalow, surrounded by a deep verandah. It was constructed of pit-sawn heart totara. Major Marshall's second wife was Jane Mary Boulter. His first wife died in 1854.

In her first year at Major Marshall's, Marion Hett was unable to repay any of her loan, since she had to spend her money buying saddlery, 'as riding is the only mode of getting off the place'. A year later, she repaid £25 and wrote on 16 July 1872: 'Things are looking up a little in New Zealand now that the price of wool is better, but there is a sad scarcity of money — everybody is complaining'. Marion Hett remained happily with the Marshall family for some years. She described her duties as almost nominal — four hours' daily teaching — and the position remained socially congenial. She reports having dinner and later staying with the Premier and Mrs Fox, whose country home was on a nearby property. By the time of her last letter, written on 21 October 1873, Marion Hett wondered whether she would ever see her 'native shores again'. According to a letter from another correspondent, she later left Major Marshall's family and, in 1879, was a partner in a school at Gisborne, Poverty Bay.

Kate Brind settled at Nelson, in the north of the South Island, in 1872 and a year after leaving home wrote on 27 July 1873 from Provincial Gardens, Nelson: 'a dreary time it has seemed . . . this province and town are so quiet that there is never anything to write about'. In a letter written earlier, on 8 May, she had mentioned receiving £100 a year as a governess in a school and the news of this high salary, combined with the failure to repay her loan, provoked a letter from Miss Lewin, threatening to take legal proceedings if the money was not paid at the proper time. Kate Brind explained that the £100 salary had been only a temporary arrangement and her salary was now £80. 'My drawback has been doctor's bills. I am still under him and likely to be for some little time as the sea voyage weakened me considerably', she wrote on 6 April 1874. Later that year, she made the final repayment of her loan. She was then living with her brother, who had taken over the Provincial Hotel at Nelson, and was expecting their mother to join them. In a letter dated 14 March 1875, she said she was engaged to be married and expected to leave her position, with a Mrs Edwards, in a year or eighteen months. In the meantime, she had to pay off her mother's fare.

Miss M. Campbell also worked in Nelson about this time. She wrote to Mrs Sunter on 1 May 1874, after a ninety-day voyage to New Zealand, saying that she had a job with Mr J. Oldham at Wernith, about three miles from Nelson.

A very unhappy emigrant was Emily Mary Hunt, who wrote to Mrs Sunter from Hill Street, Wellington, on 19 December 1874: 'I regret from my heart ever leaving England, but when Miss Lewin is paid, I shall be free, for never can I be happy in this Country ... I am perfectly disgusted and everything is so dear ... I am writing to the Duchess, perhaps she will pay out of compassion and then I will return'. The Duchess apparently was one of the guarantors of her loan. Emily Hunt does not seem to have shared the strong feeling of obligation to repay her loan herself, which many other governesses expressed.

Miss E. L. Manning had a much happier outcome to her journey to New Zealand. She arrived on 5 November 1875, on board the *Great Britain*, and in a letter written from Dunedin in February 1876, said she had married her friend's brother, Mr Buck, very shortly after arriving. Later that year, on 17 October, she wrote from Dunedin, asking for another two years to repay her loan because she and her husband had bought a home. She had recently had a son.

There is an indication, in a letter from Miss E. A. Hacon, from Timaru, Canterbury, that the amounts the governesses needed to borrow were increasing, although their salaries remained low. On 20 June 1878, Miss Hacon remitted her first quarter's salary of £15, which brought her repayments to £22, but she still was left with another £20 to repay. Nevertheless, she was happy with her move to New Zealand. 'I did very wisely in making the attempt to come out, for it is a fair grand land and there is a better chance here of making money, if you will only work hard for it, than at home', she said.

Miss Georgie Bird, who arrived on 1 July 1877 on the *William Davie*, found work at £100 a year in the same area as Miss Hacon, with Mrs Tripp, a bishop's daughter and wife of a wealthy sheep-farmer. She wrote on 21 July 1877, from Cranmer Cottage, Chester Street West, Christchurch, just before leaving with the Tripps to go to their country property at Orari Gorge, Waiki Bush, Geraldine, inland and north of Timaru, where she said she did not expect to meet with adventures similar to Lady Barker's.* Mrs Tripp later dis-

*Lady Barker, born Mary Anne Stewart in 1831 in Jamaica, married, in 1852, Captain George Barker, who in 1859 was knighted for services in the Indian Mutiny. He died two years later. In 1865, Lady Barker married a New Zealand

pensed with Miss Bird's services, since although she was an excellent teacher', she sometimes 'behaved strangely and rudely'. This information comes to light in correspondence from Harriet Herbert of Mount Herbert, Waipukurau, a sheep-raising district, forty-four miles south of Napier, Hawke's Bay, a governesses' agent and a member of the Hawke's Bay Education Board, the only woman in New Zealand to hold such a position. Miss Herbert had been appointed following the passing of the Education Act in 1877.** As did similar Acts passed in the Australian colonies, this legislation resulted in the development of the government school system. And as in Australia, it was to limit further the need for governesses in New Zealand, except in the most isolated areas.

Miss Herbert had been assisting the FMCES emigrants to obtain positions for some years. During 1879–80, she wrote a series of letters to Miss Lewin about the placement of governesses. On 8 May 1879, she asked: 'Are you sending out any Governesses now? There seems a great dearth of them all over New Zealand just now and people have had to send to Melbourne.' This encouraging news prompted the Society to send a considerable number of emigrants to New Zealand, too many in fact for Miss Herbert to place, particularly when economic conditions in the country deteriorated.

In the same letter, Miss Herbert also gave some advice on what was required of governesses in New Zealand:

> . . . (especially for Christchurch) it is as well to know something of their family and social position. In New Zealand Governesses are generally treated more as one of the family than in England and for that very reason the question is often asked, 'Is she a Lady by birth?', besides which a great many Governesses marry among the

---

sheep-farmer, Frederick Napier Broome, who bought the Steventon sheep-run on the Selwyn River in the South Island in 1866. Under the name of Lady Barker, Mary Anne Broome wrote of her life there in *Station Life in New Zealand* (Macmillan, London, 1870), followed by *Station Life, and Station Amusements in New Zealand* (1873). These books, which were widely read at the time, contain descriptions of such adventures as wild-boar hunting. Lady Barker wrote many other books, including *A Year's Housekeeping in South Africa* (1877), written while her husband was Colonial Secretary to Natal, and *Letters to Guy* (1885), written to her son while her husband was Governor of Western Australia (1882-89), during which time he was knighted. She died in London in 1911.

**Harriet Herbert was balloted to retire in December 1878 and chose not to stand for re-election.

friends of their employers and birth and good manners go a great way in that respect . . .

In our large towns there are generally High Schools for girls as well as boys, so most situations are in the country and ladies requiring the excitement of Town Life had better stay in England.

In a letter dated 13 May, and posted at the same time as her previous letter, she added:

. . . prepare anyone who comes to take whatever is vacant to begin with and to be prepared for *country life, thick* boots, muddy roads, few excitements, but most likely very pleasant employers who create a far more homelike feeling than generally falls to a governess's lot in England.

Towards the end of the year, on 8 November 1879, Miss Herbert gave the first warning of financial difficulties ahead: 'Things are not so flourishing in New Zealand as when I wrote last, the financial depression which spread a gloom over Europe has affected us too'. She also wrote of the education system:

We have High Schools for girls as well as boys in all our towns. Houses are not so large as in England very often and families not so exclusive — so all combines to make the demand for governesses in the towns less and less. The education in our public schools is now very thorough, but whether cramming girls with all the *ologies* really has a beneficial effect on their characters and helps them to make good wives and mothers remains to be proved. I don't think needlework gets sufficent attention and it is essential here . . . girls here marry early and how much happiness or misery may depend on their being able to make [a] home comfortable and pleasant for the husband.

Miss Herbert advised against the emigration of one particular woman who was over forty years of age — she was too old to be transplanted from the 'comforts and luxuries of an English home' to the 'comparative roughness of station life in New Zealand'. She added: '. . . generally speaking the houses are smaller and furniture plainer, there are fewer servants; sometimes the family is left for weeks without any and a governess who stood on her dignity and refused to help would do a foolish thing'.

By the beginning of 1880, Miss Herbert wanted the flow of

governesses, which her correspondence had initiated, stopped. On 26 January, she wrote to Miss Lewin:

You say you will go on sending Governesses till I cry 'Hold, enough', so please 'Hold' now. Since I wrote telling you of our difficulty in finding Governesses a period of great financial depression has passed over New Zealand; many families reported wealthy have reduced their establishments, paying lower salaries to teachers or doing without altogether and I fear it will be difficult to find homes for your late consignments, certainly not at the salaries they expected.

... [Governesses] will have to be content with £40 and possibly a rather rough home. Ladies, not young, and fresh from England, are almost sure to dislike this — being discontented, mutual dissatisfaction ensues.

Miss Herbert commented, in a letter dated 20 March 1880, on the fate of some of the arrivals, particularly Fraulein Woerner, who she feared would remain unemployed: 'Foreigners do not answer here ... She is *not* well educated, has only the sight of one eye and holds almost infidel opinions.' At this time, Fraulein Woerner was living off Miss Herbert's charity, since she was unable to pay the board that Miss Herbert had guaranteed. After her arrival, Fraulein Woerner went first to Dunedin, where in a letter written to Miss Lewin on 19 October 1879, from 'Kempston House', Heriot Row, she made some original observations. Instead of 'a few miserable huts as I expected to see there are very pretty houses and several of them, particularly those belonging to some wretched old bachelors, are perfect castles. Inside they are very comfortable, the house in which I am staying has even a bathroom where I can have a bath whenever I like.'

Two sisters, the Misses Long, Miss Herbert thought might be easier to place. Concerning another, Miss Blackith, she commented in a letter dated 26 January 1880:

...is it wise to bring her out? ... If Miss Blackith can cook so well she had far better put her pride in her pocket and take a cook's position ... I am sorry to send you bad tidings and assure you I have spared no pains on behalf of your protegees, only I hope you will send no more just yet; I *cannot* place them.

Miss J. Caldwell, who arrived on 31 December 1879 on the

Sobroan, and whom Miss Herbert had tried to persuade Lady Fox, the Premier's wife, to employ as a companion, managed to get a job at Christchurch at £50 a year, but she was far from happy. She wrote to Mrs Sunter on 30 January 1880:

> Everything here is so *dear* and *bad* for Governesses that several have said to me that you and Miss Lewin ought to be told *not* to send out any more ladies, at any rate for a year or so, for there is the same difficulty finding engagements as there is in dear old England; salaries are just the same (perhaps I might say not as good) as board and lodging are frightfully dear. If Miss Brooke [her cousin, who had emigrated with her] and I had not had money of our own I do not know what we should have done . . . Schools are doing the same harm here as in England to Governesses — at times I can hardly believe I am in the Colonies, for one sees in Christchurch just as much comfort and refinement as at home and everything goes on in just the same way, were it not that everything is *much dearer*. . . . The persons who make money here are working men; they and servants can live here like ladies and gentlemen. I am really sorry I cannot give you a better account of New Zealand; as to Australia [the ship had called at Melbourne on the way through], it is worse. Lots have to return home, finding nothing to do.

Others were in more difficult circumstances. Fanny Cross survived by doing home dressmaking and later got a job with a wholesale business house in Dunedin. 'This is a very monotonous life', she wrote on 25 October 1881, 'and I should not advise any single woman to come out to the Colonies without having some friends here'.

Eleanor Blackith took a position, not as a cook, but looking after the three Simcox children at the parsonage at Porangahau, thirty miles into the hills from Waipukurau. She described Porangahau in an undated (1881) letter as 'very primitive'. In a later letter, dated 2 November 1881, she said she was engaged to marry a Mr Lawes in England, but expected a long engagement.

Caroline Fox, who arrived on the *Sonkar* in about July 1879, was employed to teach six children on a station in Canterbury, the position with Mrs Tripp previously held by Georgie Bird. In an undated letter, probably written in September 1879, she described them as 'very backward and [they] require more patience than brains to be exercised on their studies'. Later, she moved to a position with the Reverend L. L. Brown, Maori Hill, Timaru, writing from there on 26 February 1880, when she repaid £25 of her loan.

Another arrival about this time, Miss I. Keith, said in a letter dated 5 September 1879 that she had had a good many situations to choose from, including two recommended by Miss Herbert, but she had gone to one in Canterbury, which she had found herself by advertising. The position was with Mr E. G. Wright at Wenslow, Mudermere, and an attraction in taking it was that her brother was working on a new line of railway about ten miles away.

Elizabeth and Mary Long were found jobs in the Hawke's Bay area by Miss Herbert, Mary with the Reverend Shearman's family at Waipukurau, near Mount Herbert, and Elizabeth on a sheep-station in isolated country at Waimarama,* twenty-two miles south-west of Hastings, along the coast from Napier. Elizabeth Long wrote on 20 May 1880:

The place is very remote and lonely and I was obliged to ride 17 miles to get here as there is no other way of coming here except by bullock dray and that only twice a year. The Meinertzhagens are people of position and I believe very well off and Mrs Meinertzhagen and her sister, who lives with her, do a great deal of work in the house, the dairy and the garden, for though there are three servants there is always plenty to do; they live very simple lives but very happy ones. I think their only real want being that there is no church nearer than Napier, 40 miles away, and that is bad for everyone. However, I make the children read the Bible a good deal and learn catechism, hymns, etc. and on Sunday I sing hymns with them at the piano, besides having more reading than on weekdays.

I have now given you an account of my life here, which I like in many ways, but one thing I must tell you which was not pleasant. When I first came Mrs Meinertzhagen wanted me to take my meals in the schoolroom with the children and I decidedly refused to do so; I offered to breakfast with them, as I should in that way ensure greater punctuality in beginning lessons and proposed to give them their tea before the late dinner hour; but for two or three days she would not agree to this, and then I said I must leave, the sooner the better, but the next morning Mrs Meinertzhagen said that if I insisted on dining with them she supposed I must do so and that

---

*Frederick Huth Meinertzhagen, whose father was a partner in the wealthy firm of Huth and Co., had purchased the leasehold of Waimarama, in partnership with Walter Lorne Campbell, in 1868. For many years, access to the property was by bullock-wagon or horseback and the first five miles of the trip to Hastings were along the beachfront, before turning inland over Maori tracks. The Meinertzhagens returned to England in 1880.

was the end of it. Contrary to my expectation she has been friendly ever since and I am very comfortable, but my ideal of New Zealand life has been spoiled; and although it is undoubtedly the paradise of servants, I am afraid the paradise for governesses has yet to be discovered.

Her sister, Mary Long, wrote at the same time an undated letter, enclosed with her sister's of 20 May, from the parsonage, where she received only £30 a year:

I do a great deal of needlework and housekeeping, as well as teach two girls, one boy and another girl I teach Music to. But as I am kindly treated and one of the family and am only 40 miles from my sister, I am content only to know I get too little pay; however it can't be helped as Mr Shearman* is very poor . . .

Now I really don't know does it pay for young ladies to come out here: it cost a lot to come and though there are not so many governesses as at home, there are also not so many situations, and though education is expensive here, still people don't seem to care to pay governesses at the same rate. But in spite of it all I *would rather be a governess here than in England.*

Those governesses who followed, found an even tougher employment market. Falling overseas prices for wool and wheat and declining gold production led to widespread unemployment in New Zealand in the 1880s.

In 1881, the Society had a letter from Mrs Charlotte Kemp, who had been asked to assist new arrivals. Her home was in Wellington, but she wrote from the Young Women's Institute, Queen Street, Auckland, where she was visiting. Writing on the employment situation in New Zealand, she said:

At the same time will you forgive my saying that I think New Zealand is not a good place to send young women to who are wishing to better themselves. I went to Miss Smith's** home last night and saw four or five educated young gentlewomen who are anxiously looking and waiting for something to do. One has gone into a milliner's shop, being tired of waiting. The salaries given are not by any means high. Unless a New Zealand Governess is really a sensible person who does not object to giving a hand at housework,

---

*Reverend J. Shearman, Church of England vicar of Waipukurau parish from 1876 to 1881. The parish included all of Hawke's Bay south of the Waipawa River, except the portion within the parish of Porangahau.

**Laura Smith, head of the Young Women's Institute, Auckland.

sometimes help with children's needlework too, she will find very few places to suit her. Schools are cheap here and many people prefer sending them there to having a resident governess. So many ladies come here thinking they are going to get just what they want and find themselves so grievously disappointed that I quite dread to hear of anyone coming.

The last emigrant to New Zealand who is recorded in the FMCES letter-books is Miss A. Russell. She wrote on 26 January 1882 from Mrs Pledger's Boarding House, Albert Street, Dunedin, to announce her safe arrival at Port Chalmers the previous day. She said:

My voyage has been a very pleasant and happy one . . . we met no homebound vessels, only a few steamers for Hamburg and foreign places.

No situation awaits me at present, but I am told that in a few days I shall probably hear of something from Mrs Turnbull of Dunedin who is at present away but expected soon.

The FMCES's report published in 1886 spoke of the hopelessness of obtaining situations in Auckland. The Society had received a report from there 'telling of one governess having gone into a factory, another as a servant in a shop, a third as housekeeper and *only* servant in a widower's family, while our informant and her family earned a meagre pittance by needlework'. The Society, however, remained confident about the prospects for governesses in the country, for the report added: 'Such are the results of persisting in ignoring the Society's warnings never to remain in the Port towns, but to accept the first well-accredited offer from inland residences'.

11 A Challenging Life in South Africa

'. . . this is the corner of the vineyard the Great Husbandman has allotted to me to labour in'.

Miss S. E. A. Hall, Graaff-Reinet, 1879

In South Africa, FMCES emigrants began arriving about the same time as in Australia and by the end of 1862, the first emigrants, Rosarie Winn and Catherine Crowe, had written to the Society. Of those who followed, though not in the numbers who emigrated to Australia and New Zealand, several went to the families of planters at the sugar estates established in Natal, others to the families of Dutch farmers (not always a happy experience) and several to schools, particularly to Miss S. E. A. Hall's school for girls at Graaff-Reinet in Cape Colony, Miss Catherine Crowe's Cheltenham House at Pinetown, near Durban, Natal, and Miss Mary Watson's Egerton House at Bedford, inland from Port Elizabeth, in the eastern part of Cape Colony. Miss Crowe was herself one of the pioneer emigrants to South Africa under the Scheme and Miss Hall was another FMCES emigrant.

The concerns of these women were similar to those of the governesses who went to Australia and New Zealand: the difficulties in obtaining a situation, the low pay (much lower on the whole than in Australia) and the problems of repaying the money loaned by the Society. In South Africa, there was the added element of accommodating to life in close proximity to the native people and, later, to the last of the frontier wars between the settlers and the native tribes, the Zulu wars, the confrontation between the British and the Boers and the excitement of the diamond finds.

The emigrant governesses were attracted primarily to Natal, which from 1856 had been a British colony. In Natal's early years, the British settlers eked out a precarious existence. Agriculture had declined with the exodus of the Boers from 1831 on the Great Treks to the interior, which led to the formation of the republics of Transvaal and the Orange Free State. However, the British government's encouragement of immigration eventually led to an improvement in the economy. Cotton and coffee were planted experimentally, but the great success was the production of sugar-cane. Production began in 1851 and by 1860, 3,000 tons were being produced yearly in Natal and by 1872 about 6,000 acres were under cultivation. Durban, named after Sir Benjamin D'Urban, Governor of Cape Colony in the 1830s, developed as the colony's sea-port and principal town.

The governesses who arrived at Natal in the 1860s found life in Durban and the surrounding districts a rather primitive existence. However, with the assistance of James Brickhill,* the bank officer husband of one of the Society's South African correspondents, they settled into jobs fairly quickly, even if most of these were very poorly paid.

The first letter from South Africa came from Rosarie Winn, who was met by her brother and taken to stay with friends. Writing on 25 June 1862 from Durban, she said she had been offered a job at £20 a year to teach four children.

I feel very happy and contented and comfortable and am not in the least afraid of getting on. I consider I have been most successful and fortunate and a kind Providence has watched over

*James Brickhill was one of the earliest settlers in Natal. He arrived on the *Conch* at Port Elizabeth in 1842 with a detachment of the 27th Regiment. A few months later, he was blinded by a cobra and pensioned out at 8½ pence a day for life. When he regained his sight, he moved to Pietermaritzburg, where he was one of the founders of Natal's first bank, the Natal Bank. In October 1855, he became manager of the Durban branch of the bank and remained in that position until 1883. He died on 13 November 1889. He was married first to a Miss Cadle and after her death, married Mary Rogers Harvey in 1855. Mary Harvey was related to T. M. Harvey, a founder of Harvey, Greenacre & Co., until 1982 a leading Durban department store.

James Brickhill was a member of the Durban Town Council, 1860–61, a prominent member of the Congregational Church and a pioneer tea-grower at his estate, Prospect Tea Estate, Umbilo, near Durban. His descendants still live in Durban.

and taken care of me from the very beginning of my new career, for which I am most thankful. It seems so strange to be surrounded by so many Kaffirs, for they are the principal persons who work for you and wait on you here and they are nearly all in a half nude state, but they are much further advanced in civilization than I expected to find them. And you have no idea of what a number of fine shops there are, but everything is very expensive in the way of living. Clothing and house rent is very high. The rent of a small cottage £70 or £80. Boots and Shoes too are very dear. I should never have thought that living would have cost so much, but they say we are a good deal further advanced than they are at the Cape.

Rosarie Winn was one of the few governesses who mentioned a shipboard romance: 'I have done *one very* foolish thing, which I did not *mean* to do. However, I am not going to do anything rash and shan't marry just yet. I am going to wait a little while first and see how the Gentleman gets on.'

Two years later and still unmarried, Rosarie Winn was governess to the children of the resident magistrate, Dr Benjamin Blaine, at Verulam, which she described as a 'nice little Colonial village', about twenty-two miles from Durban. Verulam, situated across the Umgeni River, north of Durban, was founded in 1850 by a group of Methodist ministers brought to South Africa under the patronage of the Earl of Verulam and later became the principal town of the Inanda sugar-cane region. Dr Benjamin Blaine was the first district surgeon in Natal and later magistrate at the capital, Pietermaritzburg. In her letter of 31 July 1864, Miss Winn described her surroundings:

The houses are all one storied and mostly built of thatch; some of the dwelling places consist of huts merely made of wattle and dab and thatched. There is scarcely a white servant to be had anywhere for love or money; coolies or Kaffirs compose the domestics of an establishment and it is absolutely necessary to know the Kaffir language if you wish to get on here.

Miss Winn had been hired to teach Dr Blaine's three girls music, French and English, to teach one son music, and to teach reading and writing to the small daughter of a Cornish neighbour. She received £30 a year, which she said was good money for a beginner. She believed Dr Blaine intended to bring out a governess from England on his current leave and, if so, she would move to the Cornish neighbour, if she was not married by then. However, another correspondent, Miss J. S. Fowler, reported a sad end to Rosarie Winn's romance, writing on 21 May 1866, 'the gentleman to whom Miss Winn was about to be married' had just died.

The Misses Crowe, two sisters from Dublin, travelled out to South Africa with Rosarie Winn. Catherine Crowe, in a letter dated 1 July 1862 from Berea, Durban, Port Natal, described her arrival:

> The Captain and his wife were very kind, indeed the former took us on Shore in his own boat and saw after our luggage. We came from the Port to Durban by Rail which is a distance of two miles and the next morning called on Mr Brickhill, who seemed sadly disappointed he had not heard we were coming as in that case he would have advertised for us . . . Nothing can exceed Mr Brickhill's kind interest about us; he does not appear to think *anything* a trouble he can do for us.

Within two days, Mr Brickhill had found Catherine Crowe 'a very comfortable situation as a Governess with a salary of £40 per annum, which is considered high as the people are not rich'. The situation was two miles from Durban, 'on a rising ground called the Berea, which promises in a few years to become quite a Town so many people are building on it'. Her sister obtained a position at £40 a year as governess with a family living six miles from Pietermaritzburg, about fifty miles to the west.

> I think with God's blessing we may do well here, but at the same time Governesses do not seem to be in requisition nearly as much as Servants . . . I have also been told that as a general rule females become delicate after having been here a short time. The chief diseases are Low Fever, Dysentery and Natal Sores* which have the appearance of large boils. With regard to civilisation, the Country is more forward than one would expect in such a new Colony.
>
> Maritzburg is the Chief Town in this place and as it is the Seat of Government and Government officials it is the most fashionable.

*A mosquito-induced affliction. James Brickhill is credited with discovering and marketing 'Brickhill Specific' or 'Natal Specific', a remedy for Natal sores.

Writing again on 4 October 1862, when she forwarded £11 to the Society in repayment of her loan, she added that she hoped to send money advanced to her by the Dublin Society in two months. This is an apparent reference to a scheme of Maria Rye's for involving towns and cities in the United Kingdom in raising money to lend to emigrants. In a letter to the London *Times* on 9 April 1862, Maria Rye and Jane Lewin acknowledged the receipt of donations to the FMCES and asked why the ladies of Bath, for instance, should not combine to raise funds to send middle-class women to the colonies. 'Dublin has already commenced. Will not other towns follow the good example?' they asked.

Catherine Crowe went on to report in her letter that:

> . . . my sister and I are (thank God) quite well and very comfortably settled . . . [situations] are just now hard to be got as there have been a great many heavy failures within the last few years so that people are trying to curtail their expenses as much as possible. I am told Business is still very dull. The chief advantage of the Colony seems to me to be the fine healthy climate, though we have very warm weather and very frightful thunder-storms sometimes, but chiefly in summer which is the rainy season.

Catherine Crowe later became head-mistress of Cheltenham House, a school at Pinetown, about twelve miles west of Durban.* By April 1867, she was employing another emigrant governess, Miss J. S. Fowler, and had sent for her sister, who for some years had been governess with the family of James Renault Saunders, a sugar-planter at the Tongaat Sugar Estate and a member of the Legislative Council.

From her first position teaching the Reverend Josiah and Mrs Tyler's five children at an American Mission Station at Esidumbini, Tongaat, Miss Fowler had written on 30 November 1865:

> No one should come out here unprovided with sufficient warm clothing. Winseys, Merinos and Velvets are in constant use. Nothing surprised me more on my arrival than seeing Ladies dressed in Merinos, dark shades. Everything is as fashionable as

---

*Miss Crowe was headmistress during the years 1867–68. The school was put up for sale in 1868, but failed to attract a buyer and then closed.

possible, there being three or four Mails a month and constant immigration from England and the Continent. Light clothing is of course indispensable, Muslin, Barege, etc.

She then worked for J. F. S. Tredoux, a wealthy landowner with a property at Leliefontein, near Pietermaritzburg. Mr Tredoux discharged her, she said in a letter on 20 April 1867, 'in an ungentlemanlike manner, but he is *Dutch* and that thought controlled my indignation'. Miss Fowler thought she was worth more than the salary of £50, which she was being paid by Miss Crowe, and she said she was grieved and distressed' at her present inability to repay her loan. She asked to be charged interest after the two years four months' currency of the loan had expired.

Another FMCES emigrant, Emilie Glen, also worked at an American Mission Station at Umsinduzi, Verulam, where she taught the Reverend William Mellen's four children and also in the native school, all for £24 a year. Not surprisingly, she thought the colony was in a very bad state economically. Writing on 27 October 1866, soon after her arrival, she said the scenery was truly magnificent but she had 'only seen one white man since I have been here and yet I am very happy. It seems as though the dark cloud that has hung over my life is fast disappearing.' On 16 August 1870, another correspondent, Miss M. J. Blake, reported that Emilie Glen had married a Mr Walton* and was living at Ladysmith.

Miss S. Haffenden, who arrived in May 1863 on the *Durban* and whose family lived in Kent, probably travelled more widely than any other governess who went to South Africa. In her first letter, written on 6 June 1863, she reported that she had a job at Pinetown, but received only £25 a year for teaching four children. Six months later, when she wrote on 17 December, she was with a Captain Struben** and his family at Pretoria in the Transvaal Republic, a thousand miles inland from Cape Town and three weeks' journey by wagon from Pinetown. She said

*Probably John Clarke Walton, MLC and agent, or alternatively, James Wardle Walton, a farmer.

**Johan Herman Marinus Struben, Pretoria pioneer and official of the Transvaal Republic.

she was teaching three children and was companion to Mrs Struben, for £60 a year, and reported:

> They are getting a new Piano up from Natal, but we have any amount of pleasure up in this off Country and several new English families in Pretoria, so that it is quite gay. I often ride or drive out with Mrs Struben.

By October 1864, Miss Haffenden was married to Dr S. J. Meintjes* and was living at Potchefstroom, near the southern border of the Transvaal. Her husband was one of only four qualified doctors licensed to practise in the Boer republics. Writing to the Society regarding the repayment of his wife's loan, Dr Meintjes warned, in a letter dated 18 October:

> It is not safe to send money by post from the Repub[lic] to either Natal or the Colony and when remittances are forwarded they must be done by private opportunity. At this rainy season of the year, owing to the rising of the rivers, the want of proper means of crossing them, and the Mail being carried by caffer [*sic*] runners, the Mails are more uncertain than at any other time.

Three months later, on 28 January 1865, Dr Meintjes and his wife were living at Grahamstown, in the eastern part of Cape Colony and by 24 June, they were at Burghersdorp, in the north-eastern part of Cape Colony, 200 miles inland from Port Elizabeth. Mrs Meintjes' travels over large areas of South Africa can be followed in the number of letters her husband, apparently imbued with the importance of repaying her loan, wrote to the Society, either sending money or explaining how it would be sent.

Miss A. H. Jackson, who travelled to South Africa with Miss Haffenden, wrote some vivid descriptions of the hazards of living in Natal during 1863, while she was governess to Dr Benjamin Blaine's children at Verulam. These reports are preceded in her first letter, dated May 1863, by a complaint about the Society's representative, Mr Brickhill, who, she said, had advertised the Society's emigrants as though they 'were cattle'. The advertisement,

---

*Stephanus Jacobus Meintjes, born in Graaff-Reinet in 1840 and educated in Edinburgh, who died at Bedford in 1901.

which appeared in the *Natal Mercury* of 6 March 1863, read:

GOVERNESSES.

Two ladies are expected by the *Durban*, who wish for engagements on arrival.

One is qualified to teach French, German, and Music, besides the usual branches of an English education, and has had much experience in tuition.

The other is not so accomplished, but can teach English thoroughly, and the rudiments of Music, Singing, and Dancing, and is prepared to assist in Household duties, if required.

These Ladies bear high testimonials, are healthy, and determined to give satisfaction.

Parties requiring the services of either of the above, are requested to communicate with the undersigned, stating their requirements, and amount of salary, &c., they are willing to pay, and on arrival of the vessel further communication will be made.

J. Brickhill

Durban, March 4, 1863.

Miss Jackson also reported that she found 'a great want of governesses', but the salaries were 'generally low'. Of life at Verulam, she wrote:

The insects, particularly the mosquitoes, are very troublesome. There is a small insect called the tick that inhabits the long grass, unless it can get to human arms and legs, a locality it seems much to prefer. Once established there, it burrows its way into the flesh and it is with great difficulty dislodged. The irritation they cause is something indescribable. I am all over spots and pimples and bumps from the shoulders downwards and have not had a good night's sleep since I came. All strangers are subject to this annoyance and also the prickly heat, which is a sort of rash that breaks out round the body like Shingles, and to what are called Natal Sores, which are neither more nor less than small boils which come out on the body and legs . . .

The ugliest things I ever saw in my life (except the Kaffir women) are the Kaffir men. Their faces are positively devilish and their characters answer in every respect to this description. They are great liars, very cruel among themselves and not at all honest. The Coolies are a better-looking race, but great thieves and very idle . . .

The English about here are not particularly healthy-looking; the women especially are all very pale and seem worn and languid. Nearly all the houses consist of one storey, the rooms have large low windows and canvas ceilings. The whole construction is as light as possible and in case of Fire, falls like a pack of cards.

The commonest vegetable is pumpkin, which is boiled. I ate it perseveringly for more than a week and tried to like it, but failed signally in the attempt. It tastes like nothing in particular, unless you put on a quantity of pepper and salt, in which case it tastes of pepper and salt . . .

There is a great want of Servants; neither Coolies nor Kaffirs are to be trusted and they are not fit for anything but the roughest work. English Servants are very scarce; they never stay long in a place and give themselves great airs. The most useful thing to send out would be some Maids of all work, only they nearly always marry soon after coming out . . .

The great charm of life here is I think the freedom; there is a repose and rest to it and to anyone tired of the dreadful rush for life in London it would, I should think, be very pleasant for a time. There is a total absence of excitement and the women seem to be too much occupied with their households to care for anything beyond, but after all, it is house-keeping under extreme difficulties as women feel and men know nothing of. I am not surprised that the men should want wives, but I am rather surprised at the women for marrying as they do here where there is so little inducement.

On 27 August 1863, Miss Jackson again complained of the advertisement in which Mr Brickhill had asked for work for the governesses. 'You cannot imagine the ridicule and disagreeable remarks that that advertisement caused and even now it is sometimes referred to.'

In her last letter, dated 10 October 1863, Miss Jackson commented on prospects for governesses: '. . . in nearly all the large towns there are Schools in abundance. Durban is quite overrun with them . . . I should decidedly advise your not sending out too many here.' Miss Jackson found the climate in Durban unhealthy and suffered from prickly heat.

The people all have a worn, tired look, attributable as I am told to the hot summers, but also in my opinion much more to the inferior food, and the unhealthy state of the sleeping rooms. The old Colonists build their houses without fireplaces and at night when the doors and windows are all shut you may judge what the state of air must be when there are several children in the same room. Luckily I have a room to myself, and have had the glass taken out of some of the panes and find the atmosphere much more agreeable in consequence. The prevailing complaint here is worms, adults and children alike are subject to them; the usual remedy is an emetic, which brings them up a yard long and sometimes more . . .

The Polygamy question is causing much discussion just now. Several cases have come before the public of Girls having been tortured to induce them to marry old men; one victim died lately from having been roasted over a slow fire all night, and efforts have been made to bring the father to punishment as he was the person who tied up his daughter. There have been several letters on the subject in the local papers; some people think the Queen ought to be memorialised and a stop put to polygamy at once, but others say such a thing is impossible and would bring down the Kaffirs on us at once, which would be very impolitic as we have not powder enough in the Colony to avail us in case of War.

The Kaffirs are very queer people; some writers present them as very good and some very bad. Of the goodness I have seen nothing, but the badness is perceptible enough. They are desperate liars, cowards, cruel to an awful extent, and very ungrateful, very lazy, and only work on compulsion. In the Kraals the work is all done by their slave wives. So the more wives a man has the more work he gets done and when he dies they all become the property of his eldest son, together with his oxen and other cattle.

My great bugbears here are the snakes, of which there are a good number about. I have seen four specimens, the first was a puff adder that lay coiled up on some bricks in the kitchen and which fell a victim to Dr Blaine's gun. It was about three feet long, striped brown and black and a very venomous kind. The next I saw was a small grass snake, quite harmless, about as thick as the middle finger for a few inches and then a long tapering tail nearly white and two feet long. The next I saw was much more formidable; it lay coiled up in the mulberry hedge and was found by the white servant where I had been a few minutes before gathering Mulberries; it was a green mamba, and got away without our seeing the direction in which it disappeared. The last specimen was a long brown one, which the Kaffirs killed while we were at Church. One of the little boys opened it and took out a rat which had just been swallowed.

There has been a good deal of rain lately and you have no idea how miserable the place is under such circumstances. These houses were only meant for sunshine and the doors don't fit and the windows are loose and minus a few panes of glass and part of the inhabited rooms are out of doors, so that the wet and dirt are trampled in and the floors get like a swamp, and the children take cold.

The insects here are very troublesome and some of them very

beautiful. I saw a large specimen of Spanish fly yesterday. The moths are magnificent, so are the locusts, and there is a sort of grasshopper that goes by the name of Hottentot God. It crawls to the top of a stick and nods at you like an old man, and bites too if it has a chance. There is also a white ant that repairs its lovely brown wings only for an hour. The body is eaten by the Coolies fried with rice, and is said to taste like butter.

When we were at the Tongaat last week we went over a sugar mill and saw all the operation from the first crushing of the cane to the last boiling.

The wild flowers here are magnificent, mostly like those in Greenhouses at home; the lilies are particularly fine, generally white, but sometimes streaked with pink. Oct. 22nd. We are expecting the Mail in every day and are very excited in consequence, in fact it is almost the only thing we have to look forward to from month to month. I am making a collection of dried flowers, butterflies' wings, insects, etc. to send home in case of an opportunity occurring.

We had a thunderstorm here last night, a most awful one, awful even for this place. I could never have imagined anything so dreadful. For two hours the lightning and thunder continued without one minute's pause . . .

This was the final communication from the observant, inquiring Miss Jackson. Two years later, on 30 November 1865, Miss J. S. Fowler reported that Miss Jackson had died very suddenly only a few months after marrying a Mr Armstrong. Her death was attributed to heart disease.

Sarah Henderson, who with her sister was one of the earliest arrivals, although not the first to write to the Society, was employed near Durban for a year, then moved to the Tongaat Sugar Estate, to work for Mr Saunders. On 28 September 1863, she wrote:

In reference to Governesses emigrating, I do not think Natal is the most desirable place for them; the almost entire lack of white female Servants is a great drawback. It is true we have seven black servants in the house, but even with that number everything has to be superintended by the Lady of the House. I think as the Colony progresses there will be a very fair field for Governesses, but until then it would be better to let Ladies know beforehand of the inconveniences they will have to put up with. If they cannot obtain situations in England I then think it quite right and advisable to come to Natal. Another great drawback is there is no one to receive young Ladies on their arrival, and to be obliged as we were to go to a public Hotel or boarding House is not very agreeable.

Sarah Henderson reported that her sister was in Cape Town, waiting for a steamer for Madras, where she was accompanying a family as governess, and said: 'I will endeavour to return you part of my Sister's money by the time it is due, the remainder she will send me from India. It has been quite impossible for her to send you any as she has received such very low salaries.' Later, when writing from Winvok, Natal, where she was living with a Dutch family, Sarah told Miss Rye that her brother had the opportunity of getting a job as a tutor in South Africa, but could not afford his fare out. She asked if the Society would advance his fare, the first and only request to the Society for aid on behalf of a male would-be emigrant. There is no indication that the request was successful.

By 18 February 1868, when Sarah Henderson wrote her last letter to the Society, she apparently had been in India, where her sister may have been working still. She wrote from London to Miss Rye about a misunderstanding concerning the repayment of her loan and an offer of a further loan.

I feel that I ought to write you a few lines as my character is concerned in the matter.

You said in your letter that I did not pay you the money I borrowed, it was Mr Laidlaw. If my brother-in-law did pay you, I remitted him the money to do so as I was in India at the time. It did not come out of his pocket.

Many thanks for your kind offer in saying that you would advance half the passage money second class round the Cape, but I shall not require it as my friends will pay my passage overland.

Governesses arriving in South Africa in the latter part of the 1860s were faced by a depressed economic situation very similar to that in the Australian colonies at that time. Amelia Temple is an example of the almost impossible financial situation that faced poorly paid governesses when their strong sense of duty compelled them to attempt to repay their loans to the Society. Amelia's wage was £25 a year and her debt to the Society was £36. She wrote first on 27 April 1868, from her position with Mrs Hawkins, the wife of the resident magistrate at Richmond,* about forty-five miles west of Durban, where she had five children to teach. 'Everyone is dreadfully poor out here', she reported. With her first letter, she enclosed £12 of her £36 debt and in a move that must have left her almost destitute, repaid another £12 six months later on 10 October and the final £12 on 11 February 1869. By this time, she had left Mrs Hawkins on account of her health and had a job in Durban teaching three children. Her lack of financial resources is pathetically apparent from her comment on her lack of writing paper. 'I trust you will excuse a half sheet, but I'm nearly out of paper and everything is so dear here'. Later that year, in a letter dated 13 June, she wrote: '... business is so uncertain and nearly every month you hear of some one failing'.

The lack of employment and the general economic depression led James Brickhill to advise the Society, on 8 September 1868, not to send any more governesses to Natal. He wrote to Miss Lewin:

> I have been thinking for some time past of writing to you, but have been prevented and take this opportunity of acknowledging your letter respecting the Misses Blake, who have not yet arrived, having had a long and, I fear, stormy passage.
>
> My particular object in writing to you is to advise that no more young ladies should be sent to Natal at present. This Colony (though I believe one of the finest in the world) has undergone great changes in the last few years, caused chiefly by reckless speculation induced by a multiplicity of banks and monetary institutions. This has produced bankruptcy in many and dishonest men have also brought down the better portion with them. These remarks refer chiefly to the commercial portion — the sugar and coffee planters and the agricultural portion are, in my opinion, doing well, but the unfortunate position before mentioned has so far disorganised the community that it will be some time before *full* confidence is restored — I think therefore it will be advisable for you not to send more until our circumstances improve much.
>
> I find also I am not in a position to give that attention to the young ladies that they ought to have; my house being four miles from the town takes up much time in riding to and fro daily.
>
> I regret to say that I have not been well satisfied with either

*Arthur Caesar Hawkins, magistrate during the period 1853–86.

Miss Stone* or Miss Robinson, the former I believe still in some occupation, the latter I believe is not, but I hear is going to be married. I hope it is so. Miss Temple is in a comfortable family and is doing very well. Miss Glen is just going up the country to commence in a school under the Government. She is sure to do well wherever she goes. I have had some enquiries in answer to my advertisement of the Misses Blake, but nothing satisfactory yet and I do not know how long they may have to wait for something turning up. I have had one enquiry . . . respecting them, but it amounts to little more than polite formality.

Annie Robinson, mentioned in Mr Brickhill's letter, had written to Miss Rye from Durban on 10 January 1868, soon after her arrival, saying that she was to go to a job with Captain Lloyd, brother-in-law to Miss Temple's employer.**

South Africa's economic outlook was soon to change with the discovery of diamonds in 1869 and the rush to the Northern Cape district on the Orange and Vaal Rivers. A string of tent communities sprang up on both sides of the Vaal River, until by 1870 the population numbered about 10,000. Rival claims were made to the diamond fields by the Orange Free State, the Transvaal Republic and the local Griqua chief, but the territory was taken over by the British Colonial Office and later annexed to Cape Colony.

In July 1871, all earlier discoveries were surpassed by those at the 'New Rush'. This field drew thousands of fortune-seeking diggers from all over the world, who worked their claims until they merged into the 'Big Hole', still today one of the largest man-made excavations of its kind. As further workings were established in the neighbourhood, the original camp of 'New Rush' was named Kimberley, in honour of the British Colonial Secretary, the Earl of Kimberley. By 1873, this town had a population of 50,000, making it, after Cape Town, the largest community in southern Africa.

The impact of the diamond discoveries is reported by

---

*Ellen Stone, sister of Clara Stone, who wrote from Collingwood, Vic., on 28 January 1868; see Chapter 7, page 121.

**Captain Walter Lloyd, a farmer, married Maria Grice on the same day as Arthur Hawkins married her sister, Louisa. Walter Lloyd was later a member of the Legislative Council.

several of the governesses. Miss M. J. Blake, mentioned by Mr Brickhill, wrote on 16 August 1870:

> Of course you have heard of the late discovery of diamonds in this Country, there is great excitement about it in D'Urban just now. From the good accounts which have come lately from the diamond fields numbers are going up there, some even taking their families with them.

Miss Blake worked first for Mr E. P. Lamport, founder and proprietor of the Merebank Sugar Estate, Durban (Mrs Lamport was one of the Society's representatives in Natal) and later for Richard P. King, who had a sugar farm and mill at Isipingo and was famous as the 'saviour of Natal', for an exploit in the early days of settlement.

Louisa Prentice, who arrived in July 1869, also mentions the impact of the diamond finds. She at first was employed by Mrs Moffat, widow of a son of the famous Scottish missionary, Dr Robert Moffat, who spent fifty-four years in South Africa for the London Missionary Society. In a letter to Miss Lewin dated 23 August 1869, she said she was living at Isipingo, a seaside township about twelve miles south of Durban, and was paid £25 a year to teach Mrs Moffat's three children, aged ten, eight and six. Later, in a letter dated 14 October 1871, she said she had worked for an employer who went off to the diamond fields, but was unsuccessful. She was forced to leave this situation, apparently unpaid, and so was unable to repay her loan. By October 1871, she was employed teaching music, singing and drawing at St Mary's College, Richmond, a town about twenty miles south of Pietermaritzburg, founded by British settlers in 1850.

Another emigrant, Maria Evatt, writing to Miss Lewin from St George's Plantation, Umgababa, Natal, in a letter dated 19 December 1871, said Mr Brickhill had told her he was sorry she had come, 'as everyone was either going or gone to the Diamond Fields'. She added:

> Mr Brickhill mentioned he wrote to you two or three years ago advising you not to export any more ladies until you heard from him . . . the Colony is now in an unsettled state on account of the rush to the Diamond Fields . . . I do not regret coming in the least, and I like the place very well. My brother is doing well at the 'Diamond Fields' and I hope soon to be rich.

Not all governesses were as sanguine about their prospects. Louisa Brand, who wrote from Winder's Marine Villa Hotel, Durban, on 27 May 1874, thought her trip to South Africa had been a waste: 'It does seem a long way to come on chance . . . I think it is a pity to have left England, but I shall try and hope for the best'.

A frequent correspondent from Natal in the later years of the Scheme was Celia Hooper. She wrote first on 17 July 1873, from her position at Umzinto Lodge Estate, Alexandra, forty miles south-west of Durban, where she was governess to the children of Mr Bell, the manager of the estate, teaching them English, French, music and drawing. She then went as governess to Mrs Macfarlane, wife of the Speaker* at Pietermaritzburg and later, with her mother and sister, kept a school in Pietermaritzburg, before marrying a Mr Sinclair and going to live at the Virginia Estate, Umgeni, just north of Durban. On 27 August 1880, she wrote:

> The Dutch in Natal are very anxious to have their children well educated, especially in Music. In some of their families there is a great degree of refinement and comfort . . . the Dutch in general are very rich . . . you might know of ladies willing to exchange the struggling life of a governess at home for situations like these.

Miss Lewin, always anxious to find new openings, replied to this observation with alacrity and prepared to send governesses to Natal, a situation Celia Sinclair felt unable to handle. On 3 November 1880, writing from Umgeni, she asked Miss Lewin not to send any governesses at present, since she was not settled, was moving into a small house and was not well, so would be unable to help them. However, she did contact several schools, in an unsuccessful effort to obtain positions for the governesses who had begun to arrive.

In a letter dated 26 December 1880, she added another reason why it would not be worthwhile for governesses to emigrate just then: 'The war which has just broken out between the Dutch and the English will of course greatly

---

*Walter Macfarlane, farmer and Speaker of the Natal Legislative Council, 1859–80.

retard any effort in the educational line at present'. The war she referred to had broken out in the Transvaal Republic, which had been annexed by Britain in 1877. In 1880, the Boers revolted, fighting started at Potchefstroom and in February 1881, the Boers defeated the British at Amajuba. Later that year, the Pretoria Convention was signed, under which the Transvaal gained self-government under British suzerainty.

On 1 November 1881, Celia Sinclair wrote for the last time to the Society, from a new address, 'Ambleside, Lower Umzimkulu',* which she described as 'a new seaport recently opened to traffic', a hundred miles from Durban. She explained that she now had a child and could not assist any governess who might arrive. 'There is no opening for a governess here as it is a comparatively new settlement and settlers have almost as hard a struggle as when my parents just came from England 25 years ago, so we have to begin again and in a very small way.' She added that an English gentleman, who had planted the first sugar-cane in Natal, had arrived to settle, all his property 'up country' having been 'swept away through the late war'. He was anxious to obtain land for English refugees from the Transvaal.

The governesses found salaries very low in Natal, but generally, apart from initial unemployment, seemed to find jobs, often within a tight circle of prominent citizens. Cape Colony was a tougher proposition. Founded by the Dutch East India Company as a staging-post in the seventeenth century, Cape Town was a pawn in the Napoleonic Wars, alternately being under Dutch or British control. It was finally ceded to Britain in 1814, when there was a European population of about 26,000, mainly Dutch settlers. As demand for food and provisions increased, the farmers spread northwards, coming into conflict with the Bantu tribes. Stock thefts and reprisals lead to a series of frontier wars.

At the time the governesses began arriving in 1862, Cape Colony's economy was affected by a lengthy drought and a world-wide recession. The severity of the depression led the Governor, the autocratic Sir Philip Wodehouse, to introduce taxation, an unpopular measure. Sir Philip re-

---

*An observer noted that Archibald Sinclair had a 'small American Mill', operated by two oxen, in use at Ambleside in 1881.

mained governor until 1870, but his term of office was characterised by severe economic problems, disputes over the annexation of Kaffraria and differences in the Cape and Natal over the war between the Basuto and the Orange Free State.

In 1866, with a depleted treasury, trade at a standstill and expenditure increasing, Sir Philip attempted, unsuccessfully, to get Parliament to agree to new taxation measures. Economic problems continued until 1868, when crops improved and there were encouraging rumours of gold and diamond discoveries.

Until the late 1860s, South Africa's economy was poor, backward and pastoral, wool being the only important export. There was little to attract the great stream of Europeans going to America, Australia and New Zealand, and many of the immigrants who did arrive at the Cape left during the prolonged depression of the 1860s. The diamond discoveries changed this situation dramatically. They came at an opportune time, when the opening of the Suez Canal in 1869, which provided a shorter shipping route than that around the Cape, had threatened to bankrupt Cape Colony. In the era that followed the diamond and later gold discoveries, there was unprecedented population growth and economic activity, boosted by overseas investment.

The first FMCES emigrant to write from Cape Colony, Catherine Brough, suffered the full brunt of the colony's economic problems. She found her experiences so devastating and her opportunities so limited that she wrote in bitter terms to Miss Rye. In a letter dated 20 March 1863, she said she had written two letters previously, but had destroyed them because her feelings had carried her beyond 'justice to you'.

Your intentions in sending women to various Colonies are most undoubtedly good. And the fact that in my case it is proving a failure does not alter the debt of gratitude due to you for having given me the assistance I needed in order to enable me to leave England. But your mode of proceeding is so condemned in this Colony that I have not the same hesitation in repeating to you the public opinion as I should have had if it had been *merely* my own. But I am suffering so severely from the wrong judgement on your part . . .

So much ridicule is thrown on the way in which you are sending women abroad that I am ashamed to own that I came out under the protection of Your Society and the two or three persons who knew it I have caused to give their promise that they will never mention it. I refrain from repeating to you the remarks I have heard from those who were ignorant that I had any connection with you. I am far worse off than ever I was in England: it is next to impossible to obtain employment and the pay is so low that though I have had two temporary engagements I have not earned enough to pay board and lodging and washing, though I have been so careful those three items only come to 17/6 a week . . .

My friends in England have no idea of what I have told you, nor do I intend they should be thus grieved . . . do not again send single unprotected women wandering away from friends over the strange world again without knowing what you are doing, especially young women who would have the addition of ignorance from which happily I have been saved.

At that stage, Catherine Brough had begun a school, but after only one quarter term feared she would have to close it, since she was nearly £40 in debt. A year later, on 20 February 1864, she wrote again, still in difficulties with her school and unable to pay an assistant, 'education not being understood out here, and therefore not valued, is not paid for as it ought to be . . . [there is] in England much misconception as to the state of education out here and the amount of remuneration received'. She said she had learnt by bitter experience that life for teachers was miserable in the colony, but 'I would not for the world let my sister or my friends in England know, for it would only grieve them to no purpose. But you, I think it right to let know, that you may prevent others doing the same thing.'

Catherine Brough's experiences apparently dissuaded the Society from sending further governesses to Cape Colony for several years. One who arrived in 1868, however, became one of the Society's most successful emigrants and also by far its most prolific correspondent. This was Miss S. E. A. Hall, who wrote no fewer than twenty letters, most of them in the years between 1876 and 1882, when she was running her own school at Graaff-Reinet, the third oldest town in Cape Colony, about 160 miles north-west of Port Elizabeth and today preserved as an example of early Dutch colonial architecture. Many of these letters concerned the employment of teachers recruited in England with the help of the Society, but also ranged widely over such subjects as converting Africa to Christianity and the character of the colonists.

Miss Hall (her Christian name is not disclosed in the letters*) arrived at Cape Town armed with letters of introduction to many influential people, including the Governor, Sir Philip Wodehouse. She was soon employed at Constantia, near Cape Town, by Mrs Mallett, wife of the Solicitor-General,** at a yearly salary of £50, to teach three children. In a letter dated 17 January 1868, from 44 Bury Street, Cape Town, she wrote: 'Every one thinks me very successful, for several ladies who I have no reason to think less qualified than myself have been waiting for three or four months.' She later moved to Port Elizabeth and on 21 February 1870 wrote from 1 Cora Terrace to repay £20 on her loan. She sent a further £10 from the same address on 14 April.

In her next letter, written from Graaff-Reinet on 18 August 1876, nearly nine years after her arrival in South Africa, she wrote:

> Now I have a large and flourishing school of my own in this town, which is about 160 miles inland. I should be so glad if you could send me out a good Governess. I want a nice, sensible girl, well-educated and conscientious, who would be a real help to me in teaching English and Music or Drawing . . .
>
> . . . the Cape itself is a young country, the people are kind, but the one great idea here is money; they live for it and certainly manage to obtain a great deal, but of intellectual life there is little or none. It is amazing to me that several thousand minds can be grouped together in a couple of square miles and with no intellectual result. This Colony you no doubt know belonged to the Dutch till the beginning of this Century. The majority of the people are of the same race (excepting in a few towns which have sprung up during the last 50 years) and they regard the English with much jealousy and dislike, excepting in a few exceptional cases. I believe there is a great future in store for Cape Colony, but it will have to be free from the Mother Country, not yet, but eventually.
>
> The diamond and gold discoveries have done a great deal, but the chief good has not been in lining people's pockets with the precious metal, but in opening up the country to Christian

---

*Miss Hall's initial may have been L., rather than S. A. or S. E. A., as it appears in the FMCES letter-books.

**Hugh Mallett, Secretary and Registrar, Court of Justice, Cape of Good Hope.

teachers who have now established churches and missions a thousand miles inland. I am expecting great and good results from the town, Livingstonia, which is being built quite in the heart of Africa, truly a light in a dark place. It seems as if the day were beginning to dawn on this, the most benighted continent of the world. When the Gospel light shines from Morocco to the Cape, flooding Africa with its knowledge, peace and love, then I shall think the end near. I try to do my little towards it . . .

On 4 February 1877, she said of the people of Cape Colony:

The character of the people I have more knowledge of than admiration for; as a rule it lacks those traits which we are proud to call English . . . I am always busy in my school trying to do my part in dispelling the miserable ignorance that prevails and to lift the minds of the children above eating, sleeping and dressing, which are the chief objects of interest with the majority.

A Lady (?) who lives in this town says she does 'not know what we live for, unless it is to eat *nice*'; for the credit of my country, let me add that she is a German. I know an influential man here possessing — not worth — £20,000 who says that all England together should never make him believe that the world is round. He is of Dutch descent . . . we must get the right sort of English, those distinguished for truth, intelligence and energy.

Miss Hall added that she wanted the best teachers for her school and would pay £100 a year to one who had passed the Cambridge Examination in English. She also needed one to teach the harp or guitar and piano and another to teach drawing and painting. In a letter of 30 May, she offered £100 to £120 a year for a music teacher, adding: 'I think it is a mistake for Governesses to come out here after 30 years of age unless they possess in a large degree the power of adapting themselves to change'. Miss Hall's frequent letters continued throughout the year as she sought the Society's help in obtaining teachers for her school or made arrangements for their travel, always managing to add comments on other aspects of life in the colony. On 10 June, she remarked on the openings for workwomen and seamstresses. 'We have no one who can clean a straw hat, curl a feather or dye any article.' On 9 August, she warned:

The lady who wishes to teach in a family had better not come out; she can have no conception of what life is on a Dutch farm and the majority of our farmers are Dutch. A girl must have an immense amount of energy, health and spirit with inexhaustible resources in herself to be able to bear it.

Some of the teachers recruited for Miss Hall's school did not stay long, finding the work hard and the conditions unacceptable. Caroline Haselton was one of these. Miss Hall wrote on 3 October that Miss Haselton 'professes to dislike the Colony excessively because it is not like England . . . she is too old to get into a new groove . . . We want "Willing Hearts and Ready Hands". Miss Haselton got herself much laughed at in the June holidays when staying with a friend because she put on kid gloves to make a rice pudding.'

Caroline Haselton, however, wrote to the Society on 15 August 1877: '. . . Governesses are neglected in this House. Do not let any come for a *term of years* to Miss Hall . . . I am not obliged to stay, but all Governesses are not as well off as myself'. She complained that Graaff-Reinet was 700 miles from Cape Town and 160 miles from Port Elizabeth, with no railway: 'you may imagine the buried alive feeling one has'. However, Miss Haselton continued to teach at Miss Hall's school until May 1879, when she became ill and made the decision to move to Melbourne.

Meanwhile, Miss Hall recruited some teachers herself while on a six-month trip to Europe in 1878. One of these, a Miss Jackson, had surprisingly advanced views and in a letter written from Cape Town on 18 July 1878, Miss Hall commented:

[Her] great idea is to educate women that they shall be what she calls 'emancipated' and placed on an equality with men, that they may be thoroughly independent of them. That, as you know, is not what I want, but yes, as we are both in earnest, I hope and think we shall be able to work together harmoniously.

Miss Hall's turnover of teachers continued to be high. On 30 April 1879, she wrote again, to report that her newly imported music teacher, Miss Ellis, a silver medallist from the Royal Academy of Music, had fallen in love with the ship's doctor on the way out and had left to marry him. 'She really played beautifully', said the regretful Miss Hall.

I am doing my utmost to have a thoroughly good school. But with a few exceptions the people here would be perfectly satisfied with a much lower standard, for they are very ignorant . . . in working to make girls more elevated in thought and life I am pulling against the stream! . . . this is the corner of the vineyard the Great Husbandman has allotted to me to labour in.

She added a comment about the war between the British forces and the Zulus, which had started a few months earlier:

Sir Bartle Frere is just the man we want; he has done and is doing great good and, if his warlike measures had met with success, he would have been lauded to the skies. Lord Chelmsford is not thought much of, but the experience he has gained makes it desirable that he should remain at his post. The Basutos, another tribe, have been giving some trouble, but it is reported that they have surrended. We are in no danger in our part and trade is flourishing.

Sir Henry Bartle Frere was appointed Governor of Cape Colony and High Commissioner for South Africa in 1877, charged with the task of carrying out plans for the confederation of South Africa. However, soon after his arrival the Ninth Frontier War broke out in the eastern part of Cape Colony. It lasted six months and resulted in the suppression of Xhosa resistance and the gradual annexation of the remaining African territories between Cape Colony and the frontier of Natal. Sir Bartle Frere then went to Natal, where the Zulu War began early in 1879 with overwhelming British defeats at Isandhlwana and Rorke's Drift. Frere was blamed and he was replaced as High Commissioner for the Transvaal and Natal by Sir Garnet Wolseley. The British forces under Lord Chelmsford suffered further defeats by the Zulus, but victory at Ulandi in July 1879 retrieved the initial disaster. The Zulu chief Cetshwayo was captured and deposed and Zululand was eventually annexed to Natal. After the Ulandi victory, in Miss Hall's view: 'The Zulus should receive a much more thorough beating than we have yet given them'.

On 14 May 1879, Miss Hall wrote to Miss Lewin, asking her to check the testimonials of a music teacher she planned to employ. The teacher, Miss Reimar, was a German who had recently taught in Ireland. Miss Hall commented:

'There are such hundreds of Governesses now desirous of leaving England because they are not up to the standard there, or from other worse causes, that it becomes an absolute necessity to be most careful before engaging any'. She added a request to Miss Lewin not to tell Miss Reimar that the previous music teacher had left to get married, since she 'may be fired with desire to do likewise'. On 29 July, Miss Hall wrote to thank Miss Lewin for checking Miss Reimar's credentials. She also commented on the 'fearful shock' the death of the Prince Imperial had caused in England. (The only son of Napoleon III had been killed near Ulandi, on 1 June 1879, while with the British expedition to Zululand.) She said the blame was generally thought to be 'at Lord Chelmsford's door'.

Later in the year, on 23 November, she wrote that her school was prospering, with thirty-eight boarders and a large number of day pupils, and that her pupils had had many examination successes.

I quite agree with you in thinking that the cultivation of children's moral nature is of infinitely more importance than their intellectual culture. I think education should and must, if good, embrace both. Do not think that I would fill their memories with mere facts or even teach them to think, and mistake that for education. I would rather that their minds were elevated and refined than merely crammed.

Miss Hall also reported the imminent departure of another member of her staff, Miss Sophia Evans, who had been recruited by the Society. She, Miss Hall said, was 'very ordinary with no high aims or aspirations'.

As with Caroline Haselton, Sophia Evans' views on Miss Hall and her school are revealed in letters to the Society. On 28 July 1879, she wrote that she found the work 'much heavier and more trying' than a previous job on a farm. She said in another undated (early 1881) letter that she could not get on with Miss Hall. By this time, she had a position as a governess on a farm, Hout Constant, at Sneeuberg, a mountain region north of Graaff-Reinet, which she described as 'dull as we have no English neighbours and rarely have any visitors'. She added:

I have never regretted leaving England and think of settling down here altogether, but will most likely pay the old country a visit first: it is possible that I may come home in July for six or eight months and then come back to be married to an Ostrich Farmer.

Her sister, Clara Evans, in a letter dated 25 September 1879, said Sophia was to marry a son of Jonathon Hobson, a well-to-do farmer.* Clara Evans was then employed by Mr Biggs at Wellfound Wheatlands, south of Graaff-Reinet, where she had six pupils. She wrote of her life: 'I do not think I shall ever regret coming to South Africa, as I think it is much nicer being a governess here than in England'.

Clara Evans was herself remarkable for the extreme care she displayed in repaying her loan to the Society. On 6 March 1880, she enclosed with her letter parts of two £5 Bank of England notes, because she had been 'advised to tear them in half and send one half this week and the remainder next week, which I will do, as it is a much safer way!' She dispatched the other halves of the bank-notes on 13 April.

Sophia Evans, in her letter written early in 1881, wrote of the war between the British and Boers in the Transvaal and the fighting with the Basuto in eastern Cape Colony:

Affairs in the Transvaal seem very serious: We hope when the Troops arrive from England they will soon put an end to the strife. At present many Englishmen are flying from Potchefstroom to Cape Colony and Natal. The Dutch here sympathise very much with the rebels and it is thought some of our Boers will go to help them.

The worst of the Basuto War is thought to be over now and indeed it is to be hoped so, for many of our men now fighting there can ill afford to be so long away from home. A number of Burghers were called out three months ago and some more are to be called in February. Grahamstown lost a great number of men in one engagement; a lady from that town told me you scarcely met one person in the streets who was not in deep mourning.

Miss Hall continued her correspondence about the fighting in a letter dated 14 January 1881:

*Sophia Evans later married William Hobson and lived at 'Harefield', south of Graaff-Reinet, in an area where a number of members of the Hobson family had farms. Her only son was killed in the First World War. Clara Evans married a Mr Meredith and settled in the town of Graaff-Reinet. They had a son, Norman, who died young, and a daughter, Maud, who trained as a nurse and married Arthur Kingwill. They had one son, Arthur.

Affairs here are very unsettled; we have a Colonial war going on with the Basutos, a Kaffir tribe, and 9000 Colonists are going to fight with them, which is a great drawback to agricultural and commercial prosperity. Then the Dutch Boers in the Transvaal are in open rebellion against English Government and are shooting the few troops we have there. We are looking forward anxiously to the arrival of more regiments.

During 1880, Miss Hall had obtained another recruit for her teaching staff, Alice Hart, a highly qualified music teacher, who was engaged to take advanced pupils. In a letter dated 8 October 1880, Alice Hart wrote to Mrs Sunter after being with Miss Hall for five weeks. She said she was 'happy and comfortable' and added:

I think she [Miss Hall] is a dear Mother to all around her; does *everything* in her power (which is not small) to please the pupils and teachers, and need hardly tell you she succeeds. I am indeed very attached already and am happiest when serving her. The pupils are rather dull here, but not only in music, I think, though two or three are very bright and almost make up for the others . . .

Alice Hart was probably the only FMCES emigrant who was Jewish. She mentions in her letter that another teacher at the school, Miss Myers, was also Jewish. Miss Hall raised Alice Hart's salary by £50 to £200 a year the first week she was there. In return, Alice Hart taught for 7½ hours a day instead of six, because so many girls wanted to learn from her. She wrote:

We have delightful musical evenings every Tuesday when some of the girls play and sing. They take it in turns every month; of course they are all nervous, but in time they will no doubt become courageous. At Christmas we are going to have a concert, the first part consisting of Macfarran's Cantata (Songs in a Cornfield), my choir will in that time be *very* good; last Friday they sang a part song to Miss Hall; she seemed delighted and requested them to repeat it.

Although she did not work for Miss Hall, another emigrant, one of the more unfortunate governesses, Margaret Jenvey, was encouraged to contact her for advice. Margaret Jenvey lived first at Cape Town, where she found everything dear and salaries very poor. On 1 October 1877, she wrote to the Society: 'I suspect if matters go on so, the coloured people will be masters and the English people servants. White bread often can only be obtained twice a week, frequently *no* butter owing to the drought.'

Miss Jenvey's fortunes did not improve in the next eighteen months and on 12 April 1879, she wrote to the Society, giving her address as care of H. Markham Esq., 13 Adderley Street, Cape Town, and saying that she required more time to repay her loan. She had obtained only short engagements, the longest being of eight months at £40 a year, for which she had to teach six children at five different levels in the home of a poor Dutch farmer, which was 'poor and destitute of comforts, no winter was [to me] so intensely cold'. After leaving this position, she advertised and obtained another, where she had to start work in November, although payment did not begin until the following January. She explained:

> I was obliged to submit, fearing to lose this engagement . . . The Passenger Cart journeys are fearful owing to some of the sandy roads. I have been jolted from side to side, up and down like a ball; in vain did I cling to my seat; but I was tossed so unmercifully . . . Pray excuse this hurried note, but I have been suffering from Neuralgia and worry.

Miss Hall's final letter to Miss Lewin, dated 25 March 1882, was only partly transcribed into the FMCES letter-book. According to a history of Graaff-Reinet, Miss Hall's school closed in 1886, when she was appointed lady-principal of the Port Elizabeth Collegiate School. Miss Hall had opened her 'Elite Establishment for Young Ladies', the first high school for girls in Graaff-Reinet, on 6 April 1874 at No 12 Church Square. Regarded as a finishing school,

> Emphasis was placed on the tuition of 'English in all its branches'; Music, for which she imported highly qualified ladies such as Miss Reimar and Miss Alice Hart from Germany and England respectively; French (Miss Gautier and later Miss du Toit); Drawing; and by 1876, Dr Dall for scientific subjects. High on the list was the aim 'Health, morals and deportment'.*

---

*C. G. Henning, *Graaff-Reinet: A Cultural History*, Bulpen, Cape Town, 1975, n.p.

Apart from Miss Hall's establishment, another centre for FMCES governesses was Egerton House, a school run by Mary Anna Watson at Bedford, sixty-four miles from Grahamstown, in the eastern part of Cape Colony. Miss Watson wrote twice to the Society, on each occasion to repay money on behalf of governesses who had joined the staff.

Emily Nelson wrote to the Society from Egerton House on 29 February 1876, reporting that Miss Watson was very nice and kind, and her duties at the school were not too heavy. In a letter dated 3 September 1878, Miss Watson said that Miss Nelson was leaving the school to be married to Mr Webber. Another correspondent from Egerton House, Nora Jeston, was employed as housekeeper — one of the few FMCES emigrants to have taken such a position. She wrote her only letter to the Society on 4 March 1876, while nursing a pet monkey she had bought from the natives in her lap. She said she liked Miss Watson very much and that she had a married brother who was a barrister in Western Australia.

Another teacher at Egerton House, Miss J. B. McLean, was the last arrival in South Africa to have her letter recorded in the FMCES letter-books. She arrived on the *Dublin Castle* on 31 March 1880 and on 22 February 1882, she wrote from Egerton House to refund her loan of £33. She enclosed the first bank draft with the letter and said she would send the second the following week.

Egerton House was situated in an area affected by the fighting between government forces and the tribal chiefs, and one of the governesses, Elizabeth Mitchinson, who had worked at the school, wrote of this after she had moved to work as governess to the children of a farmer near Bedford, Mr W. Fuller of 'Rockwood'.

Miss Mitchinson, who was a daughter of the Chief Clerk in the Ordinance Department at Dublin Castle, had five pupils, whom she taught English, French, music, drawing, painting and Latin, for which she was paid £60 a year. 'Painting and Singing should be paid extra, but are not . . . when one gets into a respectable family she is as a rule well treated, but I have heard there are some very peculiar Dutch families who are not at all nice and a governess before engaging should make enquiries; one cannot be too particular.'

On 29 June 1878, she reported: 'We have had a very anxious time of it since last I wrote to you, the Kaffirs being the cause; many nights we have gone to bed but partially undressed, fearing a disturbance during the night'. The next year, when she wrote again on 16 August 1879, life in Bedford still was disrupted by fighting and she asked whether the Society would assist her to get a situation in New Zealand, if she joined her brother there.

> . . . they say the Pondos have broken out, a Kaffir tribe [who] fought some time ago under Kreli, the old chief, for whose apprehension £1000 was offered. Ever since I came to the Colony I hear of nothing but 'war'. How dreadful that Zulu War! So many here have lost some member of their family. We were rather frightened last week here on the farm. Mr Fuller was away and only his son here when such a number of Kaffirs collected to dance; there were over 200 men and women. Mr Fuller said it was a sign of war, they always do so before breaking out; however, after a little while they went away singing and shouting as they went.

12 Venturers to Alien Lands

'There is a vast field here for work and I think bye and bye many openings will appear for our superabundant females . . .'

Helen Williams, Bombay, 1863

There was a starker dimension to the problems faced by the few FMCES governesses who travelled to foreign countries in their efforts to obtain work. Without even the rudimentary support available to those who migrated to the British colonies in Australia, New Zealand and South Africa, or to North America and Canada, they found themselves surrounded by alien cultures and customs. There are letters from only two of the few who did venture further afield: Helen Williams, who went to India in 1863, and Josephine Stoney, who went to Russia in 1873.

Josephine Stoney travelled widely in Russia, at first apparently happily, with the family of a colonel in the Russian Army. She lived initially at Tiflis (Tbilisi) in the Caucasus, then at Taganrog, at the head of the Sea of Azov, a small almost land-locked inland sea to the north of the Black Sea and the Crimea. Later she returned to St Petersburg (Leningrad), and after leaving this position, found herself unemployed and desperately short of money.

In the intervening years, she had experienced the contradictions of life in the semi-feudal Russian society of the 1870s. The Czar, Alexander II, closely related to the British royal family, was the autocratic ruler of the country; St Petersburg was the centre of Russian society and the higher classes and professional people moved between there and their country residences. Serfdom had been abolished in 1861, but most of the land remained in the hands of the aristocracy. During her life in Russia, Josephine Stoney observed some extraordinary contradictions: an abundance of servants, yet often very small, primitive houses into which both family and servants were crowded; a mother leading a life of leisure, unable even to mend a glove, yet her daughters were expected to undertake a more demanding education than was usual in English-speaking countries.

Josephine Stoney at first moved confidently in this society, but her last letter, when she was stranded in St Petersburg with winter approaching, without a job and no immediate prospects and with less than a pound to her name, is genuinely moving. The problems the other FMCES governesses faced seem comparatively insignificant in comparison.

Josephine Stoney seemingly was Irish by birth — her brother was the Reverend J. J. Stoney of Ballin a fagh Glebe, Donadea, County Kildare — and her family was evidently very poor. At one stage, she sent a gift of £14 to her sister out of her yearly salary of £70, from which she also repaid £10 to her brother, for the cost of the clothes she had bought to travel to Russia.

Her first letter, dated 2 October 1873, after her arrival on the *Brownlow*, was written from Tiflis. She had obtained a teaching situation three weeks after her arrival and had been travelling with the family. Her letter was short and mainly concerned with the problems of writing and dispatching money from Russia. 'It is the rule here *not* to stamp a letter for *foreign Countries*. I am told they never reach when prepaid; therefore this and others will not be prepaid stamped, but I shall remit to you the amount for Postage when I am sending the P.O.O. if you could let me know in your next what the postage is.' Her next letter, dated 20 April 1874, was written from Taganrog, in southern Russia, and she was still concerned with postal difficulties. Letters written to her had to be addressed in Russian, she said, so she enclosed a copy of her address to be pasted on any correspondence.

She received a reply from Miss Lewin and, thus encouraged, wrote a much longer letter on 20 June 1874, still at first concerned with postal difficulties, this time the problem of sending money owed to the Society. Her solution was to send the amount she was forwarding in two cheques and to ask for a prompt receipt. Finally, on her position, she wrote:

I am happy to tell you that, *as far* as I have already seen of Russia and the Russians I like them both *very much*. The people I am with are most kind. . . . the Father of my Pupils is Colonel Markosoff, whose name political Europe is well acquainted with. He undertook the command of an army during the expeditions into Kiev and under great difficulties too. I remember having read the accounts in the papers long before I had decided on going to Russia. He is a very nice man and they are not only kind but very attentive to me. I am the first Governess for *English* they have had. *This* language is entirely à la mode, especially amongst the upper class and the Military since the marriage of the Czar's only daughter with the Duke of Edinburgh, so that I should strongly recommend any young ladies seeking the position of *Governess abroad* to come to Russia. Here your time and health is not taken for nothing, as I *must* say it is in England and Ireland. The isolation is, as you say, a *great* trial, but as I am entirely depending on my own exertions, must forfeit much if I wish to gain something. The family I am in are influential. Colonel 'M' is thought much of by the Emperor.

Less than a month later, she had received another letter from Miss Lewin, who ever anxious to obtain new destinations for her governesses, was thinking of sending some to St Petersburg, to follow in the auspicious wake of the apparently happy Miss Stoney. On 15 July 1874, Josephine Stoney wrote from Taganrog:

I shall be most happy to do what I can for the ladies you mentioned, but I think the best plan would be to send them direct to St Petersburg. Any families requiring a Governess in Russia either write to St Petersburg or go there themselves for that purpose to choose one. Now is the time to go. August is late as most of the families leave the city for their Country residences and do not return till late in October. Unless people are well provided with money for board and lodging for at least six weeks or two months it does not do to leave England in the summer, much better *early* in the Spring. Of course one may chance to meet with something a week or two after they arrive, but it is *only* a chance. I was too late and had to pay two roubles (which is the equivalent to 5/—English) every day in the boarding house of an English lady . . .

Even in this town are English Governesses *besides* myself, and plenty of Englishmen come here often as it is the *chief* town in the south from which *corn* or flour is exported to England . . .

Mrs Markosoff very kindly advanced me *three* months' salary *since* I sent the Cheque. She knew it was borrowed money brought me out, and on giving it to me said that she was sure I should like to have it paid off at once. Most kind was it not? She anticipated my desire. I received it very gratefully and now beg to offer you with *very many thanks* the remaining *eight pounds* in the form of another cheque. *Then* I should be glad to see a receipt at your leisure as I mean to inform my securities that the loan has been returned.

By October 1874, Miss Stoney had returned with the Markosoffs to St Petersburg and wrote again to Mrs Sunter regarding two governesses the Society was proposing to send to Russia:

. . . one is seldom more than a month waiting for a situation, and if one comes at the right time, in a week after arriving, they get settled. I came at a bad time, when all the families had left for their Country Seats, yet in a month I got a situation, so the young ladies should come at once. Now all good families require an English Governess and any well accomplished, as you say these ladies are, shall receive from 80 to 100 guineas a year . . . Their expenses are paid to whatever part of Russia they may be going, but only beforehand, when the people come to fetch them. If sent for through an Agency, then on arriving they receive their expenses, so they should have money for this purpose, in case they should require it. I shall be happy to call on them and introduce them to a good agency . . .

In another letter to Mrs Sunter, dated 27 November, she wrote of St Petersburg:

The snowy weather has only now set in. It is rather late this year, I am told. I do not find it colder than England as yet. The streets are kept clear of the snow and little fear of slipping as sand is scattered on the pavements throughout the City. The sledges drawn by horses are like English phaetons, but without a back to lean against. Fur is very dear here, but good. Those here who are English say there is nothing cheap in Russia except black bread. Certainly there is a large quantity of that.

Josephine Stoney did not write again until August 1875, and by that time she was in a desperate financial predicament. She had left her job with the Markosoffs and had not managed to obtain another. To Mrs Sunter, she said:

I trust you will not think badly of me when I tell you that I have left my situation and am seeking another. Three times I had all packed and ready to leave and three times the family asked me to stay. The third time I could not. I had got a good situation in the family of a Countess, but at the last moment they prevailed on me to remain by saying the Countess was a very bad woman, so I lost that good position, only one little girl of eight years, and every comfort. She was just about to travel to France, Germany, England and America. Many English Governesses offered themselves for 10 to 15 roubles a month to have the delightful prospect of travelling. But they could not teach music.

I was to have had £4 a month and free two days to give lessons, which would have brought me £2 a month or more. All together I should have had £6 a month and a chance of gaining still more. However, as I before said, I remained on, they had been at the beginning very kind to me, stayed in spite of every discomfort and at reduced salary of 30 roubles a month. The children in Russia are always sent to the Gymnasium or College after a certain age. The girls are educated like men — great importance placed on a knowledge of the Sciences as being a most requisite part of a woman's education. So it was time to prepare the children to enter, and therefore a Russian Governess out of an Institute was required, who could teach German and French. They gave her 300 roubles a year and me 360. I was to continue as before to teach Music and English. In Russia foreign Governesses are taken only for language and Music — or rather the piano if they can teach it.

When I first entered my last situation the children were very young, born almost one year after each other. I had three girls, very spoilt and ignorant of everything except bon-bons — badly trained, being usually left to the care of the Russian nurses. After my two years of toil there — it was toil, I left. I had not only to teach and guide their children from 9 a.m. to 9 p.m., but to mind, and often to work for the whole of them, which I did not undertake to do on my engagement, but I did it to help the nurse who had the washing and dressing of the four children, the washing of most of the clothes and to attend on the mother, who would not even mend a glove herself. The children now speak and read English nicely, and also play pieces and exercises on the piano, and are much better children than when I went there.

The parents are quite satisfied with the progress they made. The family have been living in much discomfort for the past 18 months, because of the Father's itinerant position as an officer. There is very little domestic comfort out here. They pay liberally, but nothing of English comfort. For seven months I had to sleep in a little dark room with three children — *no* window for *fresh* air, except one for light only and looking into the Servants' apartment. A small house with but four rooms for 12 people, four of them servants.

I decided on leaving — they left it to me to do so if I chose as they were about to leave for a remote part of the Country where they have a small house close to the Soldiers' Camp, no room for a second Governess. I went with the lady (Mrs Markosoff) to Mr Thompson — the English Clergyman. She wished an introduction in order to find through him an English nurse so that the children might *not* forget their English till they went to School, where it is now taught, but he said she cannot have one for less than 25 roubles a month, recommended by him. In September they intend taking one for less — somehow. She would not give 25 roubles for a nurse.

No young lady who desires much comfort must think of Russia. If, indeed, they wish to gain a good Salary so as to be able yearly to save, no country is better for that than Russia. Things, to be sure, are dear here, but the Governess who wishes to save her money need not dress. Unfortunately for me, I was obliged to leave my Situation at an unfavourable Season, and am at the Governesses' Home for the last five weeks. All the families are in the Country, and shall not return till the end of September, when I can then procure a good Situation, but in the meantime I am losing time and spending money for my support. I found it impossible to save money out of my Salary for the past two years, I have sent so much to my family. I have no other motive for telling you this than to let you know that I have not wasted the money . . .

June, July and August are the worst months in St Petersburg for a Governess seeking a place. I knew this when I left, but I thought by chance I might hear of something, one often does even then, but I should advise none to come out at Midsummer, either the end of August or the beginning of May are the two best times to arrive here. In winter I can always find a situation in St Petersburg, for often there are not enough Governesses with English for the demands. I have written to Mr Pennie, the English Clergyman at Moscow, to kindly procure a situation in or near that Town. I know he will write to say, as others have, that I should be on the spot; one likes to see the Person one engages. In Moscow they are much richer and pay Governesses better, consequently I am told an English Governess gets from £6 to £8 a month there. It would cost about £2 second class to Moscow. I have not even half that sum at present.

After this startling disclosure of the extent of her lack of resources while stranded in a foreign city, Miss Stoney finally brought herself to the point of her letter: a request for a loan, obviously something she found very hard to do.

Do you think the Society, who have been previously so generous towards me, would for this occasion advance me a few pounds. I would return it within three months. Dear madam, I may as well tell you this is really the purport of my letter. I have a long time to wait — a month before I can procure a position in St Petersburg and then perhaps not the amount of salary I require. I am recommended by many to go up at once to Moscow — What can I do without money? A Russian lady told me I should get something worth having if on the spot — I thought I should never have had occasion to ask aid again, of you. I imagined I should have been able to have saved something during the last two years. Afterwards I found it an impossibility — I owed so much and debts *must* first be cleared. Had I found my way out here free of debts I should have had something to put by — I was obliged to borrow from home a fortnight ago. They really are too poor to lend me the sum I now require and I want it at once; after a month or two D.V. I shall not need it, just now it would be of great use to me.

You have once kindly asked me to write a line about myself to you. I am truly sorry that it is not a more cheerful letter and that I am compelled to ask in it a loan of money for present use. I hope you will understand my position. Be assured it is the last time I shall trouble the Society. I hope if I have the health to save my money for the next few years.

Will you dear Madam favour me with an answer as soon as convenient. The sum I ask is £6. Should this be kindly advanced it will be of great use and a special favour. There is an English Bank here, a cheque enclosed without registering comes quite safely. I give the same security as before and would be glad if you could let me have the money before you write to my family. It takes so long before a letter reaches and an answer is received from England and just about the time your letter may reach me, the month for the use of the room should have expired, and if I remain two days past that date I must pay again in advance . . . Hoping to hear from you soon and that you will pardon such a long letter all about myself.

There are no further letters from Josephine Stoney, and it is not possible to establish whether the Society responded to her request for a loan. Even if a loan were not forthcoming officially through the Society, it would be surprising if some unofficial way was not found to help her.

A total of thirty-three FMCES emigrants went to the United States and Canada,* but they were poor correspondents. Only two wrote to the Society, both from New York, and their experiences were mundane in comparison to those of Miss Stoney. The first letter came from Julia Hussey, who in her letter dated 4 December 1871, from 32 East 30 Street, New York, did little more than report her arrival and that of Miss Batler, who was proceeding to San Francisco. She wrote: 'I am so much obliged to you for all you have done for us. I have not a situation as yet, but I hope to have one soon.'

The other New York correspondent was Mrs M. Carruthers, who wrote on 10 June 1872, from 85 McDougal Street, on behalf of herself and her daughters, Annie, Emmeline and Marion. Two daughters had boarded at the Young Ladies' Christian Association and, through the good offices of the superintendent, all the members of the family were put in touch with employers. Mrs Carruthers became matron of an orphanage in New Jersey; Marion found a position as governess at an Orphan Institution in New York; Emmeline was placed as companion and seamstress in a family where there were three small daughters; and Annie became a useful companion to a lady, also having the care of her two small daughters. In her letter, Mrs Carruthers said: 'The supply here runs greater than the demand . . . no encouragement for us to go west . . . I felt we must return to England if we could not succeed in New York'.

Mrs Carruthers wrote again, possibly up to a year later, in an undated letter, giving her daughter Marion's address: 27 Washington Square North, New York. She had taken up her position at the orphanage in New Jersey, about forty miles distant, in an area where there was no mail delivery. She reported on the progress of her daughters: Annie had left her job, as a nurse to two girls aged five and nine at $15 a month, for 'although she had

---

*A group of seven went to Vancouver in 1862; one went to Canada in 1869 with Miss Rye; a mother, accompanied by her daughter, went to Chicago to join her husband; and two sisters went to New York in 1871. Another went to British Columbia in 1871; a Mrs Carruthers and her three daughters emigrated to New York in 1872; one went to Colorado in 1880; five to Canada in 1882; and five in 1883; and four to Canada and one to Colorado in 1884.

her meals with the family and they did their best to keep her, yet Annie was heart-broken in a few days, and I have her here with me as teacher of 20 boys, that we may have the comfort of being together'. Her daughter Emmeline was happy in her job, where she was paid $13 a month. 'She might do better in salary, but she is so much at home.' Marion had given up her position and having observed that teachers could not get on well in New York without a diploma, was being supported by her mother while she attended Head Grammar School for twelve months, a prerequisite before being admitted to a teachers college. Mrs Carruthers went on:

> Marion is delighted with their system of teaching and if we are spared it is our intention (when Marion gets her Diploma) to return to our beloved Country, though being English I am told she will have to be very well up or they will not pass her . . . through God's mercy we are all doing well and do not regret coming, although our pleasure is hoping to return to purchase a more advanced school.
>
> The heat of this summer has been most oppressive. It will be a positive dread for the next, and the Mosquitoes a perfect plague, though to the surprise of residents here our health has continued good. The daughters think I am looking much older, but the fact of taking the position of Matron of a disorganised household has been a great labour. Good servants are very difficult to get.

The only other letter from North America was a very short one from Mrs G. H. Missen, Honorary Secretary of the Women's Protective Immigration Society at 8 Prince Arthur Street, Montreal, dated 5 June 1882, announcing that Miss Hoskings, 'recommended by you to this Society, has arrived in safety and is placed'.

Several governesses mention India as a possibility for emigration, but the Society's records contain letters from only one who went there: Helen Williams, who taught at Byculla, Bombay, apart from a brief spell at Poona. Miss Williams was very conscious of the 'heathen' environment in which she lived and worked, and she felt the need to instruct her pupils in Christianity, although conscious that she should not use her position to influence them.

After teaching first at a larger school, Helen Williams moved to take charge of the Alexandria School, established in Bombay by a Parsee judge, Mr Mannoylyu Cursitjee.

He and one of his daughters had met Emily Faithfull while visiting England. His daughters were to assist Helen Williams 'to obviate the difficulty of language'. On 8 August 1863, Helen Williams wrote to Miss Lewin, explaining that she wanted to get the school in good working order and to do so, she needed the rules and regulations of some schools in England as a guide. She named the 'Missionary College' at Highbury, the 'Soldiers' Orphan Asylum', 'Foundling Hospital' and the 'Home and Colonial Schools'. She continued:

There is a vast field here for work and I think bye and bye many openings will appear for our superabundant females — but they *must* be of the very first class in morals, character and *energy* — a mere idler or dawdler here is an unmitigated evil . . .

There is another subject too in teaching these Natives upon which I should be grateful for advice. Normally there is no religious teaching. I am at present unacquainted with the traits of the Parsee — but they appear to worship God and think every visitation for good or evil ordained by His Will. They use our English lesson books, with poetry and lessons, etc. about the Saviour. I have asked permission to teach the creation of the world by the Bible record, and yesterday I had to explain to a Pupil who Christ was. Now having with my eyes open undertaken the secular training of these people, I do not feel at liberty, directly or indirectly, to inculcate our religion — Yet I cannot pass over any explanation without the hope that the small beautiful seed of Gospel truth may blossom in their hearts — I feel after a while that it will do so, but I should be most grateful for the experience of any conscientious person who *without* being a Missionary had worked in Heathen Lands — I would be unwilling to do the shadow of any action that might appear underhanded. Yet I am desirous of making our pure spotless Bible truth appear beautiful and desirable in their eyes and shall be thankful for any help.

In her next letter, dated 12 November 1863, Helen Williams' missionary zeal was apparent:

I can only burn my little feeble light, but I can see the great and glorious lustre of divine truth that will spread over this and other lands — A spirit of enquiry once started like the Parsee old superstitions falling away and our blessed and happy religion will follow . . .

The good seed is certainly being sown and if I could in justice to myself and others give up my time to the work I feel *abundant* interest in it to do so — but having other openings, I think it is not as yet my appointed work.

By this time, she had left the school run by Mr Cursitjee, at which there were by then eighteen to twenty pupils between the ages of ten and thirty, including some mothers and daughters. She had found the judge's daughters deeply read, clever girls and had not felt capable of continuing their education. She also had found difficulty in getting suitable board and had decided to take a resident position, which would enable her to save money to pay off debts in England. She had accepted an appointment at the Victoria Girls' School, a day school in Poona run by Miss Page. The patroness was Lady Frere, wife of the governor, Sir Bartle Frere. She wrote:

This Establishment is for the education of Girls in the rising ranks of Society, one for instance, is the daughter of Captain Bennett, called Moultan Bennett, from having I believe as a private first planted his standard therein. He received a commission on the Field. Others have sprung from poor but decayed families. In each case sending their children home would only associate them with a lower class and these people are more tenacious than others of their position. Therefore a good Hill School is a constant want . . .

The Girls are fairly taught; they learn English well and Music — Singing, Drawing and French too, but with less success — they dance fairly I hear — and their deportment is *good* — they can make cakes and cut up and help the Tailors with their wearing apparel. Upon the whole I am much pleased with the School, but I hope greatly to increase its numbers, as many Protestant Girl children at present attend the Nuns' Convent Day School.

I do not think there is any opening just now for women here, there are five Governesses applying for my situation [with Mr Cursitjee] and the Byculla School [where she first taught] brings out working Girls as Nursery Governesses, quite as many as the place supports. I do not think it would do yet to send out any on speculation — there is no demand — but it is just possible there might be an opening for a Lady who is acquainted with the Kinder Garten System and capable of working it out for elder Pupils. Mr M. Cursitjee said he might have to send to England for a Lady by and bye but he is very particular about manners and morals.

On 28 February 1864, Helen Williams wrote again. She had been very seriously ill with inflammation of the lungs and congestion of the liver, accompanied by fever and dysentery. She had left Poona and again gave her address as Byculla, Bombay, where she was nursed by her sister. She wrote:

I have met with extreme kindness from all with whom I have become acquainted — indeed I feel much happier here than I was in England, and when the Doctor told me if I did not rally quickly he must send me home I felt very sad. There I was never free from pecuniary difficulties, here I have none — I could hardly pay my way there, here I can lay by money.

She had received a letter from Miss Lewin and promised to reply to her questions when she was feeling stronger. She added: 'Mr Cursitjee wishes me to return to him and carry on at the Alexandria School as before'.

Helen Williams' last letter is undated, but was written in October 1864. She explained that she had not been able to remain with Miss Page at the Hill School at Poona, 'the air so entirely disagreed with me', and the school had since closed down. She went on to say: 'My health has been so very bad — after that attack of liver complaint I had a chronic dysentery for five months, which quite unfitted me for the performance of my duties'.

The final paragraph of the letter apparently concerns questions raised by Miss Lewin about prospects for sending another governess to India. Helen Williams replied:

I should have been very glad indeed if I could have rendered her any service, but at present there are more Governesses in Bombay than situations for them. If however she still requires one and wishes to come out, I will still prosecute my enquiries, but it seems to me a great risk at her age to leave England. I think her only chance of making money here would be to get into a Public School, as the salary in private families is only from £30 to £50 as in England and the prices of everything doubled. I had £85 a year at Mr Coline's when I first went.
In

The letter ends here and, according to an added note, was found among Miss Williams' papers, following her death from cholera at the island of Elephanta, after twelve hours' illness, in October 1864.

Epilogue

The sad death of Helen Williams from an epidemic disease in a foreign country is an extreme example of the risks the governesses of the Female Middle Class Emigration Society faced when, having decided to leave behind the security of home, family and friends, they endeavoured to find work and a better life in the colonies. Inspired by Maria Rye's enthusiasm, these women ventured to strange places, where they faced adversity with dignity and a great deal of integrity — as evidenced by their almost universal efforts to repay their loans.

The decision to emigrate was a daunting prospect for a young woman in her twenties (as many of them were), but perhaps deserving of more sympathy were the older women (some in their forties and even older), who uprooted themselves to start a new life, one that sometimes made demands with which they were unable to cope. Quite often, their expectations were not realised, but they faced with great courage long journeys and the particular loneliness of entering into an unknown and often alien environment.

Little has been written about governesses, though many older people remember being taught by them. They have remained shadowy figures, often excluded from or unnamed in family photographs and mentioned only incidentally in family records. It is fortunate that, in the case of the FMCES governesses, their own words describing their lives and their feelings are available to us. Through their letters and despite the limitations of a rather restricted upbringing and social background, they emerge as articulate, emotional and appealing women.

Some governesses disappeared without trace into nineteenth-century colonial life; a few returned home, defeated; others — probably many more than those whose history it has been possible to trace — married and settled into life in the colonies, mainly in Australia, New Zealand and South Africa. There were perhaps a few 'complainers', but most of these women brought diversity, strength of character and refined attainments to the task of education in strange lands.

Appendix

Female Middle Class Emigration Society Letter-books
List of Correspondents, 1862–1882

Correspondent	*Location when writing*	*Year(s) when written and numbers of letters*
from Australia		
*à Beckett, Mrs Laura Jane (FMCES representative)	Melbourne, Vic.	1864 (1)
Allen, Florence C.	Perth, WA	1880 (1)
Allen, Mrs Margaret	Hotham (North Melbourne), Vic.; & Mount Gambier, SA	1864, 1866 (3)
Atherton, Maria	South Brisbane, Qld	1862 (1)
Barlow, Miss (?Nancy)	Janefield, Vic.	1863 (1)
Barrow, Maria	South Yarra, Vic.	1862 (1)
Barton, Mrs C.	Sydney, NSW	1864 (1)
Bayly, Mary Frances (Mrs F.A. Hole)	Newtown, Sydney & Cook's River, NSW	1866–68 (8)
Bernard, Eliza	Double Bay, NSW	1865–66 (3)
Boake, Elizabeth	Richmond & Warrnambool, Vic.	1867–69 (5)
Booty, Louisa	Sandhurst (Bendigo), Vic.	1865 (1)
Carttar, Emilie Ann (Mrs John Dodds)	Narellan, NSW	1876 (1)
Cooleu, Lizzie	Fitzroy, Vic.	1873 (1)
Crowley, M.	Illabo, NSW	?1881 (1)
Davis, Annie	Glebe, NSW	1863–65, 1867 (4)

*Correspondents who were not emigrants.

Dearmer, Louisa	Sydney, NSW	1868 (2)
Finch, Jane	Redfern & Yass, NSW	1864, 1866 (2)
Ford, Eliza Maria	Ryde, NSW	1864–65 (2)
Geoghegan, Louisa Agnes (Mrs Frederick Vaughan)	Neuarpurr, Vic.	1867–68, 1870 (5)
Giles, Fanny M.	Morpeth, NSW	1864 (1)
Giraud, Omérine	Melbourne, Vic.	1866 (2)
Gooch, Gertrude	Ashfield, NSW	1862 (1)
Hammett, Sarah E.	Melbourne, Vic.	1870 (1)
Haselton, Caroline (or Lina)	Melbourne, Vic. (also from South Africa)	1879 (1)
Heawood, Caroline Maria (Mrs J.R. Löfvén)	Melbourne & Ballarat, Vic.	1862–63 (2)
Hunt, Annie M.	Melbourne, Wangaratta & Fitzroy, Vic.	1869–71 (4)
Ireland, Ellen	Newcastle, Sydney & Goulburn, NSW	1862–63 (3)
Jadis, Edith (Mrs Edward Lautour)	Melbourne & East St Kilda, Vic; Wanganella, NSW	1873–75 (3)
Jones, Laura (or Lauranna)	Melbourne, Waranga & Sandhurst (Bendigo), Vic.	1868–69 (4)
Jordan, Pauline	Melbourne, Vic.	1877 (1)
Kidson, Jane	Fitzroy, Vic.	1863 (1)
Kightley, M. A.	Maldon & Melbourne, Vic.	1865–66 (2)
Lash, Caroline M.	Miller's Point, Sydney, NSW	1864 (1)
McGillivray, Isabella	Williamstown, Vic.	1862 (1)

McGillivray, Margaret	Ballarat, Vic.	1865 (1)
Macqueen, Agnes B.	Brisbane, Qld	1865–66 (2)
Nagelle, Cécile Céline	Melbourne, Vic; Gawler & Angaston, SA	1873, 1875–77 (7)
Oberman, Miss (?J. or I.)	Manly, Sydney, NSW	?1881 (1)
Oliver, M.A.	Neuarpurr, Vic.	1871 (1)
Ollard, Ellen H.	Melbourne, Vic.	1876 (1)
Penrose, Susan G. B.	Melbourne, Vic.	1868–69 (2)
Phayne, Rosa	Melbourne & Rich Avon West, Vic.	1869–72 (4)
Phillips, Mrs Lucy	South Yarra, Vic.	1873 (1)
Phillips, Mary	Goulburn, NSW	1862 (1)
Pyman, Margaret	Sydney, NSW	1865 (1)
Richardson, Mary	Rolland's Plains, NSW	1863 (1)
Rodgerson, Isabella	Douglas Park, NSW	1867–68 (3)
*Shaw, Annie (official of Melbourne Home)	Melbourne, Vic.	1866 (1)
Stone, Clara	Collingwood, Vic.	1868 (1)
Streeter, S. Emily	Jerry's Plains & Sydney, NSW	1862 (2)
Tindall, Eleanor V.	Mt Mercer & South Yarra, Vic.	1878, 1880 (2)
Walpole, Eliza C.	Bullarook, Prahan & (?)Hayneer, Vic.	1863, 1865, 1867 (4)
Webb, Sarah F.	Sandhurst (Bendigo), Vic.	1863 (1)
White, Mrs Ida	Bowral, NSW	1881 (1)
Wilson, Mrs Hannah	Brisbane, Qld	1867, 1871–72 (3)

from Canada		
*Missen, Mrs G. H. (of the Women's Protective Immigration Society)	Montreal	1882 (1)
from India		
Williams, Helen	Byculla, Bombay	1863–64 (4)
from New Zealand		
Bird, Georgie	Christchurch	1877 (1)
Blackith, Eleanor (?Mrs Lawes)	Porangahau, Napier	1881 (2)
Braddell, Lizzie A.	Manuherikia, Otago	1864 (1)
Brind, Kate	Nelson	1873–75 (7)
Brook, Eliza C. (Mrs MacDonnell)	Dunedin	1869–70 (3)
Brook, Mary Bentley	Dunedin	1869 (1)
Caldwell, J.	Christchurch	1880 (1)
Campbell, M.	Nelson	1874 (1)
Cary (?Carey), I.M. (?J. M.)	Dunedin & Wanganui	1863–65, 1867 (4)
Cross, Fanny	Dunedin & (?) Oamaru	1880–81 (2)
Fox, Caroline	Orari Gorge & Timaru, Canterbury	1879–80 (2)
Hacon, E. A.	Timaru	1878 (1)
*Herbert, Harriet H. (Governesses' agent)	Mount Herbert, Waipukurau, Hawke's Bay; & (?) Maliswater	1879–80 (5)
Hett, Marion (?Marian)	Lyttleton, Christchurch; Napier, Hawke's Bay; & Marton, Wellington	1870–73 (6)

Hunt, Emily Mary	Wellington	1874 (1)
James, Arabella Harriett (Mrs Brown)	Auckland & Drury	1864, 1866 (2)
Keith (?Leith or Seith), Miss I. (?J.)	Canterbury	1879 (1)
*Kemp, Mrs Charlotte (reply to request from FMCES for assistance)	Auckland	1881 (1)
Long, Elizabeth	Waimarama, Hawke's Bay	1880 (1)
Long, Mary	Waipukurau, Hawke's Bay	1880 (1)
McNeill (?McNeile), Augusta G.	Christchurch; Diamond Harbour & Governor's Bay, Lyttleton	1865–67 (7)
McNeill (?McNeile), Georgina	Rhodes Bay, Lyttleton; & Hawkesbury, Christchurch	1864–66 (5)
Manning, E. L. (Mrs Buck)	Dunedin	1876 (2)
Merritt, J.	Auckland	1863 (1)
Russell, A.	Dunedin	1882 (1)
Scott, Lucy M.	Christchurch	1867 (1)
Smith, M. E.	Napier & Pihautea, Wellington	1866–67 (2)
*Spratt, Dr Henry T. (request for a governess)	Greytown, Wairarapa	1864 (1)
Starky, Barbara	Porangahau, Napier	1868 (1)
Thomas, Fanny J.	Puerua, near Dunedin	1864 (1)
Wilson, Mary C.	Masterton, Wairarapa	1871 (1)

Woerner, Fraulein S.	Dunedin	1879 (2)
Wyett, Martha	Greytown, Wairarapa	1866–68 (4)

from Russia

Stoney, Josephine E. (?C.)	Tiflis, Caucasus; Taganrog, South Russia; & St Petersburg	1873–75 (8)

from South Africa

Blake, M. J.	Durban & Isipingo, Natal	1869–71 (3)
Brand, Louisa J.	Durban, Natal	1874 (1)
*Brickhill, James (husband of FMCES representative in Natal)	Durban, Natal	1868 (1)
Brough, Catherine	Cape Town	1863–64 (2)
Crowe, Catherine	Durban, Natal	1862 (2)
Evans, Clara A. (Mrs Meredith)	Graaff-Reinet, Cape Colony	1879–80 (3)
Evans, Sophia E. (Mrs William Hobson)	Graaff-Reinet, Cape Colony	1879, 1881 (2)
Evatt, Maria A.	Umgababa, Natal	1871 (1)
Fowler, J. S. (?I. S.)	Tongaat, Pietermaritzburg & Pinetown, Natal	1865–67 (3)
Glen, Emilie (Mrs Walton)	Durban & Verulam, Natal	1866 (2)
Haffenden (?Haffendon), S. (?L.) (Mrs S. J. Meintjes)	Pinetown, Natal; Pretoria, Transvaal; & Burghersdorp, Cape Colony	1863–65 (3)
Hall, S. E. A. (?S. A.; ?L.)	Cape Town, Port Elizabeth & Graaff-Reinet, Cape Colony	1868, 1870, 1876–82 (20)

Hart, Alice M.	Graaff-Reinet, Cape Colony	1880 (1)
Haselton, Caroline (or Lina)	Graaff-Reinet, Cape Colony (later from Australia)	1877 (2)
Henderson, Sarah	Durban & Tongaat, Natal (also London)	1863, 1867–68 (4)
Hooper, Celia (Mrs Sinclair)	Umzinto, Alexandria; Umgeni and Lower Umzimkulu, Natal	1873, 1875, 1880–81 (8)
Jackson, A. H. (Mrs Armstrong)	Verulam, Natal	1863 (3)
Jenvey, Margaret E.	Cape Town	1877, 1879 (2)
Jeston, Nora F.	Bedford, Cape Colony	1876 (1)
McLean, J. B.	Bedford, Cape Colony	1882 (1)
*Meintjes, Dr S. J. (repayments of wife's loan)	Potchefstroom, Transvaal; Grahamstown, Cape Colony	1864, 1865 (2)
Mitchinson, Elizabeth	Bedford, Cape Colony	1877–79 (6)
Nelson, Emily L. (?Mrs Webber)	Bedford, Cape Colony	1876 (1)
Prentice, Louisa (?Louie)	Isipingo & Richmond, Natal	1869, 1871 (2)
Robinson, Annie A.	Durban, Natal	1868 (1)
Temple, Amelia (or Amy) M.	Richmond & Durban, Natal	1868–70 (6)
Watson, Mary Anna	Bedford, Cape Colony	1878, 1880 (2)
Winn, Rosarie	Durban & Verulam, Natal	1862, 1864 (2)

from the United States		
Carruthers, Mrs M.	New York	1872–?73 (2)
Hussey, Julia	New York	1871 (1)

Bibliography

FMCES records

(microfilmed in 1963 as part of the Australian Joint Copying Project; originals held at the Fawcett Library, City of London Polytechnic)

Annual Reports of the Society for the years 1862–1886; 4 reports, containing rules, details of finances, subscriptions, fate of emigrants, etc.; the reports were not issued yearly.

Letter-books of the Society:
Book 1, 1862–1877
Book 2 (numbered 3), 1877–1882

Jane E. Lewin, *Female Middle Class Emigration: A Paper read at the Social Science Congress in October 1863*, n.p., n.d. (?Emily Faithfull & Co., London, 1863).

Maria S. Rye, *Emigration of Educated Women: A Paper read at the Social Science Congress in Dublin, 1861*, printed and published by Emily Faithfull & Co., London, n.d. (?1861).

Books that make use of FMCES records

A. James Hammerton, *Emigrant Gentlewoman: Genteel Poverty and Female Emigration, 1830–1914*, Croom Helm, London/ Rowman & Littlefield, Totowa, NJ, 1979.

[Una Monk], *New Horizons: A Hundred Years of Women's Migration*, HMSO, London, 1963.

G. F. Plant, *A Survey of Voluntary Effort in Women's Empire Migration*, Society for the Oversea Settlement of British Women, London, 1950.

Official government reports

Report from the Select Committee on the Condition of the Working Classes of the Metropolis, ordered by the Legislative Assembly to be printed, 18 April 1860; *New South Wales Legislative Assembly, Votes and Proceedings*, 1859–60, vol. 4, pp. 1263–1461.

Report from the Select Committee of the Legislative Council: The Present System of Immigration, ordered by the Council to be printed, 13 January 1853, Government Printer, Melbourne, 1853.

Report of the Board of the Education District of Hawke's Bay, New Zealand, for the Year ended 31 December 1878, Napier, 1879.

Report of the Royal Commission appointed by His Excellency to Enquire into and Report upon the Operation of the System of Public Education, together with Minutes of Evidence and Appendices, *Victorian Parliamentary Papers*, vol. 4, 1867 (Higinbotham Report).
Victorian Parliamentary Papers, Immigration: Report to His Excellency the Lieutenant Governor by Immigration Agent, Edward Grimes, for the Year 1852. Report dated Immigration Office, Melbourne, 9 June 1853, ordered to be printed by the Legislative Council, 31 August 1853.

Newspapers and periodicals

London *Times* 1861–3, 1903
Melbourne *Age* and *Argus* 1861–81
Sydney Morning Herald and *Sydney Mail* 1861–81
Government Gazettes: New South Wales, Queensland and Victoria

Directories and gazeteers

Bailliere's Victorian Gazetteer, Melbourne, 1865.
Bailliere's New South Wales Gazette and Road Guide, Sydney, 1866.
Ballarat and Ballarat East Directory, 1865–66, comp. F. M. Dicker, Ballarat, 1865.
Butler and Stevens' Directory 1865–66, Sandhurst, Castlemaine and Echuca, comp. John W. Butler and George Stevens, Melbourne, 1865.
Cape of Good Hope Commercial Directory and General Business Guide 1868, Saul Solomon, Cape Town, 1868.
Commercial and Trades Directory of South Australia, 1882–83, Morris, Hayter & Barry, Adelaide, 1882.
Greville's Official Post Office Directory and Gazeteer of New South Wales, 1875–77, Sydney, n.d.
Natal Almanac and Yearly Register, Davis & Sons, Pietermaritzburg, 1867, 1881, 1887.
National Directory of New South Wales, 1867–68, Walter Samson & Co., Sydney, n.d.
National Directory of South Australia, 1867–68, John W. Butler, North Melbourne, n.d.
Niven's Directory of Ballarat, 1875, F. W. Niven, Ballarat, 1875.
Official Post Office Directory of Queensland, 1868, W. J. Meyer, Brisbane, 1868.
Pugh's Queensland Almanac, 1862, 1866, 1878, 1880, 1881, 1883, 1884, 1886.

Sands and Mcdougall, *Annual Register and Almanac*, Melbourne, 1864.
Sands and Mcdougall, *Melbourne Directory*, 1863 to 1879.
Sands and Mcdougall, *Sydney Directory*, 1862 to 1882.
Sands's Country Directory and Gazetter of New South Wales, 1889–1890, Sydney, 1890.
South Australian Post Directory, 1897–98, H. Wise & Co., Adelaide, 1898.
Stevens' Geelong and Western District and Squatters' Directory, George Stevens, Melbourne, 1866.
John Vann (comp.), *The Squatting Directory of New South Wales*, Sydney, 1865.
Western Australian Directory and Almanack for 1882, [Herald], Perth, n.d.
Western Australian Almanack and Directory, Stirling Bros., Perth, 1884, 1887.
Western Australia Post Office Directory, 1895–96, H. Wise & Co., Perth, n.d.
John Windle (comp.), *The Ballarat Directory, 1869*, James Curtis, Ballarat, 1869.

General references

George Wigram Dundas Allen (ed.), *Early Georgian: Extracts from the Journal of George Allen, 1800–1877*, Angus & Robertson, Sydney, 1958.
Annals of Pinetown, compiled by Pinetown Women's Institute, Pinetown, S. Africa, 1968.
A. G. Austin, *Australian Education 1788–1900*, Pitman, Melbourne, 3rd edn, 1972.
Australian Dictionary of Biography 1851–1890 (gen. ed. Douglas Pike), Melbourne University Press, Carlton, vols 3–6, 1968–76.
Lady Barker, *A Year's Housekeeping in South Africa*, Macmillan, London, 1883.
Marjorie F. Barnard, *Sydney: The Story of a City*, Melbourne University Press, Carlton, 1956.
William A. Bayley, *Lilac City: The Story of Goulburn, New South Wales*, Goulburn City Council, Goulburn, 1954.
Allan Birch and David S. Macmillan (arranged and introduced), *The Sydney Scene, 1788–1960*, Melbourne University Press, Carlton, 1962.
J. T. S. Bird, *The Early History of Rockhampton*, Morning Bulletin, Rockhampton, 1904.
Barbara I. Buchanan, *Natal Memories*, Shuter & Shooter, Pietermaritzburg, 1941.

Bernard Burke, *A Genealogical and Heraldic History of the Colonial Gentry*, Harrison & Sons, London, 1891.

John E. P. Bushby, *Saltbush Country: History of the Deniliquin District*, Library of Australian History, North Sydney, 1980.

Gordon Leslie Buxton, *The Riverina, 1861–1891: An Australian Regional Study*, Melbourne University Press, Carlton, 1967.

Ben W. Champion (comp.), *Family Entries, Births, Deaths, Marriages, etc., in the Hunter Valley District, 1843–84*, the author, [Newcastle, NSW], 1973.

Don Charlwood, *The Long Farewell*, Penguin Books Australia, Ringwood, Vic., 1981.

——, *Settlers Under Sail*, Premier's Department, Melbourne, 1978.

Church of England Children's Society, *Waifs and Strays*, London, January 1904.

T. A. Coghlan, *Labour and Industry in Australia: From the First Settlement in 1788 to the Establishment of the Commonwealth in 1901*, Macmillan, Melbourne, 1969.

Ephrain Henry Coombe (comp.), *History of Gawler, 1837 to 1908*, Austraprint, Hampstead Gardens, SA, facsimile edn, 1978.

Crockford's Clerical Dictionary 1908, Horace Cox, London, 1908.

The Cyclopedia of New Zealand, Cyclopedia Co., Christchurch, 1908.

Cyclopaedia of Victoria, James Smith, Melbourne, 1904.

Charles Daley, *The Story of Gippsland*, Whitcombe & Tombs, Melbourne, 1960.

Dictionary of National Biography, ed. Sidney Lee, London, 1897.

A Dictionary of New Zealand Biography, ed. G. H. Scholefield, Department of Internal Affairs, Wellington, 1940.

A Dictionary of South African Biography, vols 2–3, published for the Human Sciences Research Council by Tafelberg-Vitgewers, Cape Town, 1972, 1977, vol. 4, Butterworth, Durban, 1981.

Ross Fitzgerald, *From the Dreaming to 1915: A History of Queensland*, University of Queensland Press, St Lucia, 1982.

Michael Fowler, *Country Houses of New Zealand: North Island*, A. H. & A. W. Reed, Wellington, 1971.

Jonathon Gathorne-Hardy, *The Rise and Fall of the British Nanny*, Hodder & Stoughton, London, 1972.

O. S. Green, *Sale: The Early Years and Later*, Southern Newspapers, Sale, n.d.

G. Nesta Griffiths, *Point Piper: Past and Present*, Ure Smith, Sydney, 1970.

——, *Some Northern Homes of New South Wales*, Shepherd Press, Sydney, 1954.

Wilhelm Grütter, in collaboration with D. J. van Zyl, *The Story of South Africa*, Human & Rousseau, Cape Town, 1981.
J. C. Hamilton, *Pioneering Days in Western Victoria: A Narrative of Early Station Life*, Exchange Press, Melbourne, 1912.
W. P. M. Henderson, *Durban: Fifty Years of Municipal History*, Robinson, Durban, 1904.
Cosmo Grenville Henning, *Graaff-Reinet: A Cultural History*, Bulpen, Cape Town, 1975.
Georgina Hill, *Women in English Life*, Richard Bentley, London, 1896.
R. L. Jenkins, *Nepean Towers Shorthorn Herd: New Catalogue for 1871*, R. Bone, Sydney, 1871.
James A. Jervis, *A History of the Berrima District, 1798-1973*, Berrima County Council, Berrima, 1962.
W. Ross Johnston, *The Call of the Land: A History of Queensland to the Present Day*, Jacaranda Press, Brisbane, 1982.
Margaret L. Kiddle, *Men of Yesterday: A Social History of the Western District of Victoria, 1834–1890*, Melbourne University Press, Carlton, 1961.
J. K. Loney, *Wrecks around Cape Otway*, the author, Apollo Bay, 1966.
A. Basil Lubbock, *The Colonial Clippers, 1876-1944*, J. Brown, Glasgow, 1921.
'Lyth' (Mrs Thomas), *The Golden South: Memories of Australian Home Life from 1843 to 1888*, Ward & Downey, London, 1890.
Miriam Macgregor, *Early Stations of Hawke's Bay*, A. H. & A. W. Reed, Wellington, 1970.
Joseph J. Mack, *Chain of Ponds*, Neptune Press, Newtown, Vic., 1983.
George Mackay, *The History of Bendigo*, Ferguson & Mitchell, Melbourne, 1891.
John Davies Mereweather, *Life on Board an Emigrant Ship, being a Diary of a Voyage to Australia*, T. Hatchard, London, 1852.
Cecily Joan Mitchell, *Hunter's River*, Estate of the author, Newcastle West, 1973.
P. C. Mowle, *A Genealogical History of Pioneer Families of Australia*, Angus & Robertson, Sydney, 1948.
T. Muir, 'Tobacco in Early Australia', *Australian Tobacco Growers' Bulletin*, nos 15-19, 1969-71.
Natal Who's Who 1906, Durban, 1906.
NSW Department of Education, *Sydney and the Bush: A Pictorial History of Education in New South Wales*, Sydney, 1980.
W. H. Oliver (ed.), with B. R. Williams, *The Oxford History of New Zealand*, Oxford University Press, Wellington, 1981.
Robert F. Osborn, *Valiant Harvest: The Founding of the South*

African Sugar Industry, 1848–1926, South African Sugar Association, Durban, 1964.
Robert B. Ronald, *The Riverina: People and Properties,* Cheshire, Melbourne, 1960.
Watson Rosevear, *Waiapu: The Story of a Diocese,* Paul's Book Arcade, Hamilton, Auckland, 1960.
George Russell, *History of Old Durban and Reminiscences of an Emigrant of 1850,* Davis & Sons, Pietermaritzburg, 1899.
Luther A. Scammell, *A Voyage to Australia in the Barque 'William Wilson', 1849,* R. B. Scammell, Sydney, n.d. (?1966).
A. G. Serle, *The Golden Age, 1851–1861,* Melbourne University Press, Carlton, 1963.
S. W. Silver and Company's Emigration Guide and Colonial Itinerary, Emigration Warehouse, London, 1859.
South Australian Centenary, 1836–1936, Angaston and Nuriootpa Centenary Souvenir, The Leader, Angaston, 1936.
Shelagh O'Byrne Spencer, *British Settlers in Natal, 1824–1857,* University of Natal Press, Pietermaritzburg, 1981.
The Standard Encyclopaedia of Southern Africa, ed. D. J. Potgieter, Nassou, Cape Town, 1975.
Charles Swancott, *Manly 1788 to 1968,* the author, Woy Woy, 1968.
Alexander Sutherland, *Victoria and its Metropolis: Past and Present,* McCarron, Bird & Co., Melbourne, 1888; Today's Heritage, Melbourne, facsimile edn, 1977.
R. Therry, *Reminiscences of Thirty Years' Residence in New South Wales and Victoria,* Sampson Low, London, 1863.
Henry Gyles Turner, *A History of the Colony of Victoria: From its Discovery to its Absorption into the Commonwealth of Australia,* Longmans Green, London, 1904.
Sylvia Vietzen, *A History of Education for European Girls in Natal, 1837–1902,* University of Natal Press, Pietermaritzburg, 1980.
George Walker, *A Link with the Past: A Short History of Avon Plains and District,* Ruskin Press, Melbourne, 1924.
Whittaker, D. M., *Wangaratta ... 1824–1833–1963,* Wangaratta City Council, Wangaratta, 1963.
Who's Who in Natal, with which is incorporated Women of Natal, Knox Printing, Durban, 1933.
W. Allan Wood, *Dawn in the Valley,* Wentworth Books, Sydney 1972.
Ransome T. Wyatt, *The History of Goulburn, New South Wales,* Lansdowne Press, Sydney, 1972.

Index

à Beckett, Mrs Laura Jane 6–7, 11, 64, 65, 73–4, 75, 76, 77, 119, 134, 217
à Beckett, Thomas Turner 74
à Beckett, Sir William 11
Aborigines 63–4
Abraham, Bishop Charles John 153n
Abraham, Mrs — (Auckland) 153
Acutt, Mrs R. 11
Adelaide, SA 7, 11, 107, 126, 135, 137
Alexandria School, Bombay 211–12, 213, 214
'All England' XI 54, 55, 59
Allan, James R. 155
Allen, Catherine Maria (née Barlee) 138, 139
Allen, Florence C. 25, 138–9, 217
Allen, Sir George Wigram and Lady 90, 91, 92
Allen, Rev. James 138, 139
Allen, Jessie 139
Allen, Mrs Margaret 26–7, 70, 134–5, 217
American Mission Stations, Natal 178, 179
Andrews, Edward 51
Angaston, SA 136–8
Anglesey 40, 41–2, 126
Armstrong, Mr — (Natal) 184
Atherton, Maria 35–6, 129, 130–1, 217
Auckland, NZ 47, 153, 154, 158, 173

Balfour, Mrs — (Maitland) 89
Barker, Bishop Frederic 7, 11, 50, 51, 55, 60n, 82, 98, 100
Barker, Mrs Jane 11, 51, 53, 59, 82
Barker, Lady Mary Anne (Lady Broome) 166–7n
Barkly, Sir Henry 74–5
Barlow, ?Emily 68, 69
Barlow, ?Nancy 68–9, 217
Barrow, Maria 9, 27–8, 62, 63–4, 217
Barton, Mrs C. 43, 92–3, 217
Batler, Miss — (New York) 210
Bayly, Mary Frances (Mrs F. A. Hole) 26, 95–7, 217
Bayly, W. Henry 96, 97n
Beaton, Rev. P. 67–8
Bell, Robert Lewis and Mrs 144
Bell, Mr — (Natal) 189
Bendigo, Vic. 66, 69, 77, 120
Benyeo Station, nr Apsley, Vic. 103n, 104
Bernard, Eliza 94–5, 217
Bidwill, Charles Robert and Mrs 160
Biggs, Mr — (Graaff-Reinet) 198
Bird, Georgie 166–7, 170, 220
Bishop's Girls' College, Perth 138–9
Black Ball Co. 35, 36, 130
Blackith, Eleanor (?Mrs Lawes) 169, 170, 220
Blackwall Shipping Line 26, 34, 36, 37n, 38, 39
Blaine, Dr Benjamin 176, 180, 183
Blake, Charles F. 156
Blake, Julia 18
Blake, Miss M. J. 179, 186, 187, 188, 222
Blaxland, Charles and Mrs 92
Bliss, Jane Harriet 130
Bliss, Rev. John 130
Boake, Barcroft Henry Thomas 78n
Boake, Elizabeth 25–6, 44, 62, 78–81, 217
Boake, Henry 78
Booty, Conrad 77
Booty, Louisa 44, 45, 77, 217
Braddell, Lizzie A. 156, 220
Brand, Louisa J. 189, 222
Brickhill, James 175, 177, 180–1, 182, 186–7, 188, 222
Brickhill, Mary Rogers (née Harvey) 11, 175n
Brind, Kate 28, 71, 165, 220
British Columbia, emigrants to 11, 15, 17, 210n
Brook, Eliza C. (Mrs MacDonnell) 161–2, 220
Brook, Mary Bentley 161–2, 220
Brooke, Miss — (Christchurch) 170
Brough, Catherine 191–2, 222
Brougham, Lord Henry (Baron Brougham and Vaux) 11, 127n
Brougham, Patrick and Mrs 126–7
Brown, Rev. L. L. 170
Brown, Mr — (Drury, NZ) 158
Bryant, Miss — (Melbourne) 32
Buck, Mr — (Dunedin) 166
'Buckhurst', Double Bay, NSW 94
Burradoo Park, Bowral, NSW 146
Butler, Mr and Mrs — (Goulburn, NSW) 60
Butterfield, Miss — (Sydney) 50, 52, 54, 55

Caldwell, Miss J. 169–70, 220
Campbell, Miss M. 165, 220
Canada, emigrants to 11, 15, 17, 19, 122n, 203, 210, 211, 220
Cape Colony, S. Afr., 2, 190–2, 193–4; tribal wars 198, 199, 201–2
Carlow, Miss — (Sydney & Tas.) 95
Caroline Coventry, report of mutiny on board 29–31
Carruthers, Annie 209–10
Carruthers, Emmeline 209–10
Carruthers, Marion 209–10
Carruthers, Mrs M. 131, 209–10, 224
Carttar, Emilie Ann (Mrs John Dodds) 146, 217
Cary (?Carey), Miss I. M. (?J. M.) 36, 153–6, 220
Chelmsford, Lord 196, 197
Cheltenham House, Pinetown, Natal 174, 178
Chisholm, James K. 146
Churchill, Mrs — (Natal) 11
Church of England Grammar School, South Yarra, Vic. 144
'Clairville', East St Kilda, Vic. 126–7
Clapton, Mrs — (?Auckland) 47
Clarke, Mrs Stephen 99, 101
Clarke, Mrs — (Adelaide) 11
Clergy Daughters' School, Waverley, NSW 89
Cleves, Ryde, NSW 92
Close, Edward 93
Colonial Emigration Society 18
Colonial Land and Emigration Commissioners 5, 16
Colonial Sugar Refining Co. 148–9n
Cooleu, Lizzie 126, 217
Cornwallis, complaints of conditions on board 45–7
Cowan, Miss — (Melbourne) 67
Cowper, Rev. William Macquarie 51, 98, 102n
Crook, Miss — (Melbourne) 67
Cross, Fanny 37, 170, 220
Crosse, Charles Grant 161
Crosse, Elizabeth 161
Crowe, Catherine 4n, 28, 39, 174, 177–8, 179, 222
Crowe, Miss — (London) 4
Crowley, Miss M. 28–9, 149–50, 217
Cursitjee, Mannoylyu 211–12, 213, 214

Dalley, William Bede 88
Davis, Annie 32–3, 82, 83–91, 92, 217
Dearmer, Louisa 39–40, 61, 98–102, 146, 218
Devonport, inquiry into voyage of 102
Dillon, Mrs Augustus 11, 51, 52, 53, 54, 55, 59, 60, 84, 85, 89, 92, 93, 95
Dixon, Mayor J. (Wangaratta) 124
Dodds, John 146n
Doughty, Charles G. 134–5
Dover Castle (Capt. Ayles) 26–8; (Capt. R. K. Deacon) 44–5, 63, 68, 77, 134
Dudbrook 28, 38–9
Dudbrook Chronicle 38–9
Dunedin, NZ 43–4, 92, 151, 154, 155, 161, 162
Durban, S. Afr. 7, 175–6, 177, 182–4
Durham, William 87–9

'East Leigh' Ladies' Seminary, Prahran, Vic. 71
education, Aust. 140–1, 145; NSW 50, 98–9; NZ 167, 168, 174; Qld 129; SA 136; Vic. 80–1, 122n, 145
Edwards, Miss — (Sydney) 26
Edwards, Mrs — (Nelson, NZ) 165
Egerton House, Bedford, Cape Colony 174, 201
Ellis, Miss — (Graaff-Reinet) 195
Ercildoun, Burrumbeet, Vic. 111, 114n
Evans, Clara A. (Mrs Meredith) 198, 222
Evans, Sophia E. (Mrs W. Hobson) 197–8, 222
Evatt, Maria A. 188, 222

'Fairlight', Manly, NSW 150
Faithfull, Emily 4, 5, 8, 212
Female Middle Class Emigration Society (FMCES) ix, xi, 2–8, 9, 16, 23, 32, 40, 45, 49, 52, 61, 63, 65, 76, 82, 89, 95, 105, 118, 121, 122, 125, 129, 138, 140, 173, 178, 185, 191–2, 199, 201, 215; formation 3, 11, 126; colonial representatives 11; correspondents 217–24; finances 19; patrons 11; reports 13–15, 17–19, 172; rules 11–13; total emigrants sponsored 2, 19
Finch, Jane 26, 92, 93–4, 218
Ford, Eliza Maria 29–30, 90–1, 92, 218
Forrest, Mrs — (Melbourne) 67
Fowler, Miss J. S. (?I. S.) 177, 178–9, 184, 222
Fox, Caroline 170, 220
Fox, Premier and Lady (NZ) 165, 170

Franklyn, F. B. 65
Frere, Sir Bartle and Lady 196, 213
Fuller, W. 201, 202

Gawler, SA 135–6
Geoghegan, Charles Robert 106
Geoghegan, Jane 106, 107
Geoghegan, Louisa Agnes (Mrs F. Vaughan) 2, 26, 103–8, 118, 218
Gilbert, Rt Rev. Ashhurst Turner 70
Giles, Fanny M. 25, 92, 93, 218
Giraud, Omerine 77–8, 218
'Gledswood', Narellan, NSW 146
Glen, Emilie (Mrs Walton) 41, 179, 187, 222
Gooch, Gertrude 9, 50, 51, 52, 54–7, 218
Gooch, Henry 56n
Gordon, Mrs Alexander 11, 96n
Gorham, William 83
Goulburn, NSW 54, 57, 58, 59, 60
Governesses' and Servants' Home, Sydney 46, 51, 99, 101
Graaff-Reinet, Cape Colony 144, 174, 192, 193–4, 195, 197, 198, 200
Green, Edward 132
Green, Messrs Henry & Son (shipping agents) 26, 34, 39, 42
Green, Mrs — (South Brisbane) 129
Grote, George 15
'gutter (neglected) children' 23, 122

Hacon, Miss E. A. 166, 220
Haffenden (?Haffendon), Miss S. (?L.) (Mrs S. J. Meintjes) 179–80, 222
Hall, Miss S. E. A. (?S. A.; ?L.) 174, 192–9, 222
Hamilton, Matthew 149
Hammett, Sarah E. 43, 125, 218
Handfield, Rev. Henry H. P. and Mrs 72
Hart, Alice M. 199, 223
Haselton, Caroline (Lina) 140, 144–5, 195, 197, 218, 223
Hawke's Bay Education Board, NZ 167
Hawkins, Arthur Caesar 185–6, 187
Hawkins, Louisa 185–6, 187n
Heawood, Caroline Maria (Mrs J. R. Lofven) 9, 27, 62, 64–5, 218
Henderson, Sarah 184–5, 223
Herbert, Harriet H. 152, 167–71, 220
Hereford, wreck of 28–9
Hett, Marion (?Marian) 2, 36–7, 70–1, 163–5, 220
Higinbotham, George 80, 144
Hills, Annie L. 97n
Hills, Robert and Mrs 95, 96, 97n
Hines, Francis P. and Mrs 103, 104, 105, 107, 108, 109, 110
Hobson, Jonathon 198
Hobson, William 198n
Hole, Francis Henry 97n
Hooper, Celia (Mrs Sinclair) 189, 223
Hoskings, Miss — (Montreal) 211
Hout Constant farm, Sneeuberg, Cape Colony 197
Hughes, Mary 48, 70
Hunt, Annie M. 33–4, 112n, 121–5, 218
Hunt, Edward 124
Hunt, Emily Mary 70, 166, 221
Hussey, Julia 210, 224

India, emigrants to 2, 19, 112, 185, 203, 211–14, 220
Ireland, Ellen 50, 51, 52, 54, 55, 59–61, 100, 218

Jackson, Miss A. H. (Mrs Armstrong) 1, 27, 180–4, 223
Jackson, Miss — (Graaff-Reinet) 195
Jadis, Bessie 127
Jadis, Edith (Mrs E. F. Lautour) 41, 126–7, 135, 218
James, Arabella Harriett (Mrs Brown) 47, 158, 221
James, John F. and Mrs 64, 65
Janefield, Vic. 68–9
Jenkins, R. L. 98
Jenvey, Margaret E. 199–200, 223
Jerry's Plains, NSW 1, 52–3
Jeston, Nora F. 201, 223
Jones, Mrs Gatty 11, 65
Jones, Laura (Lauranna) 119–21, 218
Jones, Canon Thomas 130, 131
Jordan, Henry 35, 130, 131
Jordan, Pauline 144, 218

'Kayuga', Glebe, NSW 83, 84, 85
Keith (?Leith/Seith), I. (?J.) 171
Kemp, Mrs Charlotte 172–3, 221
Kesteven, Mr and Mrs — (Waimakariri River, NZ) 157–8
Kidson, James 73
Kidson, Jane 44, 73–4, 218
Kightley, A. 78
Kightley, Miss M. A. 78, 218
King, Richard P. ('saviour of Natal') 188

Laidlaw, Mr — (?London) 185
Laing, Miss — (Melbourne) 65
Lamport, E. L. and Mrs 11, 188
Lash, Caroline M. 29–30, 92, 93, 218

Lautour, Edward Fredericks Augustus Young 127n
Lawes, Mr — (England) 170
Learmonth, Alexander 54, 55
Learmonth, Somerville and Mrs 114
Learmonth, Thomas and Mrs 110, 111, 114
Leigh, Rev. Richard and Mrs 58, 59
Lewin, Jane ix, 1, 10, 11, 13, 15–16, 17, 23, 53, 59, 68, 71–2, 78, 79, 90, 99, 105, 106, 115, 116, 117, 118, 120, 127, 133, 152, 159, 162, 165, 167, 188, 189, 196, 197, 204, 205, 212
Lloyd, Rev. John Frederick 153
Lloyd, Captain Walter 187
Löfvén, John Robert 65n
London *Times* 8–10, 23, 151, 152, 154–5, 178
Long, Elizabeth 169, 171–2, 221
Long, Mary 169, 171, 172, 221
'Lynwood', Glebe, NSW 90

McArthur, Sherrard & Copeland, Melbourne 124
McArthur, Mrs — (Natal) 11
McBean, Miss — (Kilburn, London) 107, 109
MacDonnell, Mrs Eliza (née Brook) 161–2
Macfarlane, Walter and Mrs 189
McGillivray, Caroline 31, 66
McGillivray, Isabella 31–2, 66–7, 218
McGillivray, Margaret 66, 67–8, 219
McGillivray, Dr P. H. 66
Macintyre, Donald 83–4, 85, 87
Macintyre, Peter 83n
Mack, Helen (née Dodds) 144n
Mack, Joseph 144n
McLean, Miss J. B. 201, 223
McLeod, Hugh Lawrence 103n, 104, 108n
McNaughton, Love & Co., Melbourne 124
McNeill (?McNeile), Augusta G. 2, 156–8, 221
McNeill (?McNeile), Georgina 156, 221
Macqueen, Agnes B. 2, 131–3, 219
Macqueen, Arthur 132
Magee, Bishop William Connor 111
Maize, Miss — (Sydney) 90, 91
Mallet, Hugh and Mrs 193
Manning, Miss E. L. (Mrs Buck) 166, 221
Markham, Hugh 200
Markosoff, Colonel — and Mrs (St Petersburg) 205–6, 208
Marshall, Jane Mary (née Boulter) 163–4
Marshall, Major John Williams 163–5
Meinertzhagen, Frederick Huth and Mrs 171–2
Meintjes, Dr Stephanus Jacobus, 180, 223
Melbourne, Vic. 11, 62, 111, 112, 123, 141, 143, 145, 146, 147, 150, 152, 170
Melbourne Female Home, Collingwood, Vic. 74
Melbourne Home for Governesses, Needlewomen, Servants, etc. 74–5, 77, 110–11, 116, 119, 121, 125, 126, 134, 142, 219
Mellen, Rev. William 179
Merebank Sugar Estate, Durban 188
Meredith, Mr — (Graaff-Reinet) 198n
Merritt, Miss J. 153, 154n, 221
Miles (?Mills), Mrs — (Governor's Bay, NZ) 158n
Missen, Mrs G. H. 211, 220
Mitchinson, Elizabeth 2, 201–2, 223
Moffat, Mrs — (Natal) 188
Molly Station, nr Narrabri, NSW 127n
'Morpeth House', Morpeth, NSW 93
Morris, E. E. 144
Mounsdon, Georgiana 50, 51, 52, 54, 55
Muskett, Elizabeth 63, 64, 65
Muskett, Sarah 63, 64, 65
Myers, Miss — (Graaff-Reinet) 199

Nagelle, Cécile Céline 41–2, 126, 134, 135–8, 219
Natal, S. Afr. 11, 16, 121, 174–5, 177, 184–5, 186–7, 190
Natal Mercury 39, 181
National Association for the Promotion of Social Science 11; congresses (1861) ix, 7–8, (1863) 15–16
Nelson, Emily L. (?Mrs Webber) 28, 201, 223
'Nepean Towers', Douglas Park, NSW 98
Neuarpurr Station, nr Apsley, Vic. 103, 104, 110
Newton, Mrs — (Napier, NZ) 161
New Zealand, economic conditions 157–8, 164; emigrants to 15, 19, 151–73, 203, 216, 220–2; gold discoveries 152, 158–9; Maori wars 152–4, 158, 164n

Oberman, Miss ?J. (?I.) 149, 150, 219
Oldham, J. 165
Oliver, Miss M. A. 108–10, 219
Ollard, Ellen H. 2, 47–8, 141–3, 219
Omakau Station, Otago, NZ 156
Ord, Mr — (Puerua, NZ) 156
Osborne, Lord (Sidney) Godolphin 8
Otago, NZ 18, 151, 156, 158

Page, Miss — (Poona) 213
Parnell, Mrs Caroline 52, 53
Parnell, Edward 53
Payne, Mrs — (South Yarra) 125
Penrose, Susan G. B. 119, 219
Perry, Bishop Charles 26–7, 134
Perry, Mrs Fanny 11, 26, 64, 65, 134
Phayne, Rosa 34–5, 110–17, 118, 219
Phillips, Josey 34, 125–6
Phillips, Mrs Lucy 34, 125–6, 219
Phillips, Mary 50, 52, 54, 55, 56, 57–8, 219
Pool (?Poole), Miss — (Sydney) 45, 46
Poplar Hospital, London 38
Port Chalmers, NZ 43, 152
Port Elizabeth Collegiate School 200
Prentice, Louisa (?Louie) 188, 223
Prince of Wales Hotel, Melbourne 75
Purchas, Dr Arthur Guyon 158
Pyman, Margaret 44–5, 77, 219

Queensland, emigrants to 15, 128–34; land-order system 129–30
Queensland Colonization Society (for Irish immigration) 130
Quilton (?Quilter), Ellen 45–6

Rachel 1, 25, 50, 51, 54, 55, 58n
Redclyffe Station, nr Napier, NZ 160
Reimar, Miss — (Graaff-Reinet) 196–7, 200
Result 31–2, 37–8, 66, 71
Rhodes, Robert 156
Riccarton Roller Flour Mill, nr Christchurch, NZ 157
Rich Avon West Station, Wimmera, Vic. 112–13
Richardson, Mary 45–6, 82–3, 219
Robberds, Mrs — (Liverpool) 89
Robinson, Annie A. 187, 223
Rodgerson, Isabella 97–8, 219
Roe, Mrs — (matron, Melbourne 'Home') 42, 111, 112, 126, 142
Russell, Capt. Andrew Hamilton 160
Russell, Miss A. 173, 221
Russia, emigrants to 19, 203–10, 222
Rye, Miss B. 122n
Rye, Maria S. ix, 3, 4, 5, 6, 7–8, 9, 10–11, 13, 15, 17, 19, 20–1, 23, 28, 33, 49, 51, 59, 64, 68, 76, 78, 92, 95, 96n, 97, 110, 114, 122n, 134n, 151–2, 154–5, 178, 185, 191–2, 210n, 215

St George's Plantation, Umgababa, Natal 188
St Mary's College, Richmond, S. Afr. 188
St Paul's School, Auckland 153
Sampson, Miss — (Melbourne) 67
Saunders, James Renault 178, 184
Scott, Lucy M. 160–1, 221
Scott, Thomas King and Mrs 111, 112–13, 115, 116
Selfe (?Self), Mr — (London) 37, 40
Senner, Miss — , Ladies' School, Hackney, SA 126, 135
Shangster, Mrs — and Miss — (Sydney) 100–1
Shaw, Annie 77, 219
Shearman, Rev. J. 171, 172
Silver, S. W. & Co., London 12n, 36, 37n, 40–1, 44
Simcox, Rev. — (Porangahau, NZ) 170
Sinclair, Archibald 189, 190n
Sinclair, Celia 189–90
Smith, Capt. Cope and Miss 72
Smith, Jane 35, 129
Smith, Laura 172
Smith, Miss M. E. 160, 221
Society for Educated People in Indigent Circumstances 106
Society for Promoting the Employment of Women 4
South Africa, diamond finds 174, 187–8, 193; emigrants to 7, 19, 174–202, 203, 216, 222–3; Zulu wars 2, 174, 196, 197, 202
South Australia, emigrants to 134–8
South Brisbane Church School 129
Sowerby, Rev. William 58
Spratt, Dr Henry T. 159, 160, 221
Starky, Barbara 161, 221
Still, Miss — (London) 122n
Stone, Clara 121, 187, 219
Stone, Ellen 121, 187
Stoney, Josephine E. (?C.) 203, 204–10, 222
Strongith'arm, Miss — (London) 17
Streeter, S. Emily 1, 25, 50, 51, 52–4, 55, 59, 60, 71n, 219
Streeter, Mr — (?London) 71, 72
Struben, Johan Herman Marinus and Mrs 179, 180

Sullivan, Capt. Daniel Henry 146n
Sullivan, Mrs Mary Matilda, Ladies' College, Bowral, NSW 146
Sunter, Mrs — (London) 17
Sutton, Frederick and Mrs 163

Taylor, Rev. Robert 95
Temple, Amelia (Amy) M. 185–6, 223
Thackeray, Rev. J. R. 89, 93
Thomas, Fanny J. 156, 221
Thomas, Mrs — ('Lyth') 22–3, 87–8, 93
Tindall, Eleanor V. 143–4, 219
Tongaat Sugar Estate, Natal 178, 184
Tooth, Frederick 94
Tredoux, J. F. S. 179
Tripp, Mrs — (Prahran) 71, 72
Tripp, Mrs — (Orari Gorge, NZ) 166, 170
Turnbull, Mrs — (Dunedin) 173
Tutu Totara Station, nr Marton, NZ 2, 163
Tyler, Rev. Josiah and Mrs 178

Umzinto Lodge Estate, Alexandra, Natal 189
United States, emigrants to 19, 131, 203, 210–11, 224

Vaughan, Frederick 108n
Verulam, S. Afr. 176, 179, 180, 181–4
Victoria Girls' School, Poona 213, 214
Victoria Press, London 4, 8
Victorian Servants' Institution, Melbourne 67
Virginia Estate, Umgeni, Natal 189

Waifs and Strays Society 122n
Walcott, Stephen 10
Walker, Jane B. 144n
Walpole, Eliza C. 37–8, 71–3, 219
Walpole, Henry 71, 72
Walton, James Wardle 179n
Walton, John Clarke 179n
Wambo Station, Patrick's Plains, NSW 87–9
Watson, Mary Anna 174, 201, 223
Watts, George 91n
Webb, Sarah F. 48, 69–70, 219
Webb, William 69
Webber, Mr — (Bedford, Cape Colony) 201
White, Adam 146–9
White, Mrs Ida 146–9, 219
Williams, Helen 203, 211–14, 215, 220
Willis, Edward 6, 11, 65
Willisboro Station, Rolland's Plains, NSW 82–3
Wilson, Fletcher 133n
Wilson, Mrs Hannah 133–4, 162, 219
Wilson, Mary C. 133n, 162–3, 221
Wilson, Miss — (Brisbane) 133
Wimmera, Vic. 2, 103, 108–10, 113
Winn, Rosarie 38–9, 174, 175–7, 223
Wise, George and Mrs 92, 96
Wither, Miss — (Melbourne) 65, 75–6
Wodehouse, Sir Phillip 190–1, 193
Woerner, Fraulein S. 169, 222
Women's Protection Immigration Society, Montreal 211, 220
Woods, John and Mrs 150
Wright, E. G. 171
Wyett, Martha 18, 42–3, 159–60, 222

'Yasmar', Ashfield, NSW 54
Young, Misses — (Melbourne) 67
Young Australia, complaint of voyage in 35–6
Young Women's Institute, Auckland 172